Richard
&
Elizabeth

Richard
&
Elizabeth

by Lester David & Jhan Robbins

ARTHUR BARKER LIMITED   LONDON
A subsidiary of Weidenfeld (Publishers) Limited

ISBN 0 213 16660 7

Printed Offset Litho in Great Britain by
Cox & Wyman Ltd, London, Fakenham and Reading

FOR ELIZABETH TAYLOR AND RICHARD BURTON

We shall not look upon their like again

Foreword

THIS BOOK ORIGINATED AS A SERIES OF ARTICLES FOR *THE NEW YORK Times* Special Features. Intrigued by their subjects, the authors decided to continue the research thus begun.

There are many people that we wish to thank: Sir John Gielgud, Emlyn Williams, Brook Williams, Henry Wynberg, the late Sir Stanley Baker (who, though fatally ill, insisted on talking from his hospital bed about his boyhood friend), members of Burton's family, Jim Backus, Donna Quinn, Mickey Rooney, Henry Miller, the late Morris Ernst, Hugh French, the designer Halston, Will Geer, Michael Wilding, Professor Nevill Coghill of Oxford University, and scores of others whose names and contributions to this book appear in the text.

May we express our gratitude, also, to the individuals and staffs of film research centers. Especially helpful were the Academy of Motion Picture Arts and Sciences in Los Angeles, the British Film Institute Library in London, the Library of the Performing Arts in New York, the Queens Borough Public Library for use of special files, film officials in Leningrad and Moscow, and libraries and schools in Wales.

We are indebted to John Osenenko, manager of *The New York Times* Feature Syndicate, for his original encouragement and unstinting help. And to our wives, Sallie and Irene, who agonized with us through it all, no acknowledgement can be sufficient.

Our special thanks, too, to William Shakespeare for use of certain of his lines that, with bloodless, blameless blade, nick at the high points in the lives of our subjects. It is this, essentially, that we have tried to do with this very strange, very exciting couple for whom, we confess, we have developed strong affection. It was Shakespeare who, in the end, put it best in *The Taming of the Shrew*:

Such a mad marriage never was before.

Jhan Robbins
Lester David

Contents

A Prologue

The Passion and the Puzzle

Come, begin!
And you, the judges, bear a wary eye.
—*HAMLET*

AFTER THE FILMING OF A SCENE FOR *CLEOPATRA* IN ROME, ELIZABETH Taylor paused uncertainly just outside a building where a broad puddle of water, rainbow-splotched with oil drippings from the movie set, blocked her way.

Directly behind was her Antony, the husky 35-year-old British actor Richard Burton, who observed her dilemma. Instantly, he whisked off his heavy white cloak, spread it carefully over the water, made a courtly bow and in his rich voice invited her, "Cross, Majesty."

Elizabeth smiled radiantly, stepped onto the garment—and fell sprawling into the puddle, which was deeper than either had thought. Gallantly, he waded into the pit to help her out, ruining his costume as well as hers.

Symbolism, anyone?

The heroic Sir Walter Raleigh gesture toward a modern-day Elizabeth could well encapsule the next fifteen years in the lives of the most talked-about couple on the screen and perhaps in the world.

For Richard, hardly serious at this early stage of their relationship and seeking only to be larkishly helpful, plunged Elizabeth—and himself as well—into much deeper water than either knew about or intended.

Although they are no longer wed to each other, their romance and marriage has become one of the world's legendary loves, the most tempestuous of the century and notable because it helped alter the moral code of our times. Notable, too, because the two principals, who loved so passionately, came near to destroying one another.

Their relationship was conducted on a world stage. They were the special darlings of the women's and movie magazines; they appeared on their covers, either in photos or text, more than two thousand times between 1964 and 1974. Burton once estimated that more than one million words were written about them. He did not know, nor did anybody ever bother to figure out, how many newspaper headlines and how much television time were devoted to them.

One need not stretch too far for a reason: No other couple did so much with such panache before so many.

Their lives, separately and together, were chaotic. They still are. To allow the reader to follow their story with the proper degree of clarity, an abbreviated chronology is needed.

They met in 1951. He was married; she had recently divorced her first husband and was soon to acquire three more. In 1964, free of their spouses, they married each other. They were man and wife for eleven years, then were finally divorced after several separations. They remained apart for a year and were remarried in October 1975. Four months later, they separated once more and were divorced for a second time in early August 1976.

By that midsummer, Elizabeth, with high visibility, was playing the social circuit in Washington, and with no trouble at all, she had risen to queenship of the political-partying scene, a new role for her and an enormously successful one. Capital hostesses who could corral her for an event were themselves courted for invitations. In public, she was not mourning the loss of Richard Burton. "I've been having a very good time," she'd tell reporters.

Burton did not appear as happy that summer. Customarily outgoing, an unstoppable talker, an ebullient man, he was downright glum in public. In Hollywood, where he had gone to make a film, he was constantly in the company of a tall, beautiful former model named Susan Hunt. He returned to New York in early August, and on the twenty-first, he slipped down to Arlington, Virginia, where he and Susan were married by the same judge who had wed Henry and Nancy Kissinger.

Less than two months later, on October 11, Elizabeth announced her engagement to John William Warner, Jr., ruggedly handsome, forty-nine years old, who served as Richard Nixon's Secretary of the Navy between 1972 and 1974. He was divorced in 1973 from Catherine Mellon, daughter of the millionaire-philanthropist. Warner is wealthy, owns a three-thousand-acre cattle farm in Middleburg, Virginia, a splendid townhouse in Georgetown, and is active in the Washington social set.

They were married by year's end.

The era has ended. The razzle-dazzle, the eruptions, the often vulgar displays of passion and acrimony may no longer be spread over the front pages or shown in living color on television screens. If so, it is perhaps the best time to heed Wordsworth and recollect in tranquillity—recollect and seek to analyze this strange, incredibly talented, magnetically appealing couple who entertained (and sometimes revolted) the world for almost a generation with their off-stage behavior.

As they cavorted before us, they developed into symbols of romance, modern American style. A popular greeting card, intended to be sent to couples on wedding anniversaries by their friends, can still be found in shops: "Like Romeo and Juliet, Antony and Cleopatra, Liz and Dick—you belong together."

Each is an original. Who but Elizabeth Taylor would plunk a million-dollar gem into a salad?

One day she was dining with friends at the Lanai Restaurant in the Beverly Hills Hotel in California. Around her neck she wore the Cartier-Burton diamond, a huge 69.42-carat gem which had just been purchased for her by Richard for more than a million dollars. The gift had received worldwide publicity. Everyone in the posh place, including several movie and TV stars, craned necks, eager to see the dazzling jewel.

Elizabeth, aware of the interest she was arousing, called over the headwaiter. She removed the diamond and placed it atop her salad plate in a bed of lettuce leaves and asked him to take it around the room and show it to the diners. He did—to every table and white-leather banquette, where the patrons, many of them rich and famous, ogled it. Then the headwaiter brought it back, and Elizabeth picked it delicately out of the salad, wiped it, replaced it around her neck and continued her dinner.

Who else but Burton would pass out hot pretzels to a cluster of autograph hunters? Several years ago, on New York's Fifth Avenue, he was besieged by a throng of teenagers who pleaded for his autograph. He agreed to sign the outstretched books and papers on condition that they sign their names for him. As a crowd watched, the actor began trading signatures. Spotting a pretzel vendor, he bought out his entire supply which he distributed to his young admirers. He asked for the pretzel merchant's autograph, but the man said he couldn't write. Burton, unfazed, asked him to carve an X on a pretzel. After signing and receiving the signatures, Burton stepped into a waiting chauffeur-driven limousine. Waving the notched pretzel and the autographs, he recited from Shakespeare's *Romeo and Juliet*:

"What's in a name? That which we call a rose
"By any other name would smell as sweet."

Richard and Elizabeth scandalized the world in the early 1960s when, though each was wed to someone else, they lived together openly. Moral standards had not yet altered to accept such behavior, which many considered outrageous flouting of the norms by two persons who, because of their status, seemed to consider themselves exempt from their precepts. But currents were moving fast. The world was preparing for the most radical shift in its sexual codes in recent history; and the Burtons conducted their affair, which Richard himself has called "Le Scandale," at this moment of moral flux. Because of their enormous popularity and the tendency of the world to follow the leader—particularly glamorous leaders like Richard and Elizabeth—they were responsible, at least in part, for helping push the old morality into the discards.

There have been other sensational love affairs. King Edward VIII's passion for Wallis Warfield is more historically significant. Jacqueline Kennedy and Aristotle Onassis were a curious combination, sparking endless speculation. Gable and Lombard, Tracy and Hepburn, Bogey and his Baby, Laurence Olivier and Vivien Leigh, Douglas Fairbanks and Mary Pickford, Errol Flynn and Lily Damita—all were great, often stormy Hollywood romances. But the lives of none of these were so wildly, impetuously, passionately entwined as those of Elizabeth Taylor and Richard Burton.

None of the men would rhapsodize, as Burton has, about his wife's "wonderful bosom," buy her incredibly expensive furs and diamonds and—not very long after—scream at her to leave him and go hang herself.

None has ever admitted missing her husband so much that when he was away on location, she wandered in lonely sadness around her bedroom, found a pair of his socks the dogs had chewed, and in her words, "mooned over them." Richard told everyone Elizabeth went to bed with his socks when he wasn't there in person.

None, like Elizabeth, made it unmistakably clear that even the

6

sound of her man's voice affected her deeply and sensuously. Once Richard Burton made a recording of *Under Milk Wood*, the great poetical drama by the late Dylan Thomas, like Burton a Welshman. Elizabeth adored the recording. Uninhibitedly, she told a close friend that every time she heard Richard's voice savoring the lush imagery and rich music of the words, she would experience an orgasm.

Showy, flamboyant, exhibitionistic, they were also something quite special and, in a sense, important to us. They were, individually and together, our fantasies played out before us, even more spectacularly than we envisioned them. Many of us have scoffed at them, of course; they invited ridicule. But many, too, will, perhaps sneakily, have a pang of regret that we will probably not see another couple like them from the Hollywood mold, for the mold has been broken. Lunching at "21," the New York restaurant where jet setters and the elite of the show world gather, Morris Ernst, the outstanding civil liberties lawyer and *bon vivant* who knew Richard and Elizabeth well and who had been entertained in the homes of many top-ranking movie stars, talked about them a few weeks before he died.

Morris Ernst: "They were the last of their kind, special people who supersede nobility in the minds of Americans and much of the world. They inhabited a make-believe world into which we put them. We encouraged them to do the ridiculous and they didn't let us down. They provided the thrills that made reality disappear for a time, and made our lives a little juicier.

"Elizabeth is still a beautiful woman. I saw her only recently and can vouch for that. A man still gets a hard on when he sees those luscious breasts. [Ernst was over eighty.] And Richard does the same thing for women, who fantasize about being in bed with him."

The Times of London, in an unusual tribute, editorialized after their remarriage: "We happily join the millions of staunch Taylor-Burton subjects to wish the couple God-speed, for they have the marvellous ability to make a make-believe world even more unbelievable, but oh so delicious. Long may they be able to cast their wonderful spell."

Secretary of State Henry Kissinger threw a cocktail party for the couple in his suite at the King David Hotel in Tel Aviv when they decided to rewed. "The Burtons prove the axiom that truth is lots stranger than fiction. There's nothing bland about that couple—they're simply fabulous." Even President Gerald Ford and Governor

Ronald Reagan, when they campaigned for the nomination, were asked at press conferences about the couple. To Gerald Ford they are "extremely colorful people." And Governor Reagan observed that "unlike some Hollywood types I know, they insist on being themselves."

Henry Miller, still the indomitable literary rebel who shocked the world with his once unprintable books, *Tropic of Cancer* and *Tropic of Capricorn*, is now eighty-four, frail, blind in one eye and always accompanied by a companion. He rarely attends functions and still more rarely gives interviews. But at a meeting of the Actors and Directors Lab in Beverly Hills, he wanted to speak about Richard and Elizabeth.

Henry Miller: "They were never afraid to act out their true feelings. If she wants to wiggle her ass, she wiggles her ass. If he wants a piece of tail, he's not afraid to get a piece of tail. If they want to be cantankerous, they are cantankerous. Too many people want to do something that the public may frown on, even in these days. So they draw back—afraid of what society will say. They're mutes who are even afraid to whisper.

"The Burtons and the Taylors are getting rarer and rarer. They don't whisper—they shout. I don't believe in discipline and neither do they. They feel that nature should point the way.

"Today, when compared to most stage or movie personalities, the football star is more apt to be regarded as the great and outstanding one. But not where Taylor and Burton are concerned—they still reign supreme and are dear to the public's heart."

Stories of their marital difficulties even seeped into the Soviet Union where film fans, learning of this book, desperately wanted to learn "the latest" Burton-Taylor gossip. Personal stories never appear in Soviet newspapers or film publications. B. M. Kreshin, a member of the editorial board of *Moscow News*, a weekly published in several foreign languages for tourists, said in Moscow, "That's not our style."

Nonetheless, according to Zina Skalova, a high Soviet film-market official, "Soviet people know all about the couple. We've seen many of their films, *The Taming of the Shrew*, *The Comedians*, *Who's Afraid of Virginia Woolf*, and of course, Miss Taylor's *Blue Bird*. Even though we publish nothing of their private lives, somehow people know they are something special. It gets around."

A Russian journalist had a chance for some firsthand information in 1975 but could not take advantage of it. Richard Burton had come to Moscow for the film festival. A woman reporter for the Soviet press center asked for and was granted an interview. She was invited to his hotel room. Burton was in rare form. For two hours he talked—and talked and talked—tilting vodka, the world's best, often and freely. He talked of his early life in Wales, of his great love for Elizabeth, of Shakespeare, of life and, now and then, of how attractive the woman journalist was.

"She returned to the office laughing and told us all about her interview," says Ms. Skalova. "Unfortunately, the publication for which she wrote used only a few sentences." But before the week was out, the story of Burton's garrulous talk was repeated, doubtless with embellishments, throughout the Soviet journalistic set and, from there, out among the populace.

Comrade Kreshin may have been expressing Soviet views, but he was surely not speaking for all of the Russian people. Nina Voroshka, a small, dark-haired school teacher in the Ukraine, said, "They were so much in love. It is so beautiful, two people in love like that. I cannot believe he just wanted to adorn himself with the most lovely person in the world. Do you know them? Do you think they will marry again?"

Natasha Agroniva, large-busted and red-faced, was laying tiles on a terrace of the Hotel Roosyia in Moscow near Red Square. She was asked if she had heard of the Burton-Taylor marriage and its failure. Through an interpreter, she replied: "Liz? Dick? I'm so sorry for them. People don't let them live and be like ordinarily married people. If people would just let them alone, they would work out their happiness. But Western people and the newspapers and the television make all this noise and they are like freaks."

An Intourist guide in Kiev was avid for gossip about the pair; a couple in the lobby of the Moscow Circus was similarly intrigued. Love, and gossip about love and marriage, seeps into the Soviet Union like Western rock music.

They loved with an almost frightening intensity. "Richard and I are hardly apart," Elizabeth said in 1973, "but when we are together, it's agony." She loved him completely. "I didn't reserve anything," she has said. "I gave everything away ... my soul, my being, everything. ..." She blended her life into his. Thus she once wrote, "Just reaching out in the middle of the night and touching ... saying 'I love you' for no reason. Knowing that he'll be aware that I am there even when I am silent. *And that I matter!*" (Her emphasis.)

His need for her was equally great. In London, after one of their numerous separations, he was asked if they would get together again. His reply: "I expect so. We are flesh of one flesh, bone of one bone." Once he said, "If I were to be left without her, I should surely die. If I didn't dwindle into death from a broken heart, then I would die by my own hands. Life without Elizabeth is a desolate experience at best. I must have her to continue. I would not be a man if I did not treasure her body and mind."

In Los Angeles, Donna Quinn, a very pretty young woman with a Debbie Reynolds look and bounce, who was formerly the Burtons' West Coast representative, recalls one unpublished incident in 1974, after still another breakup. Burton was in Oroville, north of Sacramento, making *The Klansman* with Lee Marvin and Cameron Mitchell.

Donna Quinn: "Elizabeth had gone to Hollywood, but Richard was still in Oroville, Elizabeth decided to make some appearances and I was instructed to inform the press that she was going to be at the upcoming Academy Awards ceremony. The newspapers carried the story. It was then that Richard called me. It was about three A.M. He sounded very drunk, and for half an hour he kept blabbing away. It was weird. I didn't put the receiver down—just listened. At times he was incoherent: 'We got to do this right. . . . Do you hear me? Right. . . . Tell everyone that we aren't busted up . . . we're together. . . . Do you hear me? That's right. . . . I'll be at the Academy Awards with her. . . . Tell them that. . . . I'm coming to town. . . . Do you understand?'

"The next morning nothing further happened and I called Oroville, but was told that Richard was sound asleep and had posted a 'Do Not Disturb' sign on his door. He never did come to Hollywood that time. I don't think I ever told that story to Elizabeth, but I'm sure if I had she would have found some kind words of understanding. She's like that."

Their battles were as monumental as their stature in show business, some silenced by bitter name-calling and door-slamming, but often, more effectively, by other means. A London taxi driver named Basil Ward, a favorite of the couple who has driven them many times, perhaps put it best. Ward, a short, slender man with three missing front teeth, was born within the sound of the Bow bells and talks in the odd cockney-rhyme style.

"A mighty fine bloke 'e is," Ward said in a London pub over a glass of stout, "and so is his carving knife [wife]. Mostly their own chauffeur drives them, but sometimes they take me. I drive them once to the American Embassy. On the way 'e says something real loud. She says something real loud, Soon my bloody ears 'urt awful. Suddenlike, it gets quiet like the inside a bloody abbey.

"So I look in the mirror and they are sittin' real close. They're kissin', they are.

"When we gets to where they're going, 'e 'elps 'er out, arf carryin' 'er. She giggles, 'Richard, don't.' But does 'e put 'er down? She is kicking her biscuits and cheese [knees]. 'E gives me a quid tip."

At forty-five, Elizabeth is still a great beauty, though she may not appear so at times. She has never worried much about her looks, never taken great pains with them, nor even considered herself a beauty. She feels she is "lazy, shy, sloppy," and there are days when she will not look her best. But the famous violet-blue eyes are clear, the complexion smooth, the lips curved and full, the dark hair a frame for a perfect oval face. The late actor William Redfield, who played Guildenstern to Burton's Hamlet in 1964, described her face as "lozenge-shaped," a happy phrase, "which means that even when she goes a bit pudgy the face remains narrow at the chin and slightly depressed below the cheekbones." To Redfield, she was a "more striking beauty in person than on the screen," a conclusion with which most who know her agree.

But Elizabeth does not. She has always thought others were lovelier. She looks upon Jacqueline Onassis as a beautiful woman. And though she denies that she has a "complex" about her looks, she is ruthlessly objective about herself, believing her feet and arms are too large and her legs not long enough.

Burton himself, in a pixyish mood, once evaluated Elizabeth. "She has an insipid double chin, her legs are too short, and she has a slight pot belly." But again, there was praise where it was due. "She has a wonderful bosom, though." Another time he said, "You know, Elizabeth isn't particularly attractive physically. She has the shape of a Welsh village girl. Her legs are really quite stumpy." Then he added, "But she has this something which makes her the biggest star in the world."

She cannot see a child cry. Once, unrecognized in dark glasses, she was assigned to share a table with a mother and her eight-year-old daughter in the mezzanine restaurant at Fortnum & Mason, the famous London specialty shop. She ordered *vol au vent*, a

11

mushroom and shrimp dish served with a rice sauce. When the child asked for a rich dessert, her mother refused. "Do you want to be a fat lump all your life? That's what you'll be if you don't watch what you eat!" The child, who looked only a pound or two over normal weight, pleaded, but her mother would not relent. The child bowed her head and her eyes glistened. Hurting for the little girl, Elizabeth whipped off her glasses, identified herself and told the woman, "I never diet and I'm told the results are rather pleasing. Why don't you give the poor child what she wants!" And she stalked out.

She has always been a little in love with love. Once she said, "Love is such a vulnerable thing. It's a shame people don't give it more of a chance, treat it with more respect. Have you been to Pompeii? Well, there's a man and a woman holding each other, sort of frozen from the ashes that came down when the volcano erupted and buried them. It's like a piece of sculpture because it's mummified by the ashes and all gray.

"They are holding each other in an embrace of such love and affection. Their expressions are almost tranquil. They lay down and held each other and accepted death. They wanted to die together.

"To me, it's the most beautiful thing, because it's real. It happened two thousand years ago, but they hold on to each other at the moment of truth, the moment of death. And that's what life's all about—being able to hold on. How lucky they were."

She has never tolerated bias. Shortly after their first marriage, she and Richard were being escorted to a table in one of New York's most fashionable restaurants when they overheard a receptionist tell a black couple, "I'm sorry, but we have no tables." They looked at one another. Elizabeth told the maitre d' they would like a table for four. They invited the black couple to join them.

She enjoys sex and says so frankly. Once she told a reporter, "I think sex is absolutely gorgeous. I don't make any bones about sex being wonderful. Anyone who says that it isn't, is either mentally sick or afraid he or she can't measure up."

Richard is one of the world's most talked-about actors and many times a millionaire. At the Plymouth Theatre in early 1975, where Richard starred in *Equus*, a veteran traffic policeman said, "I've handled them all from Barrymore down, but there's nothing to compare with the attention Burton receives."

12

Elizabeth has called him one of the world's best-looking men. "He is the ocean. He is the sunset," she has said.

Nearing fifty-two, he is no longer a Poseidon or Apollo. The years have nibbled away at the youthful good looks. Furrows are grooved in his cheeks, and there are jowls where once was a clean jaw line. But the strong face, sturdy body and deep, rich, flexible voice are there still.

Hollywood would probably not have cast him in the role of a distinguished Shakespearean actor. He lacks the patrician nose and thin-lipped hauteur of a younger John Barrymore, the youthful male beauty of Sir John Gielgud, the dignity in maturity of Lord Laurence Olivier, the lean figure and brooding look of an Edwin Booth. In physical appearance, he is a blend of peasant and noble-man. He is self-consciously aware of the former and discounts the latter.

"Stripped, I'm a monster," he says. "I've got a body like an abandoned dressing room. When I took my clothes off to appear in bathing trunks [in *The Night of the Iguana*], strong men laughed and strangers kissed each other."

Sir John Gielgud, Richard's close friend and stage idol, referred to him as "that terribly rough boy." Once when Sir John was describing a fellow actor to him, he said, "He's built like a peasant. Just like you, Richard."

Observing him in his small, white-walled dressing room at the Plymouth Theatre, a visitor knows what Gielgud meant. Burton has a large head, barrel chest, and enormously wide shoulders. He appears to be very tall; however, he is only five foot ten, which is one inch less than he had formerly measured.

"An RAF doctor," Richard says, "used calipers to determine my height and pronounced me five foot eleven. Do you suppose that worrying over Elizabeth caused the shrinkage?"

Burton's eyes are green, set far apart beneath bushy brows. Many of his childhood friends in Wales said they used to tease him by calling them "the spooky eyes of the devil." Richard still likes to flash them in almost diabolical glee. Lauren Bacall, who has known him for years, said, "Wicked Richard is using those eyes again—making him appear wickeder than ever."

Elizabeth spoke of them as "Richard's sexy Satan eyes." Susan, his current wife, says they are "brilliant and changeable."

His unruly brown hair, worn long in the back, is flecked markedly with gray. Both cheeks are pitted, the aftermath of a severe case of adolescent acne. He weighs 160 pounds now, down from 180, but a small paunch is apparent beneath the belt of his gray trousers.

He pats it unlovingly. "I have a tendency to get flabbier than most people," he says. "I'm so afraid of getting fat. There was a man in our village in Wales who must have weighed 300 pounds. As a child, how I'd worry I'd rival him when I grew up."

The couple has often been ridiculed by the sophisticated media. *Newsweek* has derisively called them "Dickenliz," names they abominate and never use. (They are always Richard and Elizabeth to their friends and each other. Early in his career, Burton was once introduced as "Dick" at a Hollywood party. "I asked if they would please call me Richard," he said. "Dick made me feel like a symbol of some kind.") Elizabeth hates "Liz" because her brother, Howard, would tease her as a child by calling her "Lizzie the Cow" or "Lizzie the Lizard."

Their frankness was endearing. Most of the time they were open with the public, seemingly unable to dissemble. One sees a sharp distinction between the Burtons and those other world celebrities, the Kennedys. Unlike them, the Burtons seldom hid their weaknesses nor played games with the press. The Kennedys would let the world know what they wished it to know, on their own terms and their own time schedule, planning deliberately, choosing the writers, parceling out the publicity and planting it carefully. When they felt it served their purpose—the Kennedys were masters at this—they would invite a friendly newsman or woman to Hyannis Port to watch an ebullient family in action. When publicity would do no good, down came the portcullis and nothing emerged; not even the closest friend in the press was vouchsafed a word, much less an audience. Once a prominent author, who had written a best-selling book about John Kennedy that put the former President in the most favorable light in years, was assigned by a magazine to interview Senator Ted Kennedy. He was astounded when he received a curt refusal. The reason: "An article at that time would be no help."

True, the Burtons did not see all journalists who asked. But when they did, they usually unabashedly told the world through them about their feelings, their lives, their great love for one another and/or their inability to get along, their fears and their anxieties.

Elizabeth, unlike many film stars, cannot mask her feelings. She

14

has little sense of guile. She will reveal her insecurities along with her rare talents and wondrous shape. She will not—cannot—say anything she does not believe is the truth. Once publisher Hugh Hefner took her on a personally guided tour of his bunny-populated *Playboy* mansion, proudly exhibiting the tropical pool with his lounging maidens, the palatial indoor garden, the lushly decorated rooms. When he asked how she liked it, he was hardly prepared for her prompt reply: "It's crap."

Burton's sex life? Ask and he'll tell you, not pretending to take offense as some others will nor grinning as though to shock, but pondering the question as any other. Thus, speaking about himself and Elizabeth and their lives in a broad-ranging conversation, he will point out that he has now passed 50 years of age.

"The times for sex," he says, "may be slightly fewer, but when you do—oh joy! It's more exciting and ferocious than when you were a callow youth. I've always believed sex improves with age. However, you also find more time, and have to apologize less, for periods of relaxation. Not that you require a great deal of relaxation to perform properly. But at fifty you have learned to appreciate the beauty of relaxation."

Just months before his second divorce from Elizabeth, he leaned back in his dressing room at the Plymouth Theatre, closed his eyes and said softly, "My God, she is beautiful!" His opinion had not changed from that earlier time several years before when he said, "She's beautiful all the time—morning, noon and especially at night. Even when she's wet."

As for Burton, Elizabeth believes he is "a very sexy man who has jungle essence," an estimate with which millions of women won't quarrel. She said, "He's full of chutzpah, but in a classy way. He can be in the middle of dozens of other men and he's the one you'll notice."

Burton is astonishingly candid about his vulnerability. He describes it simply, with none of the hyperbolism that customarily adorns his speech, "Booze nearly killed me."

Richard Burton's brush with death, Elizabeth's anguish over his headlong rush toward self-destruction, his triumphant return to glory—all this is part of the story of the marriage of the century, perhaps the least known, obscured as it was by the stardust.

As recently as June 1976, Emlyn Williams, Burton's close friend and one of the most important influences in his life, was convinced the couple would reunite. "Elizabeth and Richard were meant for each other," he said.

Elizabeth apparently thought so, too. "We can't live without each other," she admitted that summer. So, too, did Richard. "We're apart for a time now," he said after they separated like exploding atoms. "I suppose we'll get back together."

But they married other people. Why, if they were "flesh of one flesh, bone of one bone," in Burton's phrase? Why, if life without Burton was intolerable for Elizabeth? Are they still playing games with each other, is the passion, at long last, ended for good? Finally, was it all genuinely love in the true, mature sense?

The actors are at hand; and, by their show,
You shall know all that you are like to know.
—A MIDSUMMER NIGHT'S DREAM

One

The Boy
from Pontrhydyfen

There is much care and valour in this Welshman.
—*King Henry V*

1. "Green and Grievous Was My Valley"

"WHEN RICHIE JENKINS WAS BUT A SLIP OF A BABY," SAID OCTOGENARIAN Tommy Jones as he reached a knobby, scarred hand for his pint in the Miner's Arms, oldest pub in the quiet, almost forsaken village of Pontrhydyfen. "A body could plainly see that the little bugger wasn't headed for the pits like his da and his brothers. Nay, not Richie Jenkins. Even then his babble was distinguished and full of poetry."

Tommy Jones knew the Jenkins family well. He had worked alongside Richie's father in the coal mines of South Wales outside the town limits. "I had my health and strength then," said Jones as he took a swallow of the ale. Most of his teeth are missing and he made a loud swishing sound as he drank. "Many's the time I held baby Richie in my lap while he drenched me clear through his nappy. Why, I bloody well remember once the peeing was so immense it could have flooded all of Cardiff. I was about to set the little bugger down when, Heaven be my witness, if he didn't raise his fist and babble, 'A great honor I've just bestowed on you.'

"Aye, at once I told his father, Dic, what an amazing infant he did have and that the boy, remarkable he was, would surely climb to the very top and do the valley proud. It's an astonishing gift of prophecy I have."

It was, of course, a tall story: Neither Richard's peestream nor his rhetoric were so well developed that early in life. But a legend has already grown up about Richie Jenkins—now Richard Burton—in his native village, and a visitor had best nod his head and agree " 'twas e'en so." Listen of an evening in the Miner's Arms and one hears even more outrageous tales about his accomplishments as an infant, a small boy, a lover, a husband, and especially as one of the world's most distinguished actors.

It is important to start here, in Richard's home town, to see the homes and spend many days with the people who knew him, to talk to the members of his large family, for only then can one hope to understand the man. "We may our ends by our beginnings know," Sir John Dehman wrote centuries before. Much of what Burton is today was molded here, in the harsh countryside of South Wales: his lust for language, his passion for poetry, his wild, unruly behavior, his great tenderness, his compassion for the poor of the world, his raw guts, his free spirit, his love of booze and his capacity to absorb vast quantities of it, his spells of deep melancholy, which the Welsh call the *hiraeth*, his readiness on the instant to woo any woman anywhere, and even his acting. He said years ago that he wanted to play Hamlet like a Welsh peasant, vigorously with nothing prissy about him, and he did.

Burton's birthplace is a semidetached square stucco house which was already old when he came into the world in a second-floor bedroom. It sits on a hilly street near the main road and a high viaduct spanning the Afan River, a gray, narrow ribbon of water meandering slowly through the grazing lands of the Fynddaw slopes. When his fame rose, the Welsh Tourist Board tacked a neat brass plaque alongside the steps. It was promptly stolen. Another was installed and this, too, quickly disappeared. Currently, the two-story stucco house has a simple three-by-five-inch card in the window that reads:

```
Richard Burton
Actor
10 November 1925
```

Now, as when Richie lived there, the village seems old, soiled, respectable and poor. Pontrhydyfen is bravely trying to keep up with modernity but not succeeding very well, like a runner staggering behind the pack in a marathon. Several shops line the main street, which has a name, but everyone calls it the "main road": a food store, a men's and women's clothing emporium, a tailor, an auto-supply place.

The Miner's Arms, a small stone pub, is close to the center of the village. It is only twenty-five feet from one end to the other, and just about half that length inside. A coal-burning stove stands in the center of the room, surrounded by four wooden tables and chairs. The bar is less than seven feet long, and a dart board hangs on the wall opposite. A few pictures are nailed to the other walls and there is another photo, larger than the others, of the 1923 championship Pontrhydyfen rugby team. One of the members in front, a burly, smiling young man, is Ivor Jenkins, Richard's brother.

All the close members of Burton's family but sister Hilda, who is eight years older, have either died or moved away from Pontrhydy-fen. Hilda Owen is a handsome woman, and it's easy to see the resemblance. Her brick house at 4 Penhydd Street is scrupulously clean and resembles many of the other houses in the village: slate roof, curtained windows and a squat chimney.

"Richie may have great abundance now," says Hilda, "but never for one moment has he forgotten where he came from, and he never will."

Nor will he, for Burton's loyalty to the land of his birth has never dimmed. He talks about Wales even more than he does about acting. He knows, and will sing at any invitation or without one, hundreds of Welsh songs. He commemorates St. David, the patron saint of Wales, faithfully every March 1, occasionally by wearing the tradi-tional leek, or green onion, in his hat if he can get one, but always by drinking awe-inspiring amounts in the saint's honor. He taught Elizabeth Taylor to speak some Welsh, in which he himself is fluent. Indeed, some of Elizabeth's most flavorsome comments to him contained references to his nativity. Once, when he celebrated on the eve of a birthday by downing a fifth of bourbon, she called him—endearingly—a "boozed-up, burned-out Welshman." The times when he made her really angry, she would call him—not so endearingly—a fucking Welshman.

Burton's parents were Richard and Edith Jenkins, who spoke only Welsh. His father was a bantam cock of a man, five feet two inches of jaw-jutting pugnacity when the mood was upon him, tender and nearly overwhelming in his solicitude at other times. Although small, he was well muscled, with powerful miner's hands, a Welsh edition of Sean O'Casey's irascible, hard-drinking, imaginative, and warm-hearted Fluther Good.

Richard's mother, a good deal younger and taller than her hus-band, had been a barmaid. "A very well-favored looking one," recalls Tommy Jones. "A real beauty, she was. Blonde and strong. Poured the drinks in a Cwmavan pub and sometimes Dic drank there. But then he drank everywhere. He was a man of vast drinking habits—a twelve-pints-a-day man. But he stopped long enough to woo the comely lass.

"Another gent who owned vast boarding houses wanted Edith Thomas, but she only had eyes for Dic. And why not? Although Dic was but very small, he was more than a match for most. Oh, what a lovely style he had."

"Right you are, Tommy Jones," agreed a shriveled old man who was leaning against the bar and had overheard the conversation. He appeared to be in his late seventies and bore a striking resemblance to Harry Truman. Although age and disintegration were creeping over him, he had probably been as peppery as the late President in his youth and middle age.

The coal stove in the center of the Miner's Arms was operating at full capacity, but despite the heat he was wearing a long green overcoat that was closed to the very top. Several buttons were missing and the upper part of the coat was fastened with safety pins. The peak of his gray tweed cap was safety-pinned on.

He pulled the cap closer to his forehead and said, "When they were courting, Dic took his wife-to-be to a fair. To warm her blood he signed up for the wrestling and weightlifting contests. The other men who had entered were heads taller, but no matter to him. Duh! He was always a man ready for a challenge and would take naught from nobody. With ease he won the contests, he did. And a month later, a blushing sixteen-year-old Edith married him. Still the champion lifter—although the bride was long in the legs, her bones were not heavy—Dic, who had many that wedding day, carried her over the threshold.

"Edith was a good wife and began turning out children right from the start, but sadly the first two, both named Margaret, died soon after birth. But the other eleven lived on."

The beer-drinking Miner's Arms patrons helped him name the Jenkins children: "Tom . . . David . . . Ivor . . . Will . . . Verdun . . . Graham . . . Cecilia . . . Catherine . . . Hilda . . . Edith . . . and Richard."

When they finished, one said, "What a glorious brood they turned out to be."

None of them rivaled Richard in fame, but all developed into bright, interesting and attractive adults. David became a police inspector and once turned down an invitation to join Scotland Yard in an executive capacity.

Edith, who married an eminent British physicist, had a remarkable way with figures, and neighbors pleaded with her to chart their budgets.

Verdun, who had been christened on the closing day of the World War I battle of Verdun, became a miner and helped set a record for coal removal. He lost his right leg in a mining accident and was awarded 300 pounds. He bought a grand piano with the proceeds although he couldn't play a note, explaining, "And why not? I've always wanted to own something grand!"

All the children inherited their father's love of life. Dic is still a legend at the Miner's Arms, which has remained the center of village life.

"Whenever he had more than a few," Tommy Jones says, "he'd throw back his head and sing. Very tuneful, he was. He had a favorite about a salesman who had ladies all about Wales. I must remember to teach that song to Richie when next he comes. Here's how it goes:

Billy Davies had ladies aplenty.
One in Llanbrynmair,
One in Llabelli,
One in Llaboidy,
One in Llandudno,
One in Llanrhian,
And all of them he kept so happy.
Oh, to be Billy Davies!"

Despite his advanced age, Jones had a rich baritone. He sang with an imperturbable tenderness but offered apologies. "Far better than me, he was. Dic would wink as he sang, and raise his brows something fierce and jig about. So jolly. Aye, to hear old Dic sing it again."

Second only to Dic Jenkins's weakness for liquor was the lure of gambling at a nearby dog track, and often both went hand in hand. On paydays, Dic would have a problem: Should he have a drink first and decrease his betting money, or go to the hounds where he might double or triple his pay. More often than not, the drink won. With his remaining funds he would then head for the track where, regularly as the seasons, he would lose, which would so disgust him that he would again head for the bar for more drink to ease his pain—this time his drinking was put on the tab.

On one memorable occasion, after a losing day at the track and a heavy one at the bar, Dic brought home a mangy, starving dog, "Boys," he hollered as he entered, "our troubles are over." The dog was a greyhound which, Dic said, would enter the races and make their fortune at last. Ivor Jenkins gulped and told his father that the dog was probably more than twenty years old and couldn't trot, let alone run, if a steak were across the room. Dic was indignant. He began to argue, but Edith, sighing gently, said to Ivor and his brothers, "Put the dull ha'penny who is your father to bed." They did, and by morning the dog had gone.

Daddy Ni—the children's nickname for their father—never saw Richard act in a movie. Or rather, he saw only one short scene. The story was related by another regular at the Miner's Arms, a man deep in his seventies, with a huge stomach and bald head. He wasn't wearing socks and had taken an orange out of a bag he carried. As he ate the orange, he slowly spat out the seeds.

"In those days," he said as he sent a seed flying, "there were many more pubs around here—seventeen between us and the film house. Well, one day, the film house was featuring one of Richie's movies. Dic set out to see it and visited all seventeen pubs before he got to the theater.

"But get there, he did, only to see Richie pour himself a drink in the film. That made Dic ever so thirsty again, and you know what he did? Went back to the nearest pub—and never returned!"

An old woman sitting alone in the corner kept repeating, "Such a man! Such a man!" In her long, flowing black dress and black knitted shawl, she bore a striking likeness to Queen Victoria.

"Richie's dear mother was all for religion," she said. "But not his dada—he was positively agnostic. Never set a foot in church, and on Sundays he'd drink beer instead. He was drinking beer on this very spot when he and a pal were set to arguing about God. Suddenly, Dic asks for a glass of water. One is given to him.

" 'See this glass of water,' he says to his pal. 'If God changes it into beer then I'll agree that he be!'

24

"As Dic turns his back, someone snatches the glass of water and puts down a glass full of spirits. When Dic sees it, he is at once very confused. He looks at it, sniffs it, and finally tastes it. But he stops after one sip.

" 'You must be bloody daft,' he cries out, 'if you think me that foolish! God never set foot in this place! This is not beer. It's too cabbagy-tasting. It's a wallop [ale]! But it seems a pity to waste.' So doesn't Dic finish it! I hear there is much of the father in Richie."

To which Tommy Jones added as he clicked his tongue, "Amen. Not in looks. There he favors Edith. But in all else, he's the exact copy of Dic."

Richard, the twelfth of thirteen children weighed twelve pounds at birth. His father considered that a lucky omen and celebrated the event by downing twelve whiskies with twelve beer chasers. Each time, he repeated a similar toast, "To my lovely new boyo, who is number twelve, is twelve pounds heavy and was born at twelve o'clock sharp." (Actually, Daddy Ni, as Richie himself would do later, was embroidering the facts to make a good story—Richard arrived hours earlier.)

Two years later, Richard's mother died after giving birth to her thirteenth child. His father couldn't work in the mines in addition to tending very young children, so Richard was sent off to Port Talbot, seven miles away, to live with his sister Cecilia and her husband, Elfed Jones, who also toiled in the pits.

Although Richard often returned to Pontrhydyfen to visit his family, it was a tremendous emotional shock for the two-year-old to suddenly lose his mother and be forced to leave his home. He's not given to self-pity, but in one off-guarded moment he said, "My sister Cecilia was truly magnificent in the way she reared me as her own. I loved her with a sometimes unbearable passion. But let's face it—it's different to be without a natural mother."

The Jenkins children inherited their mother's good looks. Most of the boys, including Richard, also favored their mother in height. But they acquired their father's thick-muscled body.

One hears stories of how the four Kennedy brothers, sons of Joseph and Rose, fought among themselves like warring tribesmen, yet ganged up fiercely against any who dared pick on one of them. The seven Jenkins boys, a great deal poorer, pummeled one another no more gently; as for any common enemy, Hilda shakes her head warningly and says, "To have Daddy Ni's boys against you was something to shy away from, no matter what. They were the nicest and the politest, until one of the family was picked on. Then they became a mighty rough lot."

Richard recalls that the brothers would prove their manliness by walking across the ledge of the high bridge near their house. "You'd crack your skull if you slipped," he said. "I did it, even though I was frightened. After all, I had to prove that I was a full-fledged member of the Jenkins family."

"We always were close," Hilda says, "even though we never had much money. Well do I remember the Great Strike when the miners marched two hundred miles to London to present their grievances, and many they were. The miners had to work in half a foot of freezing water, and their reward was early tuberculosis. Rich never forgot those evil times—he still speaks of them."

Growing up in an impoverished Welsh valley, however, wasn't all bleak. A boy could dream of becoming a celebrated rugby star and envisage wearing the red jersey of Wales. He would begin by memorizing the names and averages of all the professional players. Richard became proficient at this and even knew their heights, weights and personal habits.

He'd talk for hours to Elizabeth about the Welsh team, how they would drink from the backs of their beer glasses when they lost to Scotland, and balance a bottle of champagne on the manager's head when they won.

One of Richard's schoolmates, Gerwyn Williams, played rugby for Wales. Williams keeps himself in good condition and looks as though he could still step onto the field and play championship ball. "If Jenk had stuck with the game," Williams said, "he might have become a professional—had it in him. Always was one with a great deal of drive."

For two pennies, a valley kid could go to a Saturday matinee at the *Picturedrome*, the local movie house popularly known as the *Cach*— the Welsh word for "shithouse." If the projector didn't break down, Clark Gable could be seen wooing the ladies, and Groucho Marx insulting them. At the time, Richard's favorite was the cowboy star Hopalong Cassidy. After one of his movies, Richard swaggered around town drawling in lingo decidedly not Welsh, "Pardner, a man can only trust his horse. Savvy?"

26

The Port Talbot villager who told the story said, "Aye, if ye ask me, that may be the cause of all his current problems." Then, removing steel-rimmed glasses from his blade of a nose, he added, "Substituting women for horses can cause trouble!"

Port Talbot, nestled between the mountains and the sea, housed one of the largest modern steel works in Europe, whose chimneys constantly coughed clouds of black smoke. Yet nearby, sheep grazed peacefully near the ruins of an ancient Norman castle. Natives were warm and kind to each other, but distrusted outsiders. In Pontrhydyfen, everybody was poor, but here the petty cruelty of the village caste system thrived. The inhabitants of Port Talbot spoke English, but the accepted language in Pontrhydyfen, only a few miles away, was Welsh.

Richard says, "I've always been in love with the Welsh language and missed hearing it in Port Talbot. It's a wild, breathy, passionate, powerful tongue. I once heard Shakespeare's *Macbeth* recited in Welsh, and it shook me to the core."

He tried to convince Elizabeth that you could say things more effectively in Welsh than in English. He must have succeeded because she has become one of the leading exponents of the Welsh language. Recently, she told a friend, "You don't simply say that a man possesses a good voice, but that he has a 'bell in each tooth.' A lovely shading."

"To this very day Rich speaks Welsh whenever he gets the chance," says Hilda. "He missed it greatly when he lived in Port Talbot. Even though Rich was extremely fond of my sister and brother-in-law, he felt as if he was going away to far-off foreign shores. But he never was one to complain, so the stoic little lad made the best of it.

"Daddy Ni so looked forward to seeing the lad. He proudly called him, 'My true little Welshman.' In Welsh, Rich would answer, 'Daddy Ni, I'm so glad to be in our house.'

"Richie had a beautiful soprano voice, and the two of them would carry on in lovely fashion. A favorite song was about Cranshaw Bailey and his little engine. Our father knew so many songs. He was a man of little education, but he was never without a book. He read everything, good and bad. A tremendous reader, he was, and also a wonderful teller of stories. For hours, Richie would listen to him talk about the doings of wonderful characters he had invented. I'm

27

certain that Richie's love for the printed and spoken word come from Daddy Ni."

Richard agrees. Dic would obtain much of his knowledge by studying his son's textbooks, particularly the poetry books and the English-literature anthologies. He would soak up information avidly, as Richard himself did. One day Dic, seeing how intently Richie leaned over the pages, said to his son, "You don't read books, you rape them." Burton said years afterward, "He'd say that about me, but he meant it about himself."

In Port Talbot, Richard attended the local elementary and secondary schools. He was a good student and well liked by the other pupils. Several entries in *The Wayfarer*, a school magazine, attest to that:

"R. Jenkins has proved to be a most valuable member of the school. We are sure he will be so in the future."

"R. Jenkins has been a tower of strength in Rugby and under normal circumstances would probably have gained an International cap. He is without doubt worthy of the honor."

"We are proud to announce that R. Jenkins won the Scripture Reading Competition."

"R. Jenkins was prominent in four events: 1st putting, 3rd javelin, 1st 440, 4th discus."

Richard, however, failed to return to school after the 1941 Christmas holidays; that wasn't very surprising—boys from mining homes were continually dropping out. He considered going down to the pits to join his father and brothers, but instead got a job as a junior sales clerk in the local haberdashery shop.

"How he hated that job," Hilda recalls. "He did it because he felt his earnings—about thirty shillings a week—were very necessary, as money was short. Only sixteen at the time, he seemed to have given up all hope for the future. He smoked and drank and took up with girls. He felt that his prospects were dismal indeed.

"And then Rich did something that had seldom been done before—he returned for the autumn term of 194"

One of Richard's former teachers was responsible for the sudden reversal. Meredith Jones, a controversial instructor, decided that the boy belonged in school. And there was little in Port Talbot that Meredith Jones didn't have his way with.

Early one Monday morning, the rotund, red-headed man stormed into the haberdashery shop and accosted Richard. "Young man," he bellowed, "whatever are you doing here?" Before waiting for a reply he added, "Get back to school immediately! Now go! Go!"

Richard went.

Some years later a grateful Richard composed an essay to the man who came to his aid when he desperately needed help. He wrote:

"Without him I would have missed a large slice of life—I would not have gone to a great university and I would probably not have become an actor. I would not have had the courage to answer an advertisement and I would never have gone to London except possibly in a leeked red beret and with an enclosure ticket for Twickenham. I would, I suspect, in some unpleasant job, have become morose, suspicious, bitter, and impossible to live with. I might even have become a politician."

Richard Llewellyn Jones (in Wales the name Jones is even more common than Smith is in the United States), a handsome, auburn-bearded teacher of English at the Dyffryn Comprehensive School in Port Talbot, said, "Meredith Jones was always occupied with dozens of projects and asked Philip Burton, another of the boy's instructors, to look out for him. Those two teachers played important roles in the Richard Burton saga.

"Philip Burton recognized the boy's potential and took him under his wing. For years he had been teaching school, but he had never before met a youngster with so much ability. He became Richard's Professor Henry Higgins right out of Shaw's *Pygmalion*. He began to mold his at-times unwilling subject. He improved his speech, stretched his mind. Securing the permission of Richard's father, he legally made the youth his ward, and in appreciation the boy became officially known as Richard Burton. He literally changed Richard's entire life."

Richard said of his two fathers, "My real father gave me his love of beer. He was a man of extraordinary eloquence, tremendous passion, great violence. I was greatly in awe of him. He could pick you up with one hand by the seat of your pants. My adopted father is the exact opposite. A pedant, a scholar, meticulous in his speech, not given readily to passion. I'm still frightened of him. He still corrects my grammar."

In his autobiography, *Early Doors*, Philip Burton, who now lives in Florida, writes, "Once, when an interviewer for a magazine asked me in Richard's presence when I adopted him, he broke in with, 'He didn't. I adopted him.' This did not mean that he conducted a clever campaign to ensnare me. It was just that he had a hungry need which I could best satisfy: in so doing, of course, I also fulfilled myself."

Philip Burton had been a writer for the B.B.C., and a director in the professional theater. He was a brilliant scholar of classical and contemporary literature. When the boy told the portly, dignified and soft-spoken schoolmaster that he wanted to become an actor, he had initial doubts. "But I should have known better," he says. "I've never met a person before with so much determination. I discovered that Richard had quite an unusual talent. Most notable was his feeling for poetry and language. He was in love with words even before he could understand them."

Richard likes to give the impression that acting came very easy. But despite his rapid theatrical progress, he studied actively. He recited Shakespeare in front of the mirror. He'd greet friends with lines from *The Tempest* and *Hamlet*

Richard's ambitions were limitless, and as an adolescent, his reach was beyond his grasp. Once he wanted to compete in the famed Welsh music and poetry festival called *Eisteddfodau*. He wanted, he told his foster father, to learn a song by Sir Arthur Sullivan, *Orpheus with His Lute*.

But there was a problem. The song called for a soprano voice, and Richard's, in the process of change, slipped between contralto so-prano and baritone. Alone in the school's assembly hall, Richie stood on stage as Philip Burton sat at the piano. Richie started to sing. His voice fluted into all ranges, and Philip Burton reacted as anyone else would: He doubled up with laughter. Embarrassed and angry, young Burton raced off the stage crying, "I'll show you. Someday, I'll show you!"

He did. Years later, in 1961, Richard Burton won the New York Critics Circle Award for the best performance in a musical, *Camelot*. While his singing was not exceptional—"bold rather than beautiful," Kenneth Tynan had called it—he had ample reason to turn to Philip Burton in his dressing room and say, "Well, I showed you, didn't I?"

Richard is philosophical about his success. "Green was my valley," he says. "But it was also grievous. Because of that, I had to be like the Avis Rent-A-Car—I had to try harder."

2. First Curtain

THERE ARE SOME CREATIVE PEOPLE WHO ARE STIMULATED INTELLEC-
tually when they produce a work of high merit. Others, responding
viscerally, experience an inner glow that warms them inside.
Richard Burton may be unique. The first time he appeared on the
stage as a professional actor, he felt what he called "The strangest
sensation in my penis." Thereafter, he says, he has always gotten
"throbbing fervors when something important is about to happen. I
suppose it's my barometer."

Poetry, too, will bring on the fervors. Once he said, "The thing
that really excites me—if I come across it, and it is very rarely—is a
new poem that I have never read before, which is really brilliant in
all its parts. Then I become as excited as if I am seeing a fantastically
beautiful woman for the first time. And actually, in fact, become
amorous as a result of it."

The barometer began forecasting the good things on the horizon
in 1943 after he had appeared successfully in several school productions. He did exceptionally well in a Shaw revival of *Pygmalion*. A
critic for the Port Talbot *Guardian* wrote, "As the professor, he
displayed dramatic talent that made him a dominating personality."

The review turned Richard into an instant celebrity, and a natty
uniform added to his status. Philip Burton had been appointed a
flight-lieutenant in the Air Training Corps, which prepared last-
year high-school students to become Royal Air Force pilots. Flight-
lieutenant Philip Burton encouraged Richard to join his squadron.

During the training period, which only occupied part of Richard's
time, the elder Burton saw an advertisement in the Cardiff *Western
Mail*:

EMLYN WILLIAMS WANTS WELSH ACTORS

Mr. Emlyn Williams is looking for several Welsh actors and actresses for small parts in his new play which will open in the autumn. Types wanted vary from young people to character actors and actresses. A Welsh boy actor is also required. Boy applicants must be 14 years by December 1, but are expected to look younger. Those who think they can fill these roles should write within seven days to Mr. Williams at 15 Pelham Crescent, London, S.W. 7, giving age, qualifications, and enclosing a recent photograph.

Philip Burton urged Richard to apply.

In the study of his Chelsea apartment on one of London's loveliest streets, the short, white-haired actor, director and writer spoke about meeting Richard for the first time.

Emlyn Williams: "It was during the war. I was casting a play of mine called *The Druid's Rest*, which required Welsh youths, and they were hard to come by. All the boys of seventeen or eighteen were at the point of being called up—it was 1943.

"Richard's schoolmaster, Philip Burton, rang me up and said that he had this promising boy in Port Talbot. Philip spoke of him glowingly. He brought the lad to my hotel in Cardiff. I had already seen about fifteen applicants that day and I was rather discouraged.

"Then the boy arrived and I was immediately struck with this very spectacularly handsome lad. And he read—it wasn't an enormous part I had to offer, but it was a very effective one. He read a few lines and I knew at once that he would be excellent."

At the same time that Richard applied for a role in Williams's play, Welsh-born Stanley Baker was also a candidate. Although three years younger than Richard, he had appeared professionally—a small role in a film called *Undercover*—and supposedly knew "all the angles." Williams, however, chose Richard for the part and made Baker his understudy.

Baker became a highly successful British film actor and television producer. He died in the summer of 1976 of lung cancer, a month after being knighted by the Queen. The gristly-looking, square-faced theatrical personality was best known for his tough-guy roles—two of his outstanding movies were *The Cruel Sea* and *The Guns of Navarone*. Despite his serious illness, with death less than three months away, he insisted on speaking of his lifelong pal.

Sir Stanley Baker: "I met Richard when I was fourteen. He was three years older, but there were so many similarities, we became solid friends. We both came from Welsh valleys—depressed valleys. Both our fathers went down to the pits. My father, however, had but one leg. Richard was prone to steal that detail for himself. Several times I'd hear him weave stories about his one-legged father who worked in the mines. My stories!

"I was big for my age—as big as Richard. We both had sponsors who actually believed we could be actors, dedicated teachers who, for some strange reason, had taken an interest in two deprived youngsters. They were certain that without their help and guidance, we'd face an impossible life, and they were bloody well right.

"When I got resentful and told Richard he got the part in *Druid's Rest* only because he was older, he'd reply, 'No, my dear boy. It was due to talent. Sheer talent.' The way he said it, we'd both burst out laughing. It's impossible to remain angry with Richard. Once, in London, Richard did something that upset Elizabeth fiercely. She refused to talk to him. He started making weird faces and got her laughing. Soon they were in some bloody embrace.

"Both of us learned a great deal about acting from Emlyn Williams. Richard was a quick study but hated the drudgery of rehearsal. However, he would adopt the suggestions and use them for the next show. He'd gripe and tell me his father's theory: 'If you're pleased to do something—do it well. But why corrupt yourself doing it when you could drink beer?' "

Richard may have inherited some of Daddy Ni's insight. He told Baker, "Why be an actor if you can't be the best?" Then he would join Stanley, and the two youths would go carousing.

Baker: "The show opened in Liverpool and later ran in other cities. The fact that we were mere lads didn't stop us from making the rounds of pubs. There was one in Cardiff called The Six Tits that we particularly liked. Most of the times it was filled with large groups of completely worthless characters. Richard called them 'lovely, thieving thugs.'

"We had money jingling in our pockets—I received five pounds and Richard ten. A great deal more than we would have earned in the mines! Once, however, we didn't have money to buy drinks, so Richard decided to put his story-telling ability to good use. He was filled with stories—knew more fucking stories than Solomon ever did—and he could hold audiences spellbound.

33

"In his most commanding fashion, and Richard can be commanding, he started to tell a sad tale about a very powerful miner who possessed the strength of Hercules and could do the work of twenty men. We were standing near the bar, and soon all the disreputable cutthroats gathered round to listen. Richard knew he had their complete attention and went on:

" 'One day this very powerful miner found his wife cheating on him and laying for their neighbor.'

"At this point, Richard indicated he was thirsty, and one of the patrons bought him a beer. 'And one for my friend,' he said pointing to me. When the drinks were served, Richard went on. He told his eager audience how the angry miner physically pulled the bloody bugger apart. He used dramatic gestures that Emlyn had taught us. When he came to the balls being ripped off, he practically gave a blow-by-blow demonstration to a poor sailor who was standing next to him.

"I believe we got ten free beers apiece that day."

Richard credits Baker with introducing him to sex. "I knew nothing about it," Burton says. "There I was, acting in Liverpool, and met this girl, Lil, who was an usherette and who was willing. I took her home, and Stanley, who was with me in the theater, said, 'Go on, boyo, it's wonderful.' "

Richard remembers taking an interminable tram ride to Lil's home. Her parents were upstairs, and the young couple sat on the floor in front of the fire and made love. Or tried to.

"It was a painful experience," he says, "and I was filled with a blind horror and worry. I fell asleep and dreamed I was in hell. I felt guilty and I was suffering the torments of the damned in hell and I was set on fire. I awoke to find I was actually on fire. My foot was burning because it was in the fireplace. I had, needless to say, all my clothes on.

"I did not learn anything about sex from Lil. My real education in that department came later at Oxford. I met a girl student older than I was, and she showed me what to do. I have never had any problems ever since."

If his sexual performance wasn't so good, his acting was. Newspaper critics agreed he was admirable in *The Druid's Rest*:

South Wales Evening Post: "Richard Burton as Glan is an accomplished performer."

Liverpool Standard: "The part of Glan was competently played by Richard Burton."

London Express: "Richard Burton is a skillful actor."

In the spring of 1944, Richard, who was appearing in London's St. Martin's Theatre, gave notice. He was off to Exeter College at Oxford University.

3. A Taff at Oxford

RICHARD HAD BEEN AT OXFORD ONLY A FEW DAYS WHEN HE HEARD AN upperclassman refer to him as "that *Taff* from the provinces." Saying "Taff" to a Welshman is like saying "Mick" to an Irishman— and in this case the Welshman was a notorious scrapper from a brawling mining town. Although his opponent was older, bigger, and on more familiar ground than he, Richard promptly waded in.

It was a memorable fight, and a rapidly growing crowd of under-graduates gathered to enjoy it. For a long five minutes the two young men belabored each other; since most of their blows landed, the crowd had plenty to cheer about, and did so lustily. In short order, Richard's right eye was blackened, and both his cheeks were raw; the upperclassman was bleeding from nose, forehead and chin. Burton finally managed to pin his opponent and win an apology. The onlookers applauded. Richard was an actor to the bone. A performance was a performance, an ovation, an ovation, no matter what the circumstance, so he bowed—at which point, the upperclass-man swung again. A school official happened along just in time to stop the battle from resuming.

(Reminiscing about his opponent, Richard—who has a tendency to embroider a story with each telling—now maintains, "The bugger was at least seven feet tall, and must have weighed 350 pounds!")

A few weeks later, Richard had better things to think about. Professor Nevill Coghill, the much respected Merton Professor of English Literature, was casting a student performance of Shakes-peare's *Measure for Measure*. Richard rushed to Coghill's office to ask for a part.

Nevill Coghill: "I remember the very first time Richard knocked at my door. He asked if it would be possible to read some poetry for me. 'If you think me worthy,' he said, 'perhaps you could find me a part in *Measure for Measure.*'

"I can still hear his melodious Welsh voice. I was enchanted by his reading—I hadn't heard anything comparable since Gielgud did *Hamlet.* All I had left was an understudy role in the play, and I offered it to Richard. He accepted, but soon he was onstage playing the part. I thought so much of his performance that I asked Hugh Beaumont, the managing director of one of our leading theatrical production companies, to come see him. Beaumont, who was equally impressed, suggested that Richard call him in London as soon as he finished his RAF service.

"I have been most fortunate: I have taught two students of genius. W. H. Auden and Richard Burton. I still recall a note I made against Richard's name on an undergraduate list more than thirty years ago; I wrote, '*This boy is a genius and will be a great actor. He is outstandingly handsome and robust, very muscular and has deep inward fire!*' "

Coghill and Richard maintained contact throughout those thirty years. When Elizabeth Taylor was introduced to the distinguished professor, she was impressed by his academic air. "What wouldn't a casting office give," she said, "to have him play the role of a professor. Why, he has a bell in every tooth!"

Richard still remembers warmly the encouragement and help Coghill gave him. "Recently," says Coghill, "Richard invited me to a party he was giving, but I'd been ill and couldn't attend. He's always very kind and gives me some of the credit for his brilliant success. But I'm sure he would have risen to the top without my assistance."

But at Oxford, Richard was still a long way from the top. The university's accelerated course for future RAF pilots was designed to take less than a year, but according to Burton, he learned as much as most students do in four. Nonetheless, to this day, he has mixed feelings about his time at Oxford. In a black mood, angry and defensive, he is apt to announce, "I'm the best-damned educated man in the world!" On a calm day, less bombastic and more sarcastic, he changes the story: "What did I learn at Oxford? Boozing. I learned to increase my capacity and swallow a pint in less than ten seconds."

And in moments of simple honesty, he says, "I suppose I'm a bit of a snob—I enjoy saying that I went to Oxford. But I doubt that Oxford appreciates it that much!"

It was not academics, however, but service in the Royal Air Force that was of paramount importance to Richard. As his Oxford days ended, his head was full of vivid fantasies of shooting down German planes and being hailed as a hero—possibly the last air ace of World War II.

Sir Stanley Baker: "The bloody bastard won't admit it, but in his own way, he's very patriotic. He was delighted to be in the RAF, finally fighting the Nazis. From the very beginning, he had been anxious for England to stop Hitler—he called him a 'mad dog' and talked about the havoc he had caused, especially to Jewish people.

"Richard is against all kinds of oppression and injustice. One of the important things he shared with Elizabeth was a sense of concern and love for the underdog—they contributed a great deal to worthy causes, especially to Israel. You see, Richard has never really left that poverty-ridden Welsh valley where the miners were treated so unfairly. Oh, he may not spend much time in Wales any more, but his heart will always be there. Until the day they put him in a pine box—or rather, a bloody golden casket—he will still be there among the slag heaps, fighting against social wrongs."

Whether it was prompted by visions of a hero's welcome, by simple patriotism, or by the desire to associate himself with a noble undertaking, Burton's goal of becoming a war ace was not to be realized.

"I never saw action," he admits sadly.

It turned out that his eyes weren't good enough to pass an RAF pilot's physical. Reluctantly, he agreed to become a navigator instead. His training began in England and continued in Canada, where he was shipped just in time to celebrate V-E Day in 1945, with all of North America.

Friends who knew him in his Royal Air Force days still recall him as a formidable boozer, a brawler—and not always instantly likable.

Two of these friends, Warren Mitchell and Vince Caruso, are from two totally different worlds. Mitchell, whose real name is Mick Missel, is now a British television celebrity, and Caruso a district manager for a kitchen appliance company—but they paint similarly vivid portraits of the young Burton.

Mitchell is known to millions of English television viewers as the star of *Till Death Do Us Part*, the British television show which inspired Norman Lear's *All in the Family*. He plays the English equivalent of Archie Bunker, intolerant and foul-mouthed. But in real life, Mitchell, who is Jewish, is a sensitive and articulate man.

Warren Mitchell: "At first I disliked Richard intensely, and I suppose the feeling was mutual. I had a strong idea that he was anti-Semitic. But as we got to know one another better—we were together for three solid years—I realized he was nothing of the sort. In fact, after he knocked a sergeant down for making disparaging remarks about rabbis, I made Richard an honorary Jew! Richard wouldn't tolerate any kind of prejudice. But he'd hate to have you think that he did what he did for reasons of fair play. He'd try to convince you that he simply liked fighting."

Richard's other close RAF buddy, Vincent Caruso, a lean, bold six-footer who wears a short beard, is the son of an Edinburgh barber. He also remembers a first encounter which produced very negative feelings.

Vincent Caruso: "When Richard Burton discovered that I was of Italian extraction, he insisted that I sing him the Figaro aria from *The Barber of Seville*. When I said I didn't know it, he said, 'All Italian SOB's know it—especially SOB's named Caruso!'

"I was about to belt him when he added, 'SOB's—sons of barbers.' We both laughed. He told me that he could sing the aria for me, in Welsh! And he did—I think. Maybe he faked his way through it, but he sure made it sound real. A few years ago I ran into him in London while he was still married to Elizabeth Taylor. He introduced us by saying, 'Elizabeth, I want you to meet Vince Rossini.' *Rossini*. I'll always wonder if he forgot my last name, or if it was his way of letting me know he remembered our first meeting. Rossini was the composer of *The Barber of Seville*.

"Anyway, he certainly wasn't prejudiced. 'I'll prove it to you,' he used to say. 'I'll fuck any race, creed or color!'

"He was always doing strange and wacky things. He organized a Welsh choir even though he was the only Welshman in sight. He arranged standing-on-your-head-and-holding-your-breath contests. He planned drinking bouts followed by tug-of-war competitions. Once he decided to perform a scientific experiment to see if it was possible to put your hand through a pane of glass without being cut. He proved his point by running through the barracks with two other men, smashing windows. They broke more than a hundred panes before they were caught, and they ended up spending seven days in the guardhouse. I can still hear him telling me, 'It was worth it—I didn't get a single scratch!'

"I'll tell you, he may not have shot down enemy planes, but he sure kept up the morale of his friends!"

Perhaps not *all* his friends. It was during this "strange and wacky" period that Richard got his nose broken in a restaurant fight over a tough steak. He had to have the nose set by an RAF surgeon, and it is still slightly out of line. When Philip Burton heard about the damage, he was very upset. "Richard kept it from me for a long time," he remembers. "He knew it would have provoked more anger in me than sympathy, because such escapades might have jeopardized his chances as an actor."

If Richard had no opportunity in the RAF to act on a stage, he performed successfully in a military courtroom.

Vince Caruso: "There was a prisoner-of-war camp not far away, and one of the Italian POW's was accused of raping a local girl. Richard was considered the ideal man to help the defense. Furthermore, he had studied Italian at Oxford, so they asked him to talk to the man and get his story for the defense. Richard was all excited about it. But when the two men met, they found out they weren't speaking the same language at all. Richard had learned a kind of literary medieval Italian, and the other man spoke some modern dialect from the provinces. But Richard managed to understand one thing: The woman the POW was accused of raping was a local tart everybody knew as 'Docking Lil.' That did it. The defense went to court and, with Richard acting as interpreter, claimed 'Docking Lil' raped the prisoner instead of the other way around—and they won."

Richard celebrated the victory in his customary fashion: fifteen straight drinks accompanied by recitations from *King Lear*, *The Merry Wives of Windsor*, and of course, one of Shakespeare's Italian plays, *The Merchant of Venice*.

4. Sybil

BACK IN ENGLAND AND FINALLY FREE FROM MILITARY OBLIGATIONS, Richard headed for London to pursue a career in the theater. He had three excellent reasons:

1. "Acting pays well—much better than working in the mines, or even being a navigator."
2. "I'm good at it and it doesn't seem to require too much work."
3. "If Stanley Baker and Mick Missel can do it, so can I."

Remembering that while he was at Oxford, Hugh Beaumont had offered him a job when he got out of the RAF, Richard sought out Beaumont and was promptly signed to a contract with Tennent Productions that guaranteed him ten pounds a week. His first role, a small part, was in a play called *Castle Anna*. He also understudied the male lead, but alas, no miracle occurred; the star did not fall ill and give Burton his big chance to dazzle audiences and critics.

Richard's acting, however, did not entirely escape critical notice. One reviewer wrote, "One of the better features in *Castle Anna* is Richard Burton. The young man gives tangible evidence that we will soon be hearing from him."

In 1948, after one more minor stage role, Richard was invited to join the cast of *The Last Days of Dolwyn*, a film that Emlyn Williams had written and would now direct. The two men quickly developed a warm friendship, and Richard began to spend his weekends with Emlyn and Milly Williams at their London flat or their country home. The Williamses' son Brook (who is today Richard's production manager and close friend) idolized Burton. Next to Elizabeth, Brook probably knows Richard best.

Brook Williams: "I'm twelve years younger than Richard, and when we met, those years made quite a difference—he was a man and I was a child. But he's always had the ability to get on famously with people of different ages. It was fun introducing him to my friends because he became their friend, too.

"Richard once bought me an elegant, highly polished pair of roller skates. It wasn't my birthday—Richard never needs a special reason to give presents—he just thought I should have skates, and that he should show me how to use them. He produced an imitation of a trumpet flourish, strapped the skates on his own feet and hobbled out to the road. He turned out to be a fine skater. I was very impressed. I can still remember watching him disappear gracefully around the corner. But he didn't come back for hours, and when he finally did, he was carrying the skates in his hands. They were broken. He told me—with profuse apologies—that he had skated for miles when he suddenly met a tree that refused to get out of his way. He promised to buy me another pair of skates, but now that I think about it, I don't remember that he ever did. Well, if he reads this—though he doesn't usually read things about himself—I'm sure I'll find a pair of skates waiting for me. Richard is like that. Admirable."

Brook's father, Emlyn, also admired Richard—but not some of his habits. Their friendship grew during a time when Richard was spending a great deal of his time with the kind of women euphemistically called floozies. Richard insisted he saw them out of mere kindliness. "I don't like to hurt anyone's feelings, and when they smile at me I just have to respond by being nice. So, naturally, one thing leads to another."

A psychiatrist might offer a different explanation: Many people—including successful and talented individuals—often crave adulation to such an extent that they surround themselves with less impressive companions who will offer uncritical praise at all times. But Emlyn Williams didn't spend much time analyzing his hot-headed, hot-blooded young friend; instead, he took action.

Emlyn Williams: "It was high time for Richard to stop going out with floozies, and so I contrived his meeting with the girl who became his first wife. It happened like this: During the casting of *The Last Days of Dolwyn*, I rang up the London Guildhall School of Music and told them I wanted several Welsh girls for the film. Among the candidates was a pretty girl named Sybil Williams. She was charming and I engaged her for a small walk-on role.

"She was eighteen years old at the time and it was her first film.

She had such refreshing naivete—simply bubbled enthusiasm. I could also see that she had great beauty, intelligence and charm.

"I told Richard that the time had come for him to date a nice girl. 'There's one,' I said, pointing to Sybil. Richard liked what he saw and took her out.

"They had similar backgrounds. Sybil, too, was born in a Welsh mining village. Her mother had died when she was very young, and like Richard, she had been raised by an older sister. Richard saw that she was not only pretty but also a versatile conversationalist with a keen sense of humor. I was delighted to attend their wedding."

The marriage took place early on a Saturday morning in February 1951, at the Kensington Registry Office in London. A simple reception was held for the newlyweds at the home of a friend, but the just married Mrs. Burton had to leave both groom and guests to appear in a matinee performance of *Harvey*, in which she had a small role. Richard consoled himself by tuning the radio to the Scotland-Wales Championship Rugby Match.

When Sybil returned, she found Richard deep in gloom—not because his bride had left him so quickly, but because Wales had lost the match to Scotland, 6 to 5.

As it turned out, Richard's bride brought him luck. Soon after they were married, he played Henry V on the radio. The critics raved about his performance and were quite as smitten with his screen performance in *The Last Days of Dolwyn*, just then released. Typical of the ecstatic reviews was one that appeared in *News of the World*, England's mass-circulation weekend paper: "This twenty-two-year-old possesses the fire of great acting allied to good looks, a manly bearing and an innate tenderness that renders his love scenes so movingly real. . . . Richard Burton, this column salutes you. Like it or not, you are destined for the pinnacles of fame."

At the beginning, Sybil appeared with Richard in several productions, and when they played together at Stratford, some of her reviews were markedly superior to his.

"That," says Richard with a smile, "was when I told her, 'dear, the time has come for you to pack it in!'" And at the end of the run, Sybil did, saying goodbye to her promising career without a backward glance. She was an old-fashioned girl, whose real dream was wedded bliss, and she knew her husband held the Welsh belief that a wife's place was in the home. From then on, she stayed home, and she bore Richard two daughters, Kate and Jessica.

What sort of woman was Sybil at that time? Lovely to look at, slender of figure, delicate of feature, with a delightful, warming smile. (Today, at forty-four, she looks much the same, though her hair is prematurely gray.)

Richard's family adored her. Said his youngest brother, Graham Jenkins, "Sybil was a gem of a sister-in-law—I could see how deeply Richard was devoted to her." And Cecilia, the sister who raised Richard, added, "Sybil is the most amazing girl. From the beginning, it never mattered to her what Richard did, or wanted to do—she would always say, 'All right.' Rich would leave for somewhere in the morning and say he'd be home for lunch. Perhaps he wouldn't come home till late that evening. And Sybil would never chide him, the way almost any other wife would do. She understood him from the very beginning. She loved him. I couldn't have been happier when they married. Or have chosen a better girl for him."

And indeed, Richard often compared Sybil to Cecilia. "Sybil has Cissie's kindness," he'd insist. "And her goodness. And her charm."

Yet, the impetus that would eventually drive Richard to leave Sybil may have been already present. For Sybil apparently was not as much like the beloved Cissie as another woman would prove to be. In a sketch Richard wrote in longhand about his childhood in Wales, he says, "When my mother died, my sister [Cecilia] had become my mother, and more mother to me than any mother could ever have been. I was immensely proud of her. I shone in the reflection of her green-eyed, black-haired gypsy beauty. . . . She was innocent and guileless and infinitely protectable. She was naive to the point of saintliness and wept a lot at the misery of others. She felt all tragedies except her own. I knew that I had a bounden duty to protect her above all other creatures. It wasn't until thirty years later, when I saw her in another woman, that I realized I had been searching for her all my life."

The other woman was, of course, Elizabeth Taylor. When Richard left Sybil for her, Graham Jenkins asked in wonder, "Can a man love two women at the same time? Certainly Richard has lost none of his deep regard and affection for Sybil." And years later, Jim Backus (film comedian and a close friend of Richard's) was to insist that Burton was capable of loving not only one, or two women at the same time, but three, the last one being his third wife, Susan. "Richard," says Backus, "is not like other people. Even his heart is bigger. There is room in it for Sybil, Elizabeth, and Susan—although I don't think

44

that, lovely lady though Susan is, there will ever be anything to rival the fairy-tale adventure of Richard and Elizabeth."

Shortly after Sybil gave up her career to please Richard, her husband was recommended for a role in a new play by Christopher Fry, *The Lady's Not for Burning*. John Gielgud was to be the star. Richard had always regarded Gielgud as the greatest of all living actors and tried to make the Gielgud style his own. The day of his audition, Richard was talking with some acquaintances in a theater hallway and volunteered an imitation of Gielgud. His audience was delighted by Richard's letter-perfect portrayal, but all at once they fell silent and stared straight ahead.

Burton turned around and saw why: John Gielgud was standing directly behind him. The internationally known actor said icily, "My dear boy, generally speaking, very good impersonators do not make good actors!"

Despite the embarrassing start, Richard got the role and learned a good deal while working with Gielgud. "His influence on me was so profound," Burton says, "that I had a devil of a job getting rid of his particular way of speaking. To this day I still do gestures which are strictly Sir John's. . . . I so wanted to be like him."

Richard does not hesitate to add Gielgud's name to the list of others, like Professor Coghill at Oxford, who were instrumental in his success as an actor.

Sir John Gielgud: "Richard tells people that I made him a star. Rubbish! He had tremendous ability and it came through. It was simple to detect that ability in *The Lady's Not for Burning*. He gave a most marvelous performance. He has kept a quality that outstanding actors must possess—curiosity.

"He has always been splendid to work with. More recently, when we did *Hamlet* together, Richard would arrive at rehearsals early and leave late. He would constantly ask questions about the production:

" 'How tall do you envision the Ghost?'

" 'How shall I open the nunnery scene?'

" 'Are Rosencrantz and Guildenstern vicious or only weak?'

"Richard had a tendency to shout, but a simple word of caution was enough. He's a superb performer—beautiful to watch."

Not long after Richard appeared with Gielgud in *The Lady's Not for Burning*, he and Sybil purchased a house in the Hampstead section of London. Even though Richard's success seemed assured, they were extremely cautious about money and decided to live in the upper section of the house while renting out the downstairs rooms.

Sybil: "We weren't taking chances. I performed most of the household tasks like cooking and cleaning. Richard would return home late from work. He was trying to do so much. One night after I went to bed I heard voices in the parlor. Evidently Richard had brought John Gielgud home with him—I could hear them talking. There was no mistaking John's voice—it is so smooth and melodious. This time he raised it some and exclaimed, 'My dear boy, this place is a bit of a mess! I do see buckets and buckets of dust all around! Doesn't Sybil ever clean your digs?'

"I was mortified and angry. Why, I had just cleaned the place! I put on my robe and stormed out. But there was no Gielgud. Richard had fooled me utterly. He was always an outstanding mimic, and he had been impersonating John Gielgud for my benefit. With Richard, there rarely was a dull moment."

5. Burton-on-Avon

ONE NIGHT IN 1951, AFTER RICHARD BURTON HAD GIVEN A SPECTACULAR performance as Prince Hal in a Stratford-on-Avon production of Shakespeare's *Henry IV*, several members of the House of Lords came backstage to congratulate him. Richard, still in costume, greeted them, accepted their praise graciously—even bowed. So far, so good.

Then the spokesman for the titled bluebloods made a mistake. He remarked that it was most pleasant "work" to compliment an actor of Burton's excellence on his abilities. This time it was not Richard the actor but Richard the miner's boy who responded. "How refreshing," he said coolly, "to learn that you gentlemen do *some* kind of work! But perhaps you can strengthen your roles a bit. I know that your branch of Parliament has little power, but I'm sure Commons would agree to your introducing a bill forcing princes, earls and dukes to spend a year working in the mines!"

There is no record of the comments of the lords as they left Burton's dressing room. Undoubtedly, they wished that they had remained on the audience side of the footlights, from which it was possible to come away with only the most positive feelings about Richard Burton.

Even the critics were rhapsodic. Wrote Kenneth Tynan of the London *Observer*, "A shrewd Welsh boy shines out with greatness. . . . His playing of Prince Hal turned interested speculation to awe as soon as he started to speak. In the first intermission, the local critics stood agape in the lobbies. Burton is a still, brimming pool, running disturbingly deep. At 25 he commands repose and can make silence garrulous. . . . If he can sustain and vary this performance . . . we can safely send him along to swell the thin company of living actors who have shown us the mystery and the power of which heroes are capable." John Barber of the London *Daily Express* was equally enthusiastic: "A young Welsh boy jumped on the back of this play as if it were a fiery charger and rode it to triumph. His Prince Hal is noble without arrogance, graceful without effeminacy, handsome without dullness."

When Richard followed this triumph by playing Ferdinand, the young romantic hero of *The Tempest*, a critic declared that "Burton's 'Let me live here ever . . .' in Act IV galvanized last night's assemblage into hysterical applause. If their exuberance was any indication of their affection and esteem, Stratford will shortly be renamed 'Burton-on-Avon!' "

It was heady stuff for a virtual novice. But Richard Burton had larger dreams. He would appear not only at Stratford but on the legendary stage of London's Old Vic Theatre. He would not only appear at the Old Vic but would star in a production. He would not only star but would be called back for more than a dozen curtain calls.

At twenty-nine, Richard Burton made it happen. In 1954, starring at the Old Vic in *Hamlet*, he was called back for an incredible 18 curtain calls.

What made Burton so remarkable in a world peopled with great talents, many more highly trained, more experienced than he? How did he appear to a typical English theatergoer of the time? Let's listen to a quintessential Londoner, Fanny Blackburn, for nearly fifty years an Old Vic regular, who has been blessed, as she puts it, with "the eyes of an eagle and the ears of a hound dog," explain it over tea and tiny tomato sandwiches in her charming, cluttered London parlor (a photo of herself posed outside the Old Vic with Richard Burton and Elizabeth Taylor sits proudly upon a battered grand piano).

Fanny Blackburn: "I could see and hear what others could not—the slightest movement, the faintest undertone. I tell you, Richard Burton was brilliant. Everything he did was pure gold.

"I was privileged to sit up close, observing the greats. Sir John Gielgud in *The Tempest*, Sir Laurence Olivier in *King Lear*, Sir Ralph Richardson as Cyrano, Dame Sybil Thorndike in *Coriolanus*, Dame Edith Evans in *As You Like It*, Sir Alec Guinness in a modern-dress performance of *Hamlet*. I saw them all.

48

"But great as they were, none of them compared to Richard Burton. We will probably never see a more perfect performance than the one he gave as Hamlet. His presence, his voice, his movements—he never wasted a single motion. Such great gifts!

"I actually shivered when he spoke to the Ghost. And when he cried, 'I say, away!' to his friend Horatio—that was one of the most electrifying moments I have ever experienced in the theater.

"Years later, he brought Elizabeth Taylor to the Old Vic. I have to be upright and admit that I was a bit waxy at the idea of her intrusion into that world. I had heard that she had to be handled with white gloves, that she was very brittle. But when I saw them together in person, they were such a tender-looking couple. She had such magnetism, she reminded me of Edith Evans. A beautiful, glowing, sensitive woman. I thought, if only Richard and Elizabeth were a bit younger, what a magnificent Romeo and Juliet they would make. They gave me their autographs, and my friend took the photograph of the three of us."

Fanny Blackburn's final comment was particularly provocative. "All of the other great performers at the Old Vic have been knighted. Why not Richard Burton? He only has the C.B.E."

Others have asked this question. And the answer seems plain: It is not any lack in his stage performances; it is, rather, a certain excess in his off-stage behavior. The abrasiveness of his encounter with the peers after *Henry IV* would not encourage England's Queen to place Richard Burton higher on her Honors List. Nor would Richard's penchant for repeating an irreverent tale of his meeting with a far greater personage: Sir Winston Churchill.

Churchill, a lover of Shakespeare's plays, came to see Burton in *Hamlet*. Knowing the play by heart, the great English Prime Minister followed the drama word by word, and after it was over, he pronounced Richard's Prince Hamlet "the most virile and exciting performance I've ever seen."

But what happened between the acts?

According to Richard Burton: "The 'Old Man' was sitting up front in the stalls, and during one of the intermissions, he came backstage. He entered my dressing room. I was prepared for plaudits.

"Churchill was not one to shilly-shally. He came straight to the point, and in a most distinguished tone, he asked, 'My Lord Hamlet, may I use your lavatory?'

49

"When Churchill finished and buttoned his trousers, I was on the point of asking a prop man to erect a sign over the toilet: *Here's Where Churchill Sat*!"

Many years later, when he told the story to Elizabeth Taylor, she was not amused. "Richard," she said in annoyance, "you make it impossible for them to give you a knighthood! You seem to want to be made Lord Richard of the Men's Room!"

Even when Richard wasn't doing outrageous things, or telling outrageous stories, strange things had a way of happening to him. In 1965, when he reviewed a biography of Dylan Thomas for the New York *Herald Tribune*, he wrote of one such incident. Burton was backstage at the Old Vic one night when he received a phone call from the great—but dissolute—Welsh poet, Dylan Thomas.

Richard wrote, "I was thrilled, for I was still in awe of his overwhelming personality and macroscopic genius. He said he was with my father, my foster father, and that my foster father had suggested that he, Dylan, ring me and ask for two hundred pounds for the education of his children.

"I was quite poor—I was earning forty-five pounds a week and had been saving for a car. In awe and agony, I debated whether to sell my flat and get two hundred pounds for Dylan. Of course, I should have, for Dylan died in New York shortly afterwards, and he might not have if I'd given him two hundred pounds and he had, may be, stayed in Britain.

"I told him I didn't have the money, but perhaps I could get it—but it would take time. However, he wanted it immediately, and he talked for a long time and said he would give me the rights to his new play for the two hundred pounds. When I asked if I could read it, he said he was surprised and delighted to find I could read, but in any case, he hadn't written it yet, and that it was about a love affair between two streets.

"He told me about it on the telephone, and it was marvelous. But unfortunately, it went with Dylan to New York and stays stuffed in his head with him in Langharne. It was moving and Godlike and beautiful, not in retrospect and because he was five feet six inches and is now six feet deep, but it was magnificent wrought magic then, at that time, in Hampstead, at midnight."

In the meantime, stories about Richard Burton were spreading beyond the London-Stratford theater world. In Hollywood, they heard intriguing tales of the virile, exciting young Welshman who

50

was winning critical raves, enticing theatergoers by the hundreds to queue up for increasingly hard-to-get tickets to his performances, and keeping the gossips busy as well. Twentieth Century-Fox offered to sign him for three films at $50,000 each.

Richard accepted the contract and celebrated, as always, with too many drinks and a poetry recitation—this time a gloomy speech ("Here, upon this bank and shoal of time . . .") from *Macbeth*, which expressed (more or less) the misgivings he had about abandoning Shakespeare for movies, London for Hollywood, and art for money.

The next morning Sybil poured him onto the transatlantic plane; she planned to join him in several weeks. He waved a weak goodbye. His last, whispered words were, "No more whisky for me. From now on I'm going to fit into the Hollywood life. I'll change my drink to bourbon."

6. "Glorious, Funky Hollywood"

THE FILM CAPITAL WAS ACCUSTOMED TO UNUSUAL PERSONALITIES, BUT this young Welshman was an original. One publicist for Twentieth Century-Fox said, "I swear on my mother's grave this guy is for real! His own shtick is a thousand times better than anything I could dream up in my wildest nightmare!"

With his unpressed blue tweed trousers, catchpenny green corduroy jacket, unshined black shoes and shaggy brown hair, Burton quickly became the focal point for endless gossip. He was tagged as the nonconformist's nonconformist. Fellow actors discussed his exploits. Hard-shelled bartenders were awed by his drinking performances. Beverly Hills hostesses compared notes about his antics.

Here are some of his choicest gambols:

• Frugal by nature, he recoiled at the high prices in Hollywood. On the set of *My Cousin Rachel*, a Daphne du Maurier thriller in which he co-starred with Olivia de Havilland, he addressed the female members of the cast: "My good ladies," he told them, "I can ill afford these Herculean exactments. To offset them, I beseech you to put something extra in your lunchbags that is intended for me. For your troubles, you will have my undying affection."

The next day he received three Swiss cheese sandwiches, four hard-boiled eggs, a thermos of vichyssoise, three pieces of apple pie, six bananas and five peaches. Each donor received a kiss.

• At a party in the home of producer Nunnally Johnson, Burton spotted Greta Garbo and sat next to her. "May I squeeze your knee?" he asked.

The great lady was flabbergasted, but before she could reply, Burton placed his hand on her right knee and squeezed. Then he smiled, bowed and departed.

Later he explained to Sybil, "When I was a child, Miss Garbo was regarded as the Queen of Moviedom. Now when I tell my sister that I exerted delightful pressure on Miss Garbo's knee, she'll know that I've really arrived!"

● While *The Robe* was being filmed, gossip about his relationships with other women bounced like a rubber ball around the studios. His reply? "I was recently accused of breaking up ten happy homes. Why, I hardly know some of those women. I don't want to appear seeking the role of a swaggering egotist, but after all, there's little I can do to prevent Hollywood females from seeking me out."

● At a cocktail party, he and Humphrey Bogart, well lubricated, ran into a dignified-looking guest who said that he had been raised by an English nanny. Bogey asked him, "Did you fuck her?"

Before the startled man could answer, Burton said, "Unless you did, you can't possibly lay claim to being a proper member of the bloody ruling class!"

Bogey and Burton walked off guffawing loudly. Bogart then asked a blue-haired *grande dame* type, "I've got to take a leak—can you direct me to the men's room?"

Burton winked as he added, "The real truth is that we are *that way* about each other and we need privacy!" Guffaws and another round followed.

● Dining with Kenneth Tynan, the producer and critic, he talked about the possibility of appearing in a forthcoming Tynan film. Burton explained why it didn't work out. "He offered me a role in his movie but warned me, 'You'll have to show your ass.' I asked him how much that would be worth?

" 'Not much,' Tynan replied. 'It's a low-budget picture.'

"All of me reddened," said Burton, "including my posterior. End of deal."

● At the Stewart Grangers', Vivien Leigh was astonished to hear the voice of her husband, Laurence Olivier. She thought he was back home in London. She rushed into the next room and discovered it was Richard Burton mimicking the world-renowned actor. "Richard was letter-perfect," said the British beauty. "His tone, enunciation, dialect were superb."

● While filming Edna Ferber's *Ice Palace* in Alaska, Burton was having a few quiet drinks with Jim Backus in his hotel room. Suddenly a huge chunk of ice slid down a mountainside and crashed into the side of their hotel. Burton looked out, surveyed the damage and called the room clerk. "I say, my dear fellow, I asked room service for some ice for our drinks, but don't you think this is a bit much?"

● One evening, at a benefit for hemophilia, he told the audience, "I've been a bleeder all my life. Acting in Shakespeare, I was constantly called upon to duel, and although I know which end of the sword has the point, I occasionally was cut. That was why I came to Hollywood, where I hoped to escape from those sanguineous roles. But what did I find? In glorious, funky Hollywood, you don't resort to dueling to draw blood—you do it in more subtle ways." But to show that he didn't bear any grudges, he borrowed a cane and gave the audience a lesson in dueling.

Burton earned more than a half-million dollars for his first eight movies, and that sum soon soared. Five years from the day he started filming *My Cousin Rachel*, he returned to Pontrhydyfen in a shiny new Rolls Royce, bought drinks for everybody in the Miner's Arms and confided that he also owned a Cadillac convertible. He pointed out that it was a bit difficult, even for him, to be in both vehicles at the same time. While the appreciative patrons guzzled their free beer, he told them about his villa in low-taxed Switzerland, where he now made his home between movies.

He was doing well—very well. But the feeling that he was compromising his integrity as an actor had begun to gnaw at him. Some perceptive miners in his home town saw this clearly enough through his posturing. Years later, one lank, pale old man, long since retired from the pits, would say, "He may have accumulated great abundance, but in spite of the great joy he had in showing off, some of us could see a wee bit of sadness in the boyo. Although he cock-a-hooped about having plenty in Swiss banks and the cars and homes, he was like a candle, a candle that puffs up real bright, and then, the next minute, a wind blows and the flame gets low."

Generally, Burton would ignore or ridicule gossip columnist Louella O. Parsons's movie criticism, but he went into a black funk when she wrote, "What Welsh actor has gone Hollywood and forgotten about his Stratford-on-Avon days? Soon his Shakespearean talents will surely slip away and never return!" He remembered that Louella had once called him "one of the most delightful and unaffected actors ever to come to our town."

At the time, Richard's agent was Hugh French, an Englishman who could be cast as a distinguished country squire in a West End

54

play. In his early sixties, he has retired from the agency business and is currently a film producer. Sipping hot coffee in a Hollywood hotel, he recalls a talk he had with Sir John Gielgud in Rome many years ago. French said, "John has been my friend for a long time and has never been one to avoid telling the truth. 'I think that Richard is possibly the greatest young actor of our time,' he told me, 'but I do hope he doesn't forsake the stage.'

"Richard settled for films," French said. "It pays a great deal more, and he's been wonderful in them, but still they are two different mediums, and during those years, he missed appearing live each night. He would often talk of turning to the stage while making a movie. Time after time he would say to me, 'Hugh, when I finish this one, I'll definitely do a play.' But somehow he never did."

Burton knew that much of what he did in Hollywood was cinematic junk. But he reasoned that even junk could be gilded and made to seem brilliance. "If you're going to make rubbish," he said, "be the best rubbish in it." He tried and often succeeded, though a number of his films were box-office flops: *Seawife*, *The Prince of Players*, *Bitter Victory*, *The Bramble Bush*, *The Rains of Ranchipur*, *Ice Palace*.

He took the money, the Cadillacs and the best dressing rooms, but he never rationalized, as many film stars do, that the pictures he was making were "entertainment for the masses." When a film stank, he knew it and showed it. He would actually hold his nose while reciting his lines. Once, to dramatize how he felt about a movie, he came on the set wearing a gas mask.

In 1960, Alan Jay Lerner and Frederick Loewe, authors of the long-running *My Fair Lady*, planned to turn T. H. White's *Once and Future King* into a musical called *Jenny Kissed Me*—later changed to *Camelot*. They wanted Richard to play King Arthur in their version.

Burton protested that he could only sing bawdy Welsh ditties in barrooms, but he bowed to their persistence and the promise of $4,000 a week. *Camelot* came to New York with a three-million dollar advance, the largest ever in show business.

The first-night audience at the Majestic Theatre and the critics agreed that Burton was sensational. A critic for the Associated Press wrote, "Hurrah! Richard Burton has come home and we're the winners!"

For the next eight months, Richard was Broadway's fair-haired boy, and enthusiastic crowds gathered outside the theater when he entered or emerged. They applauded, cheered and stamped their feet in approval. He acknowledged their praise but sometimes replied in mock horror, "What, no whistles?"

Inside his dressing room Burton had a full-stocked bar. Holding his customary vodka and tonic, he traded witticisms with a steady stream of distinguished visitors: Laurence Olivier, co-star Julie Andrews, Alec Guinness, Mike Nichols, Alfred Lunt, Lynn Fontanne and other theatrical luminaries.

Mayor Robert Wagner made him an honorary fireman after he had doused a backstage fire with tonic water. The New York Botanical Garden named a rose after him, and the zoo called a baby fox "Richie." He won a Tony award for the best actor in a musical. A columnist wrote, "The greatest Welshman to ever hit New York."

Once again, however, the movies beckoned. Soon, Burton would be tapped to play Mark Antony to Elizabeth Taylor's Cleopatra, and one of the most bizarre episodes in film history would be played out as the world watched.

Two

The Girl from Hampstead

Far more beautiful than any woman in this waning age.
—*The Taming of the Shrew*

1. From Hampstead to Hollywood

"DID IT ALL START WAY BACK IN OUR CRADLES?" ELIZABETH WONDERS. "Perhaps the reason Richard and I couldn't make it work was that, although we were both born in Great Britain, maybe we were really born worlds apart."

Indeed, Elizabeth's childhood was the antithesis of Richard's. While he had to fight poverty, Elizabeth was born into a world of comfort, art and beauty—and rapidly became that world's most cherished treasure.

She began life on February 27, 1932, in the fashionable upper-middle-class section of London called Hampstead. Her parents, Sara and Francis Taylor, had one older child, two-year-old Howard. Howard was an extremely attractive youngster, but he was promptly and permanently eclipsed by his violet-eyed baby sister. The doctor who delivered the 8-1/2-pound Elizabeth called her "the most enchanting baby I'd ever seen," adding that "by the time she was six months old, she was a beauty."

The beauty was welcomed into an interesting and ambitious family. Her parents were Americans by birth and upbringing, English residents by choice. Francis Taylor was a successful art dealer; Sara had been an actress of considerable promise, appearing on the stage in Los Angeles, New York and London. When she retired to marry, a critic wrote, "Marriage has robbed the theatre of the beauty, grace and ability of Sara Sothern."

So it had, but Sara had every intention of restoring those lost charms via her daughter, who was obviously born to be the star her mother had not become. Elizabeth was certainly beautiful—people often told Sara that her little girl looked like Vivien Leigh—and grace and theatrical ability could be cultivated.

59

Accordingly, the Taylor daughter was enrolled in voice and ballet classes at the age of three. And not in just any little neighborhood school, but in the kind that performed for royalty. On one occasion, when Elizabeth was not yet four years old, she and her classmates danced for Princesses Elizabeth and Margaret Rose. At the end, Elizabeth Taylor, clad in a white satin tutu, curtsied to the distinguished guests. And curtsied again—and again—and again. When, despite urgent whispers from the wings, she refused to leave the stage, the director brought the curtain down on her.

"Elizabeth, what *were* you doing out there?"

"Oh—they looked so nice, I just kept on!"

Despite the evident interest of mother and daughter, Francis Taylor did not suspect that his wife was planning a theatrical career for their little girl. He himself had a different vision. "That child," he commented once, when Elizabeth was still very young, "has such a remarkable knowledge of art that I wouldn't be a bit surprised if she ended up as curator of the British Museum!"

His appraisal was shared by others. One of them, Mrs. Nanette Bachmann, who was then a client of Francis Taylor's Bond Street gallery, had more respect for Elizabeth's artistic judgment than for her father's. Now in her seventies, Mrs. Bachmann still takes pride in telling visitors that one of the paintings hanging in her extravagantly furnished duplex London apartment was selected for her by Elizabeth Taylor at the age of six!

It happened on a day when Mrs. Bachmann was seated in Taylor's gallery, indecisively contemplating a painting recommended by Francis Taylor. "I had grave doubts about it," she recalls, "but he liked it and I was wavering. Then Elizabeth came in with her mother, just a wee slip of a child—but exquisite. She took one look at the painting I was considering—it was an outdoor scene, a forest in the snow—and burst into tears. It was obvious that she didn't like it at all; in fact, her tears just flowed and flowed. That was all I required. I refused the purchase.

"Then Elizabeth walked over to another painting, a picture of a man and woman looking at a bowl of fruit. She started smiling. I bought it at once. Imagine, the child was barely six, and she already had such definite ideas!"

(Years later, hearing the story, Richard Burton reacted with his usual mixture of admiration and resentment. "When *I* was six, I did lots better than Elizabeth. I was *paid* for my skill. My father taught me a song about a blind beggar, and his friends would give me a whole penny if I could sing it through without a mistake. Elizabeth was just a rank amateur. But I suppose it wasn't all her fault. At the time, art didn't pay too well.")

Elizabeth, however, was not a poor little rich girl pushed into precocity on a steady regimen of culture. Although her parents employed two servants and a governess and delighted in dressing their daughter in fashionable, expensive clothes, they also owned a very modest country house in the Kentish farmlands. There Elizabeth rode the pony they gave her one memorable Christmas, and lived an outdoor life.

"I had the most idyllic childhood," she remembers. "In Kent there were hundreds of acres to roam, and my brother and I made pets of all the animals we had—pet rabbits, pet turtles, pet goats, pet chickens. When the adults wanted to eat chicken, they had to buy one in town because we wouldn't let them kill any of ours. I loved them all—in fact, my plan at the time was to become a veterinarian. I wanted that quite desperately."

Whatever chance she might have had to fulfill either her own or her father's ambition for her vanished in 1939, when the outbreak of World War II impelled the Taylors to leave England for the safety of Los Angeles, where life revolved around the great film studios.

While Francis Taylor took over the management of a gallery, Sara established her family in a new home, quickly replacing their first house in Pacific Palisades with an immense Spanish-style mansion in Beverly Hills. Elizabeth entered the Hawthorn Grammar School, where most of the male students, after one look, offered to carry her books. Too shy to accept, she did her own lugging.

Among those who still remember volunteering their services is Tommy Tannenbaum, now a senior vice president at Universal Studios.

Tommy Tannenbaum: "Since both our last names began with *Ta*, Elizabeth and I were assigned to seats next to each other. Every day she'd smile at me and say, 'Good morning,' but that was far as it went.

"It wasn't enough for me, because I had a real crush on her. She was so beautiful, like a delicate doll. And that English accent! Finally I asked her brother, Howard, how I could make an impression on her. He suggested that I ride my bicycle past the house with my feet on the handlebars.

"So I dashed right home after school, changed my shirt, combed my hair, rode my bike to the Taylors' house and put my feet up on the handlebars. To make sure I would make an impression, I turned around on the bike and rode backwards. I thought I could see Elizabeth's shadow at the window.

"Of course, right in front of her door, I fell off. I bruised my bottom, but it was my pride that was really hurt, and the next day at school I planned to avoid Elizabeth altogether. But I had to sit next to her. You know what she said to me? 'You poor thing. I hear you cried. Did you hurt yourself?'

"I would have protested, but she said it so kindly, not poking fun at me but geniunely solicitous. We became friends, and I even got to carry her books. Then she left Hawthorn for a professional children's school, and that was the end of that."

And the beginning of a new life for Elizabeth.

It had to happen, of course. Even in Hollywood, Elizabeth's beauty was remarkable, and since juvenile stars like Shirley Temple, Deanna Durbin and Judy Garland were then very popular, it was not surprising that scouts for MGM and Universal sought out the Taylors, urging them to "put your daughter in pictures." Francis Taylor demurred, but when Elizabeth was nine years old, MGM offered her a contract at $100 a week ("a bloody fortune," according to Richard Burton. "At that age I'd never seen anything bigger than a bob!"). Universal topped MGM's bid by offering $200 a week in return for a seven-year option. By then Elizabeth's own ambitions had shifted. She wanted to be an actress "like my mother." For her part, Sara Taylor honestly believed that her daughter could combine a movie career with a reasonably normal childhood. Francis Taylor reluctantly agreed to let her try. The contract with Universal was signed.

Elizabeth's first film, *There's One Born Every Minute*, was a comedy about a much harassed inventor. Elizabeth played the tiny part of the inventor's bratty daughter, and the critics who panned the movie never mentioned her name. Universal was equally unimpressed. At the end of the year, the studio dropped its option, gave her a dismissal notice and sent her home—a ten-year-old has-been.

Perhaps it was because he couldn't bear to see his daughter hurt and rejected that Francis Taylor played an active role in renewing Elizabeth's career a few months later. One night, when he was on duty as an air-raid warden, his co-warden, producer Sam Marx of MGM, mentioned his difficulty casting a role in an upcoming film.

Marx needed a pretty little girl with an English accent. "That's my daughter," said Francis Taylor, who went home to tell Elizabeth she would be screen-tested the next morning.

No one in the family slept that night, which may be why Elizabeth and her mother turned up late for the test. Annoyed, Marx told them to forget it, but Sara Taylor was not to be put off. She begged for another chance until Marx irritably handed Elizabeth a script, telling her she had exactly five minutes in which to memorize several pages of dialogue. Presumably he expected her to fail. However, Elizabeth, who along with her many visible attributes possessed the hidden one of an excellent memory, came through brilliantly and was awarded the part.

The film was called *Lassie Come Home*. It wasn't really Elizabeth's film but even against the competition offered by a heroic collie and a long-suffering young boy (Roddy McDowall) she stood out. This time she was not only reviewed but praised.

Chicago Tribune: "A lovely-looking youngster named Elizabeth Taylor is a refreshing newcomer to films. Her eyes show glowingly in Technicolor sparkle. She makes a delightful companion for Lassie. Both are slated for a glorious future."

In terms of Elizabeth's career, the critic was right: she was assigned, in rapid succession, to small but interesting roles in *The White Cliffs of Dover* and *Jane Eyre*. *The Hollywood Reporter* observed that "young Elizabeth Taylor gets better and better with each succeeding movie."

School, however, was a very different and far less pleasant matter. California law required all children to receive at least three hours of schooling a day, and MGM provided classes for their young actors and actresses in what had once been producer Irving Thalberg's bungalow. Between films, the children assembled there; while they were actually working, they were visited on the set by teachers who attempted to cram ten or twenty minutes of instruction into breaks between takes, vanishing when the cameras started to roll and reappearing at the end of the scene to quiz the tired youngsters on what they had supposedly learned an hour earlier. On the set or in the bungalow, classes were often tense and strained.

One of Elizabeth's MGM schoolmates was George Crowley, a juvenile whose option was dropped when he "grew too rapidly" at the age of thirteen. Today Crowley looks back with gratitude upon his dismissal from MGM, and with pity upon Elizabeth.

George Crowley: "As a studio kid I had stomach trouble; the day I left, the stomach pains left. But Elizabeth stuck it out. She'd arrive early every morning with her homework done, all prepared, but too shy to speak up in class. The teacher would bawl her out in front of the rest of us because she thought Elizabeth hadn't studied. Then Elizabeth's lips would start to quiver as if she was going to cry.

"Once, I stopped those tears. It was a scorcher of a morning and I sneaked a bottle of soda out of my desk. Elizabeth was sitting in front of me. I still remember the starched yellow striped dress she was wearing. I don't know how it happened, but as I opened the bottle it slipped and the soda sprayed all over the back of Elizabeth's dress. She turned around, horrified, and I thought sure I was really going to get it, but she just burst out laughing. When the teacher asked what was going on, Elizabeth said, 'Nothing.' Both of us got double work as punishment.

"Well, Elizabeth became a big star. She's made lots of money, but I'll bet she has a separate heartache for every dollar. I ran into her a couple of months ago and she looked as if she had the weight of the world on her shoulders. I got the feeling she was worrying about which worry to worry about next."

Despite her shyness, Elizabeth was an excellent all-round student, with a flair for writing. Her most memorable achievement at the MGM school was a seventy-seven-page story, later published in book form as *Nibbles and Me*, about her adventures with a chipmunk given her by Lassie's trainer. Elizabeth, who never allowed the chipmunk out of her sight, kept him attached to her by day by a long string she wore around her neck, and let him sleep at the foot of her bed all night.

The chipmunk could be useful as well as amusing. On one occasion, bored to exhaustion by an endless studio interview with Hollywood gossip columnist Hedda Hopper, Elizabeth decided to introduce the reporter to Nibbles. Nibbles promptly darted up the columnist's sleeve, and Miss Hopper's shrieks of terror brought a studio guard to the rescue. Elizabeth apologized for Nibbles' "outrageous behavior." But when the shaken Miss Hopper ended the interview and went home, Elizabeth presented Nibbles with a goodie as a reward for "ingenuity."

It was her love for animals (who invariably returned her affection) that propelled Elizabeth out of her usual reticence when she heard that MGM was going to film *National Velvet*, the best-selling novel about a young English girl who rides a home-trained horse to victory in the Grand National Sweepstakes. To the millions of moviegoers who eventually cheered and wept over Velvet's moment of glory, it seemed that the role must have been designed for Elizabeth, but in fact, she had to fight the studio and her own body to get it. During her first interview with producer Pandro S. Berman, she was uncharacteristically insistent that she should play Velvet because she "so loved horses!" Berman turned her down. She was much too short, he explained, to be believable as a girl who must pass for an adult male jockey in the climactic scenes. "I'll grow!" Elizabeth retorted, and Berman, amused, told her that if she could grow three full inches before shooting was to begin in ninety days, he would consider her for the role.

Elizabeth accepted the challenge. For the next three months she gorged herself, did stretching exercises and prayed. Three months later, when she returned to Berman's office, she had grown exactly three inches! On February 4, 1944, Elizabeth began work as Velvet. Mickey Rooney, who also starred in the film, remembers Velvet—and Elizabeth—well.

Mickey Rooney: "She was terrific, but then she always is. That girl is a born actress. I know because I've worked with the best. Ninety-nine percent of the time you'd tell Elizabeth something about acting, and a minute later she'd get it right. That's what I call being an honest-to-God professional. In *National Velvet* I played the part of a former jockey who lets a bad riding accident sour him. Actually, in real life, I was pretty fond of horses and knew a little something about them. I knew that the Pi, the horse Elizabeth had to ride as Velvet, was pretty ornery. He was a splendid-looking gelding, a grandson of Man o' War, but he was downright mean. I advised Elizabeth to steer clear of him when the trainer wasn't around. But what I said went in one ear and out the other. Even when the cameras weren't rolling she'd ride the Pi bareback. And he'd do things for her that he wouldn't even do for the trainer.

"The Pi and Elizabeth became so inseparable that the horse would follow her around the lot. For her thirteenth birthday, darned if the studio didn't give her the Pi for a present! Elizabeth was good with horses, but I suppose not so good with marriages. But then neither was I."

2. Velvet and Beyond

NATIONAL VELVET CHANGED ELIZABETH'S LIFE. A FINE FILM, IT WAS A box-office smash and established Elizabeth as a first-rank performer. MGM suddenly began treating the little girl like a great big star. At first Elizabeth scarcely seemed to notice her new status. Will Geer, the 73-year-old actor who plays the grandfather on *The Waltons* and who recently renewed his acquaintance with Elizabeth when both worked on *The Blue Bird* in Russia, remembers her fondly.

Will Geer: "Everyone who works with Elizabeth falls in love with her—she's quite a person. I was first smitten when she turned twelve, back when she was making *National Velvet*. I'd be on MGM's back lot and I'd see her going in and out of the schoolhouse—petite, lovely, charming, so well put together—and always so cheerful. She still is, you know—in Russia she even made the Russians laugh—and back then she'd prance all over the lot being cheerful. I guess I've always been a frustrated grandfather, and I sort of kept an eye on her. When *National Velvet* was released I preened all over the place as if I really were her grandfather. She didn't get a swelled head, though. She stayed a decent, lovable youngster in spite of all the praise."

The praise was heady stuff indeed. Clark Gable called Elizabeth's performance, "The best ever given by a juvenile," and Frank Morgan said the only possible response to it was, "applause, applause and more applause!" Irene Dunne described Elizabeth as "an enchanting child possessing an abundance of enchanting ability," while Agnes Moorehead predicted "a very glorious tomorrow" for her. Even Orson Welles climbed on the Elizabeth Taylor bandwagon. With perhaps only half his tongue in his cheek, he announced,

"The gods are elated at what they see, and smile down on our Elizabeth!"

Sara Taylor must have taken Welles's comment to heart, for the Taylor home on Elm Drive in Beverly Hills rapidly took on the aspect of a shrine. Every room contained large pictures of Elizabeth, scrapbooks filled with interviews and favorable reviews, plus costumes Elizabeth had worn in her films. As high priestess, Mrs. Taylor was her daughter's constant—and sole—companion, driving her to the studio each morning and remaining in attendance until Elizabeth was ready to go home. Sara Taylor even had her own special seat in the studio schoolhouse. Outside the studio, Sara was the ultimate arbiter of everything Elizabeth ate, wore and did; at the family dinner table, she invariably steered the conversation to Elizabeth's latest exploits and triumphs.

One of her favorite tales was of Elizabeth's confrontation with MGM boss Louis B. Mayer, the most feared of all movie moguls. Elizabeth and Sara had gone to Mayer's office to question him about Elizabeth's next film, and Mayer had taken offense. "How dare you come into this office," he screamed, "and tell me how to run my business? You," he bellowed at the shaken Sara, "and your daughter are guttersnipes. I took you out of the gutter and I can put you back there!" If Mayer had addressed himself solely to Elizabeth, she might have endured it in silence. But he had raised his voice to her mother, and that was not to be tolerated. Shy Elizabeth stormed across the room, leaned as far as she could over Mayer's massive desk, and shook her finger in his face. "Don't you dare to speak to my mother like that!" she shouted, burst into tears and ran from the room.

Sara stayed behind to patch things up. Evidently she succeeded. Elizabeth was cast in *Courage of Lassie*, *A Date With Judy*, *Julia Misbehaves* and *Little Women*.

How did the rest of the family react to Elizabeth's growing fame and the increasingly dominant role her career was playing in all their lives?

Her brother, Howard, tolerated the situation—as long as it did not impinge too directly on his own privacy. An extremely good-looking young man, he turned down numerous film offers, and once, when words would not discourage an especially aggressive talent agent, he shaved his head completely to avoid any chance of being cast in a movie.

67

Elizabeth's father worried, not about the impact of Elizabeth's career on his own life, but on Elizabeth's. Concerned that his daughter wasn't having a normal childhood, he tried to shield her from excessive publicity and intrusion. On Sundays he would take the phone off the hook, explaining, "The child is entitled to one day without interruption!" Francis and Sara Taylor separated briefly when Elizabeth was fifteen. When they reconciled, Hollywood assumed that their differences had been over the direction of their daughter's life and that Sara's view had prevailed.

And how did Elizabeth feel about her new-found fame? Behind the cheerful smile, the rarely broken facade of shy good manners, what was happening to the wide-eyed girl from Hampstead?

Remembering from the vantage point of many years later, Elizabeth called her childhood at MGM "a gauze-wrapped cotton-candy cloud. . . . I was so totally chaperoned that I couldn't go to the bathroom alone." Her parents, she said, with obvious sincerity, "thought they were doing the right thing and it was what I wanted. They're lovely people, and I'm deeply grateful to them." But she was all too aware that it hadn't really been "the right thing." When you live in a make-believe world, carefully protected from reality and responsibility, she discovered, "you're going to get hurt much easier because you haven't learned to take care of yourself." And once, looking back over all of the bruises, all of the mistakes, she cried out, "Why—why couldn't they let me grow up like Suzy Smith with a house in the suburbs, a husband who takes the 8:10, and three fat, saucy kids?"

Why indeed? Perhaps there was a point during Elizabeth's adolescence when her parents would have welcomed the chance to start all over, to guide their child along a different path. But in truth, ever since *National Velvet*, Elizabeth's life had not been securely in their control. She belonged less to her family than to a studio, to agents, publicity people, photographers, costumers, directors, coaches, makeup artists, fan clubs, and the huge, adoring and insistent public. Elizabeth, one might say, no longer had a career—rather, the career had her.

And a very nice career it was, too. It even impressed Louis B. Mayer. "She could play Dracula's daughter and draw crowds," he once mused. "I used to wonder why, and now I know. If the moviegoers are married, they want exactly that kind of daughter. If the moviegoer is a single girl, she wants to be just like Elizabeth. And if it's a single man, then he wants to meet an Elizabeth. It's that simple."

The fans didn't have to be American to love Elizabeth. A letter from Australia, addressed simply to "Elizabeth Taylor, U.S.A.," was delivered with no difficulty. So were thousands of more completely addressed letters from every corner of the globe. Louella Parsons, the syndicated movie columnist, wrote that "my mail has always been heavy, but no one has ever caused the letter writers to work overtime as has Elizabeth Taylor."

And in February 1947, when a newspaper headline blared LIZ GETS FIRST KISS, Clark Gable commented that "everyone knows immediately which Liz they're referring to!" The "King" added, with his usual wry grin, that Elizabeth was climbing very fast indeed. "I remember when she was just starting out and she came over to get my autograph. Well, the tables have turned. Now I want hers!"

That first famous screen kiss, which occurred in *Cynthia*, was bestowed upon a nervous Elizabeth by a young actor named James Lydon, star of the *Henry Aldrich* series. (Elizabeth's memory is at fault when she credits Marshall Thompson with the embrace.) Actually, the filmed kiss was not only Elizabeth's first, but her second, third and fourth, since director Robert Leonard insisted on numerous takes. "Elizabeth is a fine actress," he said, straight-faced, "but she's not yet well versed in puckering."

(Many years later, during one of the separations that marked the last years of their marriage, Richard Burton talked about Elizabeth's difficulties with her first kissing scene. "I'm not a bit surprised that she was reluctant; she's so very shy. And to kiss an outsider— horrors! But she's learned a lot since those days. How I miss her sensual, seductive lips. They could make a man feel like a king who had conquered the world!")

The *Cynthia* kiss might have been amateurish, but it made the picture the most popular film shown at U.S. military bases all over the post-World War II world. According to Alfred Ferris, who served as recreation officer and was responsible for morale at an American base in Tokyo, "I was charged with 'furnishing amusements in such a manner that soldiers enjoy themselves while on the post'—and Liz's smooching in *Cynthia* was all the entertainment the men needed. When she got kissed, the entire camp went wild. The noise was so loud and enthusiastic it made the artillery fire seem like nothing. In the end, I just threw the army regulations to the winds and gave the guys what they wanted—I had that kiss shown over and over and over again!"

Back home, movie theaters across the country were conducting "Why I Deserve to Be Kissed by Liz" contests. In Spokane, Washington, a 17-year-old boy decked out in his father's tuxedo told an audience, "I deserve to win because I hardly ever bathe, and after Liz kisses me I promise *never* to wash again!" He was topped by a 20-year-old sailor who claimed that although he had sailed all over the world—Hong Kong, Pago Pago, the Fiji Islands and Suez—and had had plenty of chances, "I kept my lips pure for Elizabeth." The sailor brought along a buddy to testify to the truth of his story, and the audience loved it, but Elizabeth turned it down. She knew exactly where her next kiss was going: to Peter Lawford, the young British actor who played opposite her in *Julia Misbehaves*.

"Peter," says Elizabeth, "was the last word in sophistication as far as I was concerned. He was terribly handsome, and I had a tremendous crush on him. The whole cast knew how I felt. In the scene where he had to kiss me, I was supposed to say, 'Oh, Rock, what are we going to do?' and instead I said, 'Oh, Peter, what am I going to do?' The whole company fell down laughing."

By the time she was sixteen, two important things happened to Elizabeth. First, she became one of MGM's biggest moneymakers, enabling her mother to talk the studio into raising her salary to $1000 a week. (When Richard Burton was sixteen, his *yearly* salary was less than half that amount.) Second, she became—to all outward appearances—a woman, five feet three inches tall, 105 pounds—and stacked. "Our child star," said Louis B. Mayer, "has suddenly developed an elegant bosom and become a fully formed lady." He ordered her clothed and photographed in plunging necklines and was delighted to discover that "the fans loved her even more."

Elizabeth's next role was a far cry from the timorous adolescents she had been portraying. She was to play the wife of thirty-eight-year-old Robert Taylor in a melodrama about a young woman who discovers that her husband is a Communist. The film was called *Conspirator*. It is one Elizabeth would like to forget, partly because it was a flop (although she got good reviews. *Variety* said, "Elizabeth Taylor . . . is given a big opportunity for an emotional and romantic lead and comes out with flying colors"), but mostly because she was on an emotional roller coaster while making it. "What I remember," she says, "is the MGM teacher taking me by the ear and leading me to the schoolroom. I would get so angry. After about fifteen minutes of high-school 'learning,' I would return to the set and play the part of Robert Taylor's wife, doing a torrid love scene with him."

The inner conflict was complicated by the fact that off-screen Elizabeth had no social life appropriate to her age; in fact, the most popular and beautiful young woman in America had barely had a date. "I was so busy working," she remembers, "that I simply didn't have time. Not even to think about it. In the studio school we weren't allowed to daydream, so I used to escape to the girls' room and do my daydreaming there. I was going to meet a tall, handsome prince, and he'd carry me away."

In short order, the tall, handsome prince showed up; he was army officer Glenn Davis, the former West Point football star. An MGM publicist arranged to have them meet at Malibu Beach; by no coincidence at all, Elizabeth was playing touch football when Davis arrived on the scene and was urged to join her team. The two struck up a conversation, and Elizabeth invited Davis to come to dinner at her house.

"I don't remember much about that night," Davis said later. "I just stared at Elizabeth—and I think she stared back."

Certainly there was something to stare at. They were both young, outrageously good-looking, and shared the problems and privileges of living in the limelight. The romance flourished. Hedda Hopper called them "the All-American couple." After a half-dozen dates, Davis offered Elizabeth an engagement ring, but her parents intervened. "A sixteen-year-old is too young!" Instead of the ring, Elizabeth wore Davis's gold All-American football on a chain around her neck. When the army shipped him off to Korea, she wrote to him faithfully every night.

But sixteen was indeed too young, and the prince never carried the princess away. Instead, William Pawley, Jr., son of the millionaire former ambassador to Brazil, appeared at the castle gate. Elizabeth, reveling in her new-found ability to play the part of a pretty, popular young girl off-screen, tearfully broke up with Davis and fell in love with Pawley.

At the same time, older men began to take note that the enchanting Miss Taylor was available for romance. Most prominent among them was multimillionaire Howard Hughes, who spotted Elizabeth one day in the lobby of the Beverly Hills Hotel and asked one of his entourage to arrange an introduction. To his surprise, Elizabeth, who was still dating Pawley, wasn't interested.

To Hughes, who was not only wealthy and famous but a major power in Hollywood, Elizabeth's disinterest represented a challenge. He promptly bought several paintings from her father's art gallery. Elizabeth couldn't have cared less. Hughes invited the whole family out to dinner. Elizabeth wasn't hungry. Hughes mobilized his network of informants. Whenever Elizabeth accepted an invitation to a party, Hughes made sure his name was added to the guest list. Elizabeth found out what was going on and countered by calling her hostesses to ask, "Is Mr. Hughes going to be there?" If the answer was yes for Howard, it was no for Elizabeth. Finally, Hughes gave up.

Bill Pawley, Jr., outlasted the great Howard Hughes—but not for long. Elizabeth was getting ready to give up dating for something she hoped—and expected—would be vastly more satisfying, something that would indeed "take her away from all this," providing her with the stability and emotional fulfillment she could not seem to achieve in the dizzying confusion of make-believe love scenes and schoolhouse restrictions.

Elizabeth wanted to get married.

3. The Marriage-Go-Round

Richard Burton: "Granted, Elizabeth has had many husbands. But she remains one of the most moral persons I know. Her severest critics may call her a scarlet woman, but they know her not in the least and therefore do her a grave injustice. In many ways, she is the last of the Victorian prudes!"

Number One: Nicky Hilton

THE FIRST SUITOR TO WIN ELIZABETH'S HAND WAS CONRAD Nicholson Hilton, Jr., son of the millionaire socialite hotel owner. Nicky, like so many other young men, fell in love with Elizabeth via her films and photographs; unlike the others, he had friends at MGM and hounded them unmercifully until he was introduced to Elizabeth. Elizabeth was soon as smitten as he was.

And with just as little substance to go on. "What do the two of you have in common?" a reporter asked as the romance became public property. "Oh, lots," Elizabeth replied blithely. "We both love hamburgers with onions, oversized sweaters and Ezio Pinza." To demonstrate their absolute compatibility, she and Nicky placed a Pinza record on the phonograph and posed for photographers in floppy Irish-knit sweaters, a pair of hamburgers at the ready. As the photographers were about to snap the first pictures, Elizabeth stopped them. "These hamburgers," she announced, "don't have onions on them! Let's be authentic!"

She wanted very desperately to be authentic when she and Nicky became officially engaged. She spent endless hours planning a storybook, middle-class future for the two of them. When it was pointed out that Nicky had a well-deserved reputation as a spoiled international playboy, Elizabeth nodded. "After we're married," she said firmly, "he's sure to change. I'll see to that."

In her heart, she wasn't so sure. As she got to know Nicky's family and friends, she saw clearly the gulf that separated their social worlds, their expectations of what life could offer. She was stunned to discover that the Roman Catholic Church, to which Nicky belonged, would not countenance their marriage unless she, raised a Christian Scientist, agreed to bring up their children as Catholics. At first she balked. Pressure promptly was exerted from the Hilton side of the aisle. To her astonishment, MGM took their side, urging her to give in. Elizabeth finally agreed, but a little of the bloom was off the rose. "I *want* my marriage to work," she confessed to a Hilton family friend. "It must work—we love each other. But oh, everything is against us!"

No one was listening. The whole world was getting ready for the wedding. MGM apparently saw it as heaven-sent publicity for Elizabeth's latest movie, *Father of the Bride*. The studio volunteered to produce and direct the nuptials and assigned top talent to the extravaganza: Helen Rose to create Elizabeth's bridal gown, Edith Head her going-away suit, and Ceil Chapman her trousseau. On the great day, May 6, 1950, studio guards and a cordon of police held back throngs of spectators outside the fashionable Church of the Good Shepherd in Beverly Hills. Studio limousines pulled up to disgorge stars as if for a premiere: Ginger Rogers, Fred Astaire, Spencer Tracy, Janet Leigh, Alice Faye, Dick Powell, June Allyson— it seemed as though all Hollywood was there.

And Elizabeth Taylor was just two months past her eighteenth birthday.

Spencer Tracy (Elizabeth's doting dad in *Father of the Bride*) summed up the ceremony: "I've been to many weddings, but this was the flossiest. Elizabeth and young Hilton made a charming couple—he's handsome and she was even lovelier than in our movie. Elizabeth had a cold and a slight fever and had to wipe her brow occasionally—but then, everyone was using a handkerchief. Ginger Rogers, Greer Garson—even I had to reach for mine. When it was all over, I heard a studio publicist say, 'I wish I'd had the hankie concession—that wedding was the tearjerker of all time!' "

MGM's official comment was briefer. The wedding, they said, was "made in heaven."

Throughout the courtship, Elizabeth had been as closely chaperoned as ever by her mother. Now, suddenly, she was on her own. The newlyweds left for a three-month European honeymoon paid for by Papa Hilton. They sailed aboard the Queen Mary, where the Duke and Duchess of Windsor were occupying the bridal suite. The Hiltons took another palatial suite, and one night dined with the Windsors.

One passenger who paid a great deal of attention to Elizabeth was Helen Williams, who felt that she and the young star had a great deal in common. Both were young (Helen was barely seventeen), both were newly married to extremely wealthy men (Helen's groom was heir to a fortune) embarking on an in-law-financed honeymoon, and both exhibited the same touch of defiance by wearing blue jeans (which were not yet fashionable) on the ultrachic Queen Mary.

Today, Helen Williams recalls that although she was frightened of Elizabeth, she was determined to make her acquaintance—not an easy job, since the young star was usually surrounded by people. Crowds of passengers collected wherever she and Nicky went, and there were several photographers who were making the crossing only because it would afford them the chance to take pictures of Mr. and Mrs. Hilton. On the next to last day of the voyage, Helen found Elizabeth unexpectedly alone, and quickly discovered that Elizabeth seemed even more frightened of her. Once they began talking, however, all barriers fell; Elizabeth, it turned out, was only too happy to have a young female friend in whom to confide.

"How many children are you going to have?" she asked Helen.

"I haven't thought about it much," Helen replied.

"Oh, *I* have," Elizabeth said eagerly. "I want at least four. Two boys and two girls." Laughing a little, she went on to detail other aspects of the fantasy she and Nicky were to share. "We want a house in the country, not the big white one with a picket fence that most people want, but a little gray shingled one with no fence at all. We want it to be in a wooded area, with a big lawn, lots of trees and a huge sandbox for the children. I'm going to do the housework—most of it—and the cooking."

Helen, who was finding Elizabeth disarmingly sweet and absolutely sincere about her dreams, was sorry when the conversation ended.

A few weeks later Helen had a far different impression of Elizabeth. Both were then on the French Riviera, and one night in a casino Helen spotted Nicky Hilton at the gaming tables. "He was playing for what looked like high stakes," she recalls. "After a moment, I saw Elizabeth sitting nearby, watching. I was struck by how different she looked. She had been so happy on the ship and now she just seemed melancholy. I wanted to go over to her, but something held me back. Maybe because I didn't know why she should look so unhappy."

Helen was not the only person wondering what had gone wrong so very quickly. Rumors were spreading from one side of the Atlantic to the other: The young couple was in bad trouble. Louella Parsons wrote, "The fights get nastier and nastier . . . the biggest blow-up came when they were in the south of France. Nicky left his bride alone night after night in favor of the gambling tables. This was a new and unbearable situation for Elizabeth. No man had ever ignored her before, chosen to be elsewhere when he could be at her side."

Elizabeth's father-in-law saw it differently. The big problem, Conrad Hilton believed, was that Nicky was not prepared for the crowds, the photographers and reporters who bedeviled him and his bride. Nicky wanted to ignore them; Elizabeth insisted on giving interviews. As a result, said the elder Hilton, "Nick was resentful, hot-tempered, and handled himself accordingly. Sometimes his temper really flared and he stalked out."

In September, Elizabeth and Nicky returned to California where she was scheduled to make *Father's Little Dividend*, a sequel to *Father of the Bride*. The Hiltons rented a house near the studio; it wasn't gray shingle, and there was a staff to do the cleaning and cooking. When Elizabeth reported to the set, producer Pandro Berman was shocked at what he saw.

"That girl looked so weary and forlorn," he says. "I remembered her as having a keen sense of humor. but she no longer thought anything was funny. She didn't laugh. She had lost twenty pounds and had become a chain smoker. She complained of pains, and doctors diagnosed colitis and an incipient ulcer."

Despite her misery, Elizabeth tried to put up a good show. She called the rumors of marital trouble "malicious gossip" and insisted

A Taylor family portrait. Elizabeth, age two, with her mother and brother. (Sygma)

The twelve-year-old Elizabeth with her co-stars in National Velvet, Mickey Rooney and Butch Jenkins. (Sygma)

Aboard the Queen Elizabeth, *Mr. and Mrs. Conrad Hilton, Jr., the most noted honeymoon couple of the 1950s.* (UPI)

Richard Burton and his wife Sybil in their first appearance in a Hollywood night spot in 1953. (Keystone)

*lizabeth with her second husband, Michael Wilding, and young Michael
*oward Wilding, Jr., in 1953. (UPI)

Richard in the 1953 Old Vic production of Hamlet. (UPI)

Elizabeth and husband number three, Mike Todd, at the International Film Festival in Cannes, 1957, where Todd's Around the World in Eighty Days *was shown. (UPI)*

The Burtons with one of their daughters in Rome during the film Cleopatra. (Keystone)

Elizabeth and Eddie Fisher, husband number four, in Italy during the ing of Cleopatra. (Sygma)

Mark Antony and Cleopatra, 1962.

Newlyweds Mr. and Mrs. Richard Burton attend the Tony Awards in New York, 1964. (UPI)

hat her fights with Nicky were nothing but "the harmless little spats all newlyweds have." But neither the marriage nor the coverup was tenable, and seven months after the "made-in-heaven" wedding, MGM released a statement in Elizabeth's name:

"I am sorry that Nick and I are unable to adjust our differences, and that we have come to a final parting of the ways. We both regret this decision, but after personal discussion we realize there is no possibility of a reconciliation."

Elizabeth might have realized it, but Nicky didn't. Stunned by his wife's departure, he tried to win her back by sending dozens of long-stemmed roses and making dozens of phone calls to her. Elizabeth would not be swayed. Furious, Nick told her off in abusive language.

Elizabeth moved in with her stand-in, Margery Dillon. To reporters who complained that she had not been frank with them, she said, "I suppose that ever since I was a child star I've been very secretive about my problems. Until the actual separation, I didn't admit there *was* a problem. I hope you understand."

At her divorce hearing, she said that Nicky had told her to go to hell and insulted her mother and friends. She wouldn't say much more and refused to allow her lawyer to offer further evidence. "I don't want to hurt Nick more than necessary," she said. "I don't want to sound like the wronged woman."

The divorce was granted on February 1, 1952; the grounds were mental cruelty, and no alimony was awarded; Elizabeth had requested none.

Nicky, still hurt and angry, said, "It was life in a goldfish bowl. One time a battery of reporters and photographers invaded our suite—it happened all the time—and one of the photographers said to me, 'Hey, Mac, get out of the way, I want to snap a picture!' "

Conrad Hilton said sadly, "They never had a chance. . . . Beauty was the prime cause of the breakup. Elizabeth is a princess who isn't allowed to lead a normal life, and those near her are affected, too. . . . If Elizabeth had been just a shade less beautiful. . . . if she had been a counter girl at Macy's instead of a movie star . . . if Nicky had been older, wiser, less headstrong . . ."

None of those things was true, and so the marriage was over. Seventeen years later, at the age of 42, Nicky Hilton died of a heart attack. Elizabeth grieved for him. "We were much too young," she said. "I'm so sorry I hurt him." Richard Burton offered an epitaph:

"His life couldn't have been totally unhappy. After all, he did live with Elizabeth for a while."

To keep Elizabeth from brooding over her shattered marriage MGM cast her in a romantic comedy titled, unfortunately, *Love I Better Than Ever*. Filming was delayed when Elizabeth caught the flu and had to spend a week in Cedars of Lebanon Hospital.

She returned to the set looking unhappier than ever. Louis B. Mayer's prescription was "Keep her busy at all times," and studio officials obediently began to pressure other stars to invite her to their parties.

It was at one of these gatherings, a brunch at the Bel Air home of Stewart Granger, that Richard Burton first saw Elizabeth. She was sitting by the pool, chatting with another guest. As if hypnotized, the twenty-five-year-old Burton made his way to her side. Elizabeth then nineteen, seemed to him "the most astonishing, self-contained pulchritudinous, remote, removed, inaccessible woman I had ever seen." Her face, he decided, was divine, but her breasts were nothing short of "apocalyptic, they would topple empires before they withered. Indeed, her body was a miracle of construction."

In fact, Elizabeth seemed to Burton so perfect that he abruptly became aware of his own physical shortcomings. "Every pockmark on my face became a crater of the moon." He lifted his hand to cover his cheek, and as he did so, it occurred to him that Elizabeth would probably find the hand "as ugly as the face." He lowered it and went on staring.

Eventually, he began to listen as well. Elizabeth was talking about an MGM producer she disliked intensely, and to Burton's astonishment, from those Mona Lisa lips emerged language that would have done credit to a dock walloper.

Burton's face must have registered his surprise and dismay, for Elizabeth finally acknowledged his presence. "Don't they use words like that at the Old Vic?" Taken aback, Burton heard himself reply that *they* did, but *he* didn't, having come from a family that believed such language indicated an impoverished vocabulary. When he walked away, he silently bemoaned the fact that Elizabeth Taylor's beauty was only skin deep.

His was a minority opinion, however. According to Louella Parsons, as soon as Elizabeth filed for divorce, "every male wanted to get into the act—including Howard Hughes."

This time, Hughes succeeded in getting a date with Elizabeth. It was not a great success. When he sent a car to pick her up and take her to the Beverly Hills restaurant he had selected, Elizabeth refused to budge unless Hughes came to her door in person. He came, escorted her to the restaurant, and asked the maitre d' to describe the vast variety of Continental dishes on the menu. After each description, Hughes added his own comments: "From the western part of the country, a great French dish," or "From the south, a great French dish." Elizabeth listened carefully. Then she ordered a hamburger. "From all over the United States," she said solemnly, "a great American dish." At the sight of the maitre d's stricken face, she added, "and a side order of French fries!"

Hughes was not put off by the putdown. He asked Louella Parsons and Sheilah Graham to tell Elizabeth what a nice fellow he was and how anxious he was to be considered a serious suitor. Elizabeth remained unimpressed. "I don't want to hurt Howard's feelings," she said, "but he and the others don't interest me in the least."

Stanley Donen, however, interested her mightily. She found the twenty-seven-year-old director of *Love Is Better Than Ever* sympathetic, witty and wise. The more she saw of him, the better she felt about herself. But when it became clear that she was considering marrying Donen, her family and the studio objected. Donen was Jewish. She had been badly hurt by one mixed marriage, they told her with supreme irrelevance—surely she didn't want it to happen again.

Elizabeth was bewildered. Until her divorce, she had rarely made an important decision in her life without leaning on others. Now she didn't know what to do. "This is so difficult to resolve," she said unhappily, and while she struggled with this dilemma, MGM came to the rescue with the suggestion that she go to England to star in *Ivanhoe*. Elizabeth was reluctant to leave Donen, but after much urging, she agreed to go to England "for a very short spell."

It was true that she would not stay long. But she would bring home with her a souvenir.

Number Two: Michael Wilding

ELIZABETH MET MICHAEL WILDING IN LONDON AND KNEW AT once that he was "everything I admire in a man!" Asked for

87

specifics, she spoke of Wilding's "trusting blue eyes," his aristocratic ancestry, his established position as one of Britain's most talented and popular stars, his ability to combine "sophistication with a warm, boyish quality" and concluded that above all "he possesses an abundance of tranquility, security and maturity—all of which I desperately need."

The fact that Wilding was twice her age was immaterial or, if anything, a virtue. Elizabeth, madly in love, could not understand why the debonair Wilding treated her like a charming but unimportant child. She began to load her face with cosmetics in an attempt to appear adult. He noticed. "Why," he asked, "does such a beautiful girl feel she needs all that makeup?"

Elizabeth was hurt, but not discouraged. In the end, she proposed to Wilding and he—rather to his own surprise—accepted. But not because he had begun to think of her as the mature woman she wanted to be. He felt, he said later, that she was a beautiful, helpless child whom he could protect and cherish.

On February 21, 1952, twenty days after her divorce from Nicky Hilton became final, Elizabeth became Mrs. Michael Wilding. The ten-minute ceremony took place in London's Claxton Hall, but the crowd outside was even larger than the one that had cheered her on her way to her first, disastrous honeymoon.

This honeymoon was different in every way. It lasted only eight days, and it was far from lavish. A waiter who served the honeymooners in the hotel in the French Alps where they celebrated Elizabeth's twentieth birthday recalls, "Mr. Wilding put a candle in a cup of *crème caramel* and sang ten choruses of *Happy Birthday*."

For a while they were very happy. They settled in Hollywood and, according to Elizabeth, had "a delightful and simple life. Even though there was a large difference in age, we were so much alike in so many ways. We both loved animals and nature. We both were babes in the woods where economics was concerned. We worried constantly about money and had to borrow from the studio and practically put our careers in hock."

A gynecologist had once told Elizabeth that she could not bear children, but when she had been married to Wilding for three months, she discovered that she was pregnant. Overjoyed, Elizabeth bought a closetful of infant clothes for both a boy and girl, and Michael, equally pleased, purchased toy electric trains and a roomful of frilly dolls.

MGM, however, was not amused. It was expensive when a major star took time out to have a baby. After hurried top-level discussions, studio executives decided to rush Elizabeth through a movie, *The Girl Who Had Everything*, "before she showed."

The script called for Elizabeth to play the daughter of a wealthy criminal lawyer (William Powell) who falls in love with one of her father's clients (Fernando Lamas), the boss of a gambling syndicate. It was a poor film, as the studio knew it would be, and Elizabeth was upset at having to work through her pregnancy, but, said one unconcerned MGM executive, "Anything starring Liz makes money, and that's what counts." To the young star, he said, "Can't you possibly speed things up and have the kid in six months, or seven?"

Elizabeth was planning on the conventional nine months, and she got them. She was not so fortunate in the delivery room of Santa Monica Hospital, where she had a Caesarian section rather than the natural delivery she had hoped for. Her doctor, however, did give in to her plea that she be allowed to see her baby born, and anesthetized her with a saddle block which allowed her to be awake during the delivery. And certainly Michael Howard Wilding, Jr., born on January 6, 1953, was worth staying awake for; like his mother at her birth, he was an extraordinarily beautiful baby. Elizabeth was delighted with him. All the unaffected warmth that had gone into her relationships with pet animals was now lavished on her infant son. She and her husband played with Mike, Jr., bathed him, fed him and adored him as if no one in the world had ever had a child before.

But the idyl could not last. The Wildings were rapidly running out of money. Michael's type of sophisticated, romantic humor, so popular in England, was of little interest in Hollywood—his career simply vanished. So, a few months after she brought her baby home from the hospital, Elizabeth reluctantly offered to return to work. MGM sent her a script at once. Elizabeth and Michael read it in dismay. They agreed that it was impossibly bad and that several critical flops in a row would damage Elizabeth's career. She turned down the film, and MGM promptly suspended her.

It would have been a financial disaster for the Wildings, but six weeks later Paramount Pictures asked MGM to let them borrow Elizabeth to replace Vivien Leigh, who had collapsed while shooting *Elephant Walk* in Ceylon. Elizabeth would make an ideal substitute because she was not only a box-office draw in her own right but remarkably similar to Vivien Leigh (as many people had observed when Elizabeth was a child) in coloring and stance, a fact which would enable Paramount to salvage a good deal of footage.

Elizabeth, who had done the finest acting of her life while on loan to Paramount for *A Place in the Sun* when she was seventeen, was delighted to work for them again. MGM, of course, played hard to get, agreeing to the loan only in return for $150,000 (paid to them, not Elizabeth) and an indemnity of $3,500 a day for "production delays" on a film they claimed the suspended Elizabeth was due to begin. In the end, *Elephant Walk* cost Paramount three million dollars and reaped uniformly dismal reviews. Elizabeth, however, was praised. "The movie is bad," wrote *Look* magazine's critic, "but [Elizabeth Taylor] is an honest actress, who can make an audience believe just about anything."

After *Elephant Walk*, Elizabeth made *Rhapsody*. Then, with their bank balance a little healthier, Elizabeth, Michael and their baby went to Europe for a vacation. "She badly needs some rest," said Michael. "In fact, it's that or a breakdown. She's never stopped working since she was a child."

(Years later, Richard Burton contemplated his wife's work schedule and said in honest awe, "Sometimes I wonder how she does it, day in, day out. I can't think of a star who is a more dedicated worker. It has become her way of life.")

Feeling better, the Wildings returned to Hollywood, where Elizabeth made two more films in rapid succession, *Beau Brummel* and *The Last Time I Saw Paris*. Elizabeth's reviews for the latter were excellent. *The New York Times* called her "delectable," and *Film Daily* said she "looked incredibly lovely." *Variety* called her performance "her best work to date . . . shows a thorough grasp of the character." And the *New York Herald Tribune* said that Elizabeth was not only "stunning" but "vibrant," and best of all, "she has a massive talent!"

On February 27, 1955, her twenty-third birthday, Elizabeth gave birth to a second son, Christopher Edward, born, like his brother, by Caesarian section. The Wilding menage now included two children, a horse, a golden retriever, a wire-haired terrior, two poodles, two Siamese cats, two Maltese cats, seven rabbits and one duck. Louella

Parsons called the family "celestial." Hedda Hopper said they were "blissful."

Actually, the Wilding family was falling apart.

Many factors entered into the dissolution of what had once been a happy marriage. For one thing, Elizabeth no longer wished to play the role of little girl to Michael's older man. For another, her career was flourishing while his languished. An article in *Confidential*, a scandal magazine, alleged that while Elizabeth was on location filming *Giant* with Rock Hudson and James Dean, Wilding and his drinking pals had visited a notorious strip joint and brought some of the girls home for a party. The magazine was widely read in Hollywood, and although Elizabeth said, "You can't let an article like that break up your marriage," she was clearly upset.

Not long after, MGM's publicity department did for the Wildings what had been done for the Hiltons: It issued a press release announcing the end of the marriage. "Much thought has been given to the step we are taking," the Wildings were quoted as saying. "It is being done so that we will have an opportunity to thoroughly work out our personal situation.

"We are in complete accord in making this amicable decision."

Amicable it was, and so it remained. Elizabeth, sad but by no means bitter or angry, realized that the marriage had failed completely. "This wasn't a sudden, impetuous decision," she told Art Cohn, Mike Todd's friend and biographer. "We had been thinking about it for three years. It was something both of us agreed on. Life had no more meaning. I was dead, old at 24. It was just smog and no sunshine. We would wake up in the morning without hope, with nothing to do or talk about, with no reason for living out the day. At last we decided to separate and we took the step."

No reconciliation took place.

Number Three: Mike Todd

THE DAY AFTER THE PRESS REPORTED HER SEPARATION FROM Mike Wilding, another Mike entered Elizabeth's life—a man very different from the urbane, gentle Wilding. He was Mike Todd, the tempestuous, erratic and fascinating man who had just produced

91

Around the World in Eighty Days. He telephoned Elizabeth, insisting that he had to see her on "serious" business. Elizabeth, who had met Todd several times, assumed he wanted her to appear in his next film and agreed to meet him at MGM. But it wasn't a movie Todd had in mind. He met her in an outer office at the studio. Mike asked her to accompany him to an old office he had used in the Thalberg Building. There, he sat at his desk while Elizabeth perched on a couch, a coffee table between them.

There, in a gentle voice, nervous though he didn't show it, Todd told her he loved her, that she had hardly ever been out of his thoughts and that he was going to marry her. And all the while, he never reached out to touch her hand.

Elizabeth could not believe what was being told her. She sat as though mesmerized by the unreal proposal, or statement of purpose. "And yet," she would say afterward, "I knew it was like a prophesy and that every word would come true."

A week later, when Elizabeth left for Danville, Kentucky, where she was to star in *Raintree County*, Todd continued his strange courtship over the miles. Several times a day Elizabeth was summoned to the telephone to receive a long distance call from Todd; when she was not on the set, the calls sometimes lasted three or four hours and often concluded around five in the morning. Elizabeth could have refused them, of course, but by then, she was fascinated.

During these lengthy conversations she learned a lot about Mike Todd, a kind of man entirely new to her. Todd had been born sometime between 1907 and 1911 (he claimed he didn't know his age) as Avron Hirsch Goldbogen, the son of a rabbi. He considered himself essentially a peddler and had been selling since he was five years old—everything from newspapers, shoeshines and vegetables to real estate, talent and hit shows like *Mexican Hayride*, *Star and Garter*, *The Hot Mikado* and a dozen others. He had made, and lost, a million dollars before he was nineteen years old, had gone into bankruptcy in his mid-thirties, and expected to gross at least a hundred million dollars for *Around the World in Eighty Days*. He had been married twice (once to actress Joan Blondell), had a son who was at least Elizabeth's age, and a grandson. Although he had never graduated from high school, he liked poetry, literature, history and philosophy; he liked big cigars because they made him look affluent even when he was broke, and he loved Elizabeth because the two of them made the right kind of chemistry.

92

He was best of all at selling himself.

Home from location, Elizabeth began to see Todd regularly—and secretly, since she was by then wary of publicity. Mike, who usually relished seeing his name in the papers, deferred to her request for privacy and, in his usual style, made a flamboyant joke of it. On one occasion he took her to a dinner party and introduced her to the room full of strangers as Miss Lizzie Schwarzkopf (Yiddish for "black head"). During cocktails, one of Todd's friends examined Mike's date with interest and told her, "You know, you look a lot like Elizabeth Taylor, only heavier."

Todd roared and slapped Elizabeth's bottom. "See, Lizzie, I told you you're getting fat!"

(When Elizabeth told that story during her years with Burton, she often remarked that it was just the kind of thing Richard would do, too, which invariably brought from Burton a cheerful "What a backside to slap!" and of course, a whack.)

On November 14, 1956, Elizabeth filed for divorce from Michael Wilding on the *pro forma* grounds of mental cruelty. She requested $250 a month in child support, but no alimony. Then she and Mike Todd flew to Miami, where Todd chartered a yacht to take them to dinner on Nassau with the British newspaper magnate, Lord Beaverbrook. On the return crossing, Elizabeth slipped on a flight of stairs and crashed to the deck, landing on her spine.

She was, by then, accustomed to accident and illness, both of which plagued her continually. Todd, however, refused to take the incident lightly. He flew Elizabeth to New York and checked her into the Columbia-Presbyterian Medical Center, where x-rays revealed a mass of crushed spinal discs. Immediate surgery was recommended, and in the course of a five-hour operation, three spinal discs were removed and replacements fashioned from bone taken from Elizabeth's pelvis and hip.

Todd refused to leave her side for a moment. He moved into the hospital, and since he considered Elizabeth's room dreary, he dispatched an aide to purchase original paintings by Monet, Renoir and Pissarro—one for each of the walls Elizabeth could see from her bed.

Elizabeth was in the hospital for almost two months and left on January 21, still confined to a wheelchair. Her California divorce was not to be final until February, but she and Todd were in no mood to wait. (There was no longer anyone in Elizabeth's life capable of persuading her that interfaith marriages were doomed.) They flew to Acapulco, were granted a divorce there on January 30, and were married by Acapulco's mayor on February 2.

It was a very simple ceremony attended only by close friends, although half of Mexico seemed to show up later that evening when the Todds gave a tremendous reception. The highlight of the party was a brilliant fireworks display which the guests watched from a grandstand decorated with red satin bunting and fresh orchids. The pyrotechnic *pièce de résistance* lit up the sky with intertwined hearts bearing the initials E.T. and M.T.

Elizabeth was still in fragile health when the Todds returned to the United States, but clearly very much in love. Actor Ernie Kovacs summed up public opinion when he said, "Even by Hollywood standards this marriage seems to be for keeps. It should last forever—or at least three years. All kidding aside, they really like each other."

They really did. They traveled the world together, spending incredible sums of money, laughing, making love, poking fun at each other and themselves, everybody's favorite larger-than-life lovers. Even their spats were colossal. "Sure," Mike said cheerfully, "we have some hellish fights. This girl's been looking for trouble all her life, but everybody was always too nice to fight back—they kept her on a milktoast diet. With me it's the reverse—I'm good red meat. When Elizabeth flies into a tantrum, I fly into a bigger one. We fight because we love it. When she's mad she looks so beautiful that I want to take her in my arms and smother her with kisses. But I control myself—I fight—because it's so much fun to make up again."

With Mike Todd, Elizabeth was probably deeply happy for the first time since she left the farm in Kent.

(When Richard Burton would speak about Elizabeth's husbands, he rarely had anything but good to say about Mike Todd and often quoted a *New York Times* article describing the producer as a fascinating mixture of toughness and softness, business acumen and generosity. "May his soul rest in peace," Burton would conclude with unusual gentleness. And once, in a seedy pub on London's waterfront, he intervened in a fight between two strangers solely because "that chap that was getting his lumps looked like Mike Todd, and Elizabeth would never forgive me if I didn't help him out.")

When Elizabeth became pregnant, she and Todd were both

94

delighted and frightened, since Elizabeth's physical condition was still poor. Toward the end of a very difficult pregnancy during which she nearly lost the baby several times, Elizabeth was rushed from Westport, Connecticut, where she and Mike had been living, to Columbia-Presbyterian Hospital in New York, in premature labor. A nurse who attended remembers that Elizabeth was "in severe pain, and we were worried about the possibility of a ruptured uterus."

Again, Mike Todd simply moved into the hospital with Elizabeth. He begged the medical staff to give him something to do—anything at all—which might help. The nurse remembers opening the door to Elizabeth's room one night and seeing Mike, deep in prayer, reciting remembered Hebrew words from his boyhood.

Eventually, Elizabeth, sedated and exhausted, opened her eyes and spoke coherently—in fact, she made some trivial complaint about the flowers with which her room was crowded. "That was the first time I saw Mr. Todd smile," the nurse remembers, "and you'd have thought he was just made president of the world. He was just in ecstasy."

Elizabeth was sent home, but a week later she was back. Over her desperate protests—she feared the baby was not fully developed yet—doctors performed an emergency Caesarian and delivered a motionless infant girl who was miraculously coaxed to breathe and live.

"I never saw anything like Mr. Todd when we told him, finally, that both his wife and daughter were all right," recalls the nurse. "He kept shouting and picking me up in the air. I don't think I'll ever see anyone happier than that as long as I live."

Todd was so happy that he had to share it. While Elizabeth recuperated, he sat at her bedside and planned a party to celebrate his private joy and the first anniversary of *Around the World*'s premiere. "A small, dignified party," suggested Elizabeth. "Right!" Todd agreed, and arranged to invite 18,000 guests to Madison Square Garden. The sign on the marquee was in keeping with Elizabeth's notion. It read: A LITTLE PRIVATE PARTY TONIGHT.

Inside the Garden, everything was in readiness. There were 15,000 hot dogs, 10,000 egg rolls, 15,000 doughnuts, 10,000 slices of pizza, 2,000 gallons of vichyssoise, and a 14-foot-high birthday cake baked from 2,000 eggs and 1,000 pounds of cake mix. There was champagne and gifts (donated by publicity-minded businessmen) for the lucky; one Cessna airplane, six automobiles, 10 motor scooters, 25 hi-fi sets, 20 automatic toasters, 500 phonograph records, 10 ladies' revolvers (daintily tinted), 10 hot-water bags, 50 elephant bells, 400 boxes of imported cigars, 35 hundred-pound barbells, and 50 harmonicas. George Jessel was the master of ceremonies, and a kilted fife-and-drum corps was hired to pipe the 15,000 elegantly clad guests who had accepted the invitation, into the arena.

Unfortunately, thousands of gatecrashers were also piped in, and once inside, almost everyone became part of a screaming, clawing, furious—and above all, greedy—mob. The food, set up buffet style, disappeared before most of the guests could elbow their way to the tables. Waiters watered down the champagne and sold it to guests for $10 a bottle. Thousands rushed for the gift corner in such an onslaught that Elizabeth, seeing fragile, elderly Sir Cedric Hardwicke caught in the crush, dived into the mob to rescue him from injury. CBS-TV, which had paid Todd $300,000 for the right to film his "little private party," devoted an hour and a half to the debacle, the announcer later commenting, "I've worked in war zones, so I should have been prepared. But this scene of utter chaos defied me. Perhaps it can best be compared to mass battlefield desertions by both the winning and losing sides."

Among the earlier deserters were Mike and Elizabeth, who beat a retreat long before the fiasco ended. They went home—Mike in his black tie, Elizabeth in her diamond tiara—and toasted each other in genuine privacy, with real champagne. As long as they were together, they could still laugh, even when the joke was on them.

But they were not together long. Thirteen months after their wedding, Todd reluctantly left Elizabeth home in bed with bronchitis and flew in his private plane—*The Lucky Liz*—from Los Angeles toward New York, where he was to be honored at a Frairs Club dinner. The plane crashed in New Mexico; Mike and the crew were killed instantly.

Word was flashed to Todd's secretary, Dick Hanley, and Elizabeth's doctor, Rex Kennamer. Together, the two men went to Elizabeth's house, and up to her bedroom. She took one look at their faces, and knew. She ran screaming into the street in her night-clothes. Dr. Kennamer followed, caught her and led her back into the house where, mercifully, he put her under sedation.

Calls, letters and telegrams poured in. One wire read, "The President and I extend our deepest sympathy," and was signed Mamie Eisenhower. Twenty-four ambassadors sent condolences. Upwards of 10,000 people, according to police estimates, attended the burial in a Chicago cemetery, sitting on tombstones and jamming every inch of space. But most of them had not come to mourn. When Elizabeth knelt by the open grave to pray, the mob rushed her, screaming her name, trying to touch her and tear pieces from her clothes for souvenirs. The police could not protect her. Screaming hysterically, Elizabeth fought her way back to her limousine; it took ten agonizing minutes to reach it.

Home again in Beverly Hills she went briefly into seclusion and then emerged to finish the movie she had been making just before Mike's death; it was Tennessee Williams's *Cat on a Hot Tin Roof*, and Mike had been very proud of the serious and difficult acting job she was doing.

Clark Gable, who had lost his own great love, Carole Lombard, in a plane crash, was one of many who reached out to Elizabeth. "I know what it's like to lose someone you love," he said, "and I can tell you that Elizabeth is a real trouper. Three weeks later, she was back on the set. I hope she never knows trouble again."

It was a good hope, but a forlorn one.

Number Four: Eddie Fisher

BY NO COINCIDENCE AT ALL, ELIZABETH'S NEXT HUSBAND WAS Mike Todd's best friend. It was the only thing they had going for them, and it wasn't enough.

Eddie Fisher, born in 1928, was only a few years older than Elizabeth. He was a singer who, after comedian Eddie Cantor heard him in a Catskill hotel, rose rapidly in popularity. Good-looking, boyish and charming, he soon had a number of hit records, a large following of teenage girls and the ability to command as much as $250,000 for a single recording session. He became even more popular when he married another youthful star, perky Debbie Reynolds. "Never," said Hedda Hopper, "have I seen a more patriotic match than these two clean-cut, clean-living youngsters. When I think of them, I see flags flying and hear bands playing."

Eddie, however, was not much interested in flags and bands. His idol was flamboyant, incorrigible Mike Todd. Mike liked the boy twenty years his junior, and accepted his worship graciously. Elizabeth was less enthusiastic, especially about Debbie. Nonetheless, Eddie and Debbie were among the favored few invited to the Mike-Liz wedding, Eddie serving as best man and Debbie as matron of honor. When the Fishers' second child was born, they named the boy Todd Emmanuel in honor of Mike.

The relationship of the two couples is perhaps best described by a waiter who often served them at Chasen's restaurant in Beverly Hills. "It was a real ritual," he says, "always the same. First the women would order, then Todd, then Fisher. Whatever Todd selected, Fisher would ask for exactly the same. If Todd said steak medium rare, Eddie wanted steak medium rare. If Todd ordered sole slightly underdone, Eddie wanted the same thing. Then he would talk Debbie into changing *her* order to what he and Todd were eating, and when it came, Fisher even ate the way Todd did—fast. Liz Taylor, though, was something else. She had a mind of her own. Nobody dared to tell her what to have!"

It was not surprising that Eddie's reverence for Mike Todd increased after the showman's death and found its outlet in a protective attitude toward Mike's stunned and grieving widow. Leaving Debbie in Los Angeles to look after Elizabeth's children (as well as their own), Eddie accompanied Elizabeth to the Chicago funeral, talking incessantly about Mike. A grateful Elizabeth called him "a good friend and a tower of strength." She said, "I don't know how I would have gotten through without him. We both loved Mike so much, and Eddie showed it over and over. I suppose he became a link to my past with Mike."

Unfortunately, the link to the past soon became more than a present comfort. On her way to Europe after finishing *Cat on a Hot Tin Roof*, Elizabeth stopped over in New York and found Eddie there on business, without Debbie. At some point in the next few days they realized they were more than friends, and since reporters and photographers got the drift, too, the whole world quickly had a ringside seat.

And all hell broke loose. It might not have happened if the public had understood that the Eddie-Debbie marriage had not been a happy one for some time, but that was a well-kept secret. And so Debbie was cast in the role of the deceived and wronged wife. (Her sagging film career got a new lease on life.) Eddie was the cad who had taken up with another woman. (His career as an entertainer would never recover.) And Elizabeth (who lost the Oscar she deserved for *Cat on a Hot Tin Roof*) was instantly metamorphosed from an object of affection and sympathy to "Jezebel," "viper," "harlot," "thief," "destroyer," "cannibal," and "barbarian." A Swedish newspaper topped all others with the headline BLOOD THIRSTY WIDOW LIZ VAMPIRES EDDIE, but closer to home, serious newspaper editorials denounced her, fan magazines urged their readers to boycott her films, a California minister told his congregation that she should be "burned in effigy," and a Texas clergyman assured his followers that her soul would be "forever tormented in hell." Hedda Hopper took Liz to task for forgetting Mike, and when the badgered Elizabeth retorted that "Mike is dead and I'm alive!" and that "No woman can steal a happily married man," even Hollywood turned away from her. So memorable was the scandal that many years later when the widowed Jacqueline Kennedy was in the midst of an acrimonious public dispute with *Look* magazine, she summed up her own position by saying, "Anyone who is against me will look like a rat—unless I run off with Eddie Fisher!"

Despite the furor—or perhaps because of it—Elizabeth decided to marry the adoring Eddie as soon as Debbie divorced him. Shortly before their wedding, Elizabeth converted to Judaism—it was a step she had considered during Mike Todd's lifetime—and the Arab League promptly banned her movies. "I'm proud to be a Jew," Elizabeth announced. "Eddie and I have so much in common now. I love him dearly and plan to be Mrs. Fisher forever."

She surely meant it. Roddy McDowall, who had been her friend since *Lassie Come Home*, says, "Elizabeth has *never* entered a marriage without thinking it would last till death." But the situation with Eddie was a mistake from the start. During the ceremony which united her to Eddie on May 12, 1959, (and which was picketed by their angry ex-fans), Elizabeth was lovely in green chiffon, and it was Mike's son who served as best man. The newlyweds sailed on a honeymoon to Spain while "homewrecker" charges still appeared in newspaper headlines.

Elizabeth's next film, scheduled to be shot in London, was *Suddenly Last Summer*. The movie, based on a long one-act play by Tennessee Williams, dealt with homosexuality, insanity and cannibalism, and Elizabeth was strongly advised not to jeopardize what was left of her reputation by making it. But she respected Williams, and

London offered comparative privacy and peace for her and Eddie, so she accepted the assignment. It proved a great success with the critics.

Saturday Review: "Elizabeth Taylor works with an intensity beyond belief; hers is unquestionably one of the finest performances of this or any year."

New York Herald Tribune: "If there were ever any doubts about the ability of Miss Taylor to express complex and devious emotions, to deliver a flexible and deep performance, this ought to remove them."

Los Angeles Examiner: "Elizabeth Taylor plays with a beauty and passion which make her, in my opinion, the commanding young actress of the screen."

The next script MGM offered was entirely different. She was to play a call girl in *Butterfield 8*—which may have been an attempt to cash in on the still fresh scandal of *l'affaire Fisher*. Elizabeth indignantly refused, calling the script "pornographic." When Eddie pointed out that her expiring contract with MGM called for one more film, and that she could be prevented from working for two years if she refused to make it, Elizabeth began to suggest revisions which would make the movie less objectionable. After much battling and several suspensions, she yielded. She had won one important point: Eddie was cast in the movie as her song-writing Platonic friend.

If the Fishers hoped the film would mark the beginning of a new career for Eddie, they were disappointed. He would probably have been unacceptable to the public had he the acting talent of Olivier. He spent more than a year without a singing engagement before he was finally offered a two-week stint at the Desert Inn in Las Vegas. There was gossip that he was hired on condition that Elizabeth would be in the audience regularly, drawing the crowds, who were more interested in gaping at a "scarlet woman" than listening to a disgraced baritone—and certainly there was a pattern to Elizabeth's appearances. Promptly at 11:48 each night, two minutes before show time, she would enter the club and take her seat at a ringside table. After a few songs, Eddie would introduce her to the audience.

Elizabeth, looking cool and beautiful, would then rise and blow him a kiss. That was the cue for Eddie to sing directly to her.

But the melodies were not to last because the century's most sensational scandal was about to erupt.

Three

The Scandal That Shook the World

Double, double toil and trouble;
Fire burn, and cauldron bubble.
—*MACBETH*

1. New Sexual Honesty

YOUNG PEOPLE TODAY FIND IT HARD TO BELIEVE THAT BECAUSE Elizabeth Taylor and Richard Burton openly displayed their illicit love affair in 1962, reenacting in real life the romance of Cleopatra and Mark Antony that they were playing before movie cameras at the same time, they created a public scandal that became the biggest news story of that year. The blatantly unconcealed Taylor-Burton entanglement made even more headlines than the Cuban missile crisis, which brought the United States and the Soviet Union to the brink of nuclear war a few months later.

An extracurricular affair between two married celebrities would hardly be likely to stir up such an uproar today. In the much more relaxed moral and social climate of the 1970s, show-business stars can enjoy an open sexual relationship without the formality of matrimony and remain quite free from public disapproval. When Barbra Streisand, Hollywood's current big female box-office attraction, took a young former hairstylist, Jon Peters, into her house, she heard few complaints from the front office, and Peters was named producer of her six-million-dollar remake of *A Star Is Born*. Dinah Shore's national popularity as a television talk-show hostess was unblemished by her unconcealed romance with the much younger Burt Reynolds. Vanessa Redgrave never hid the fact that Italian actor Franco Nero was the father of her out-of-wedlock child in 1970. Liv Ullmann has talked freely about her five-year relationship with Ingmar Bergman, which began in the mid-1960s. "Living with him enriched me," she said. "I matured." Soon after their meeting, Liv became pregnant, but she said, "I wasn't afraid. I felt it was very right." Their baby, Linn, was born while she was making a film with

Bergman. While Liv was denounced in Norway, where she originally rose to prominence, for her unmarried motherhood, the Swedish people were far less upset and her career suffered not at all. By 1972, she was on *Time* magazine's cover, hailed as "Hollywood's Nordic star."

The list of other film stars who make their unmarried sex lives public without censor is almost as long as Sunset Boulevard. Some show-business people are even revealing themselves as bisexuals. Maria Schneider, the actress who starred with Marlon Brando in *Last Tango in Paris* and with Jack Nicholson in *The Passenger*, has admitted (in *The New York Times*, no less) that "I'm bisexual completely." Several major stars have publicly admitted having had bisexual experiences. The late Janis Joplin made no effort to hide her bisexuality and few cared. Actress-model Marisa Berenson has admitted she "adores" the company of homosexuals, that "I'd rather go out with a fag than a boring man any day. They are talented, sensitive, refined people who make the best friends." Such a statement two decades ago would have sent the public into deep shock, and a career into deep freeze, but today it barely ruffles anyone. Nor does posing in the nude present any problems; in many cases, it enhances a career. Marisa Berenson posed for *Vogue* wearing nothing but gold link chains.

Young people who are perplexed when they read about the shock waves stirred up throughout the world by the Taylor-Burton scandal do not understand the standards of moral and social respectability that all public figures, and especially the moving-picture industry's celebrities, were expected to observe in those more conventional times. Back in the early days of the silent movies, lurid newspaper stories about Hollywood stars being involved in divorce cases, sex orgies and dope addiction brought strong attacks on the film business from church leaders and other guardians of moral behavior.

Throughout the Bible Belt of the South and the Midwest, respectable families refused to let their children go to the movies because of the "perpetual sin." Along with the scandalous reports of bad behavior in Hollywood, the goings-on seen in the pictures themselves—loose women smoking cigarettes, drinking liquor and indulging in long and passionate kisses—were indeed strong stuff for those strait-laced and strictly conventional times. Box-office figures declined. The moving-picture makers panicked.

To save their image, the film companies banded together in 1922

106

and hired the highly respectable and conservative Will H. Hays, a former national chairman of the Republican Party, to clean up the industry. Ruling as president of the Motion Picture Producers and Distributors of America until 1945, he enforced the Hays Code of movie decency. The Hays Office refused to allow scenes showing a man and woman in bed, even if they were married and doing nothing except reading the Sunday newspapers.

The outspoken John Barrymore may have been prophetic when he said of the Hays Code, "Kind and good lecherous men like me will only be able to perform properly when the Hays nonsense evaporates into thin air. That time will come. Someone will defy the false and narrow morals. Oh, to be around on that glorious day—or night."

While the Hays Office was policing the movies, the studio bosses did their best to police the private sex lives of their stars in order to keep Hollywood's image wholesome and untarnished. Panic seized the movie companies again in the 1930s when *Photoplay*, the leading fan magazine, published an article entitled *Hollywood's Unmarried Husbands and Wives*, an exposé which revealed, among other shack-ups, the domestic bliss of Carole Lombard and Clark Gable, who was still married at that time to his much older second wife, Ria Gable.

David Niven wrote later in his memoirs, *Bring On the Empty Horses*, "It is difficult to imagine in these permissive days that such a dreary piece of journalism could so easily have put the cat among the local pigeons, but the cluck-clucking of disapproval first heard in the Bible Belt of mid-America became a rising crescendo of threats to box-office receipts by the time it reached California, and the big studio brass soon hauled their emancipated stars onto the mat and bludgeoned them into reorganizing their nesting habits. Clark and Carole, Constance Bennett and Gilbert Roland, George Raft and Virginia Pine, Robert Taylor and Barbara Stanwyck, Paulette Goddard and Charlie Chaplin were all mentioned in the article, and most of them bustled briskly off to their nearest priest, minister, or rabbi and toed the party line.

"Ria Gable played a cool hand with good cards, and Clark paid a stiff price to become respectable, so stiff in fact that whenever thereafter he criticized Carole, she was apt to crack, 'Well, what did you expect for a lousy half million, for chrissake—perfection?' "

The facade of conventional respectability in Hollywood endured unblemished for another thirty years. Ingrid Bergman, then the biggest box-office attraction in the industry, was blackballed and exiled from the film capital when she left her husband, Peter Lindstrom, in 1949 and ran off to Italy to make a movie for Roberto Rossellini and to become the mother of Rossellini's illegitimate son and namesake. Ingrid remained on the blacklist for many years.

At first the Burtons suffered the penalties of ostracism, too. Richard admitted, "We couldn't get the time of day from anybody. Nobody asked us out. The real friends, they stayed, but everybody else put us good and firmly on the outside."

Twentieth Century-Fox had invested a fortune in *Cleopatra* and insisted that their stars "cool it," but Richard and Elizabeth ignored the warning and continued their blazing love affair.

Dr. Ira L. Reiss, professor of sociology at the University of Minnesota and longtime student of marital and sex relationships, points out that the Burtons reflected the worldwide changes then underway in sexual mores. "They were a sign of the times," he says, "people who were fitting in with the currents then moving in a more permissive direction. The changes in sexual mores had deep roots in altering male and female roles, and the Burtons were a reflection of those changes as they embodied themselves in a couple of wealth and high professional standing."

Dr. George O'Neill and Nena O'Neill, the husband and wife anthropology team who wrote *Open Marriage*, which describes a new sexual life-style for couples, believe that Richard Burton and Elizabeth Taylor spearheaded the new honesty in sexual behavior. "Of course," Dr. O'Neill points out, "the basic changes were already underway; the old morality was slipping away though many were unaware that the revolution had arrived. Had they done what they did a decade before, their popularity would almost surely have been severely damaged. The *Cleopatra* scandal came along when our institutions were altering; we were questioning old values and trying on new ones for size. Because they were so much in the public eye, and because it is still true that all the world loves a lover, they were not only able to ride over the turmoil but to help speed up the revolution in moral standards."

In agreement is Dr. Joyce Wike, professor of sociology and anthropology at Nebraska Wesleyan University, and distinguished authority on changing sexual customs. She says, "Men and women have long engaged in society-frowned-upon activities like extramar-

tal affairs but were fearful of the consequences if they were discovered; loss of prestige and loss of job were certain to follow.

"Then along came Elizabeth Taylor and Richard Burton, who
were not only found out but readily admitted it. They didn't change
sexual standards overnight. However, they helped supply the
needed impetus. Celebrity leaders—even those who don't profess to
influence—are very necessary. We reason, 'If they can do it, why
can't I?' "

2. Fifteen Minutes to Live

A FIVE-HOUR FILM ABOUT THE WHOLE TORTUOUS STORY OF THE PRO-
duction of *Cleopatra*, the most troublesome, the longest and the
costliest moving picture ever made, would be much more interesting
than the show itself. Such a documentary account would start on
September 30, 1958, when Walter Wanger, the veteran producer of
many famous and successful movies, first discussed a Cleopatra
movie with Spyros Skouras, the president of Twentieth Century-
Fox in the company's New York office. Wanger had just joined Fox,
and he had brought with him an option on a book by C. M. Franzero,
called *The Life and Times of Cleopatra*, which he had bought for
$15,000.

(For years Wanger had been thinking about filming a picture
about Cleopatra with Elizabeth Taylor in the title role. He had talked
with her about it earlier that year, shortly before her husband, Mike
Todd, was killed. She said that the character of Cleopatra had always
fascinated her, but Mike was making her business decisions, and
Wanger would have to talk to him. Wanger met with Todd, who was
not then ready to make such a commitment.)

Wanger was about to bring up his idea for a Cleopatra movie with
Skouras, when, to his surprise, Skouras mentioned it first. He recalled that a silent version of *Cleopatra*, starring Theda Bara, had
been one of the most successful pictures that Fox had ever made. He
called a secretary and asked for a script of the ancient Bara movie.

"Just give me this again and we'll make a lot of money," Skouras
said, handing the script to Wanger. "All this needs is a little
rewriting."

When Wanger mentioned Elizabeth Taylor for the Cleopatra
role, Skouras was not overly enthusiastic. He felt that dealing with

110

her would bring the company a lot of trouble; he preferred one of the stars already under contract to Fox. Wanger went out to have lunch with Joe Moskowitz, the vice president of the company.

"Who needs Liz Taylor?" Moskowitz said. "Any hundred-dollar-a-week girl can play Cleopatra."

Wanger didn't argue, but he still wanted Elizabeth Taylor and gave her a copy of *The Life and Times of Cleopatra*. He did not talk to her again about doing the role until almost a year later, when she was in London working with Katharine Hepburn and Montgomery Clift on *Suddenly Last Summer*. Now he was more convinced that she would make an excellent Cleopatra. He also wanted Laurence Olivier as Caesar and Richard Burton as Mark Antony. The Fox casting department preferred Cary Grant as Caesar and Burt Lancaster as Antony. Among the actresses suggested for the role of Cleopatra were Brigitte Bardot, Marilyn Monroe, Jennifer Jones, Kim Novak, Audrey Hepburn, Sophia Loren, Gina Lollobrigida, Susan Hayward, Joan Collins, Dolores Michaels, Millie Perkins and Suzy Parker.

Wanger still held out for Elizabeth and phoned her in London. Jokingly, she said that she would take the role for one million dollars. Up to that time, her usual pay for a movie was around $125,000. Wanger was astounded, but to Elizabeth's surprise, he said that he would see what he could do and get back to her. She also said that she would not appear in the picture unless it was filmed abroad, which did not disturb Wanger because he knew that Fox was already planning, for financial reasons, to make the film in England.

Meanwhile, back in New York, Spyros Skouras conducted an opinion poll among the employees in his office and found that Susan Hayward was their favorite candidate for the Cleopatra role. He told Wanger that he was planning to give Miss Hayward the part. Wanger telephoned Elizabeth to tell her that she was out of the running. She started to weep.

"I want to do it," she said. "Why don't they want me?"

"They won't pay your price," Wanger said.

"I'll do it for a guarantee of seven hundred and fifty thousand against ten percent of the gross," she said.

Wanger called Buddy Adler, who was then the head of the studio. Adler said, "See if you can get her for six hundred thousand."

But when the negotiations were completed, Elizabeth ended up with a contract that gave her one million dollars outright, plus

111

$50,000 a week for overtime, plus a $3,000 a week living allowance, plus a big percentage of the picture's gross earnings. After *Cleopatra* was finally completed, Darryl Zanuck, the then boss of the company, told a Fox stockholders' meeting that if the picture earned $62 million worldwide, as it apparently did, Taylor's share of the earnings would be $7,125,000. But before she could start work, she was forced to fulfill her previous commitment to Metro-Goldwyn-Mayer and appear in *Butterfield 8* for only $125,000.

Rouben Mamoulian was appointed as the director of *Cleopatra* and went to England with Wanger to look at the facilities at the Pinewood studios where they were to film the picture. "Pinewood doesn't look like Egypt," Wanger wrote. "The stages are small and there aren't enough of them. The disappointment was so great that I became physically ill."

Another disappointment was Wanger's failure to sign up Olivier for the role of Caesar. Olivier had played in George Bernard Shaw's *Caesar and Cleopatra* and he felt that he had had it as far as playing Caesar was concerned. Richard Burton, then tied up in the leading role of *Camelot* on the Broadway stage, was also unavailable. Wanger reluctantly signed Peter Finch as Caesar and Stephen Boyd as Antony.

On August 31, 1960, Elizabeth finally arrived in London to begin work on *Cleopatra*. There was a hassle with the unionized British hairdressers, who threatened to quit work at the Pinewood studios if Sidney Guilaroff, Elizabeth's favorite hairdresser from Hollywood, appeared on the set. She refused to let anybody else touch her hair. A compromise was worked out; Guilaroff could prepare her hairdo privately in the morning but he could not appear on the set at any time.

Filming was scheduled to start on September 30, but cold and bad weather made work impossible. Worst of all, Elizabeth came down with a virus infection and a fever. Bed rest was advised, but she continued to run a high temperature. By the end of October, Fox had lost more than two million dollars because production work was stalled by the weather and Elizabeth's illness. Mamoulian was embroiled in disagreements with the script writers. Lord Evans, the Queen's physician, ordered Elizabeth into a hospital for tests. On November 10, it was discovered that she had been poisoned by an abscessed tooth. The tooth was extracted. She returned to her enthouse suite at the Dorchester Hotel, and for a few days, things emed bright again.

Then, on November 14, Elizabeth was rushed back into the hospital, suffering from meningism, a spinal cord or brain irritation. She ecovered after a week, but no more work could be done on the *Cleopatra* set without her. She had been in London for three months ithout being able to do one day's work. Lloyd's of London, carrying nsurance on the production, asked to have her replaced by Marilyn Monroe, Kim Novak, or Shirley MacLaine. Wanger angrily prosted that nobody but Elizabeth would play the Cleopatra role.

The film had now lost a great deal of money due to wasted time, ith an overhead of $40,000 a day. Skouras took Lloyd's to court laiming three million dollars—he later settled for two million. By he end of January 1961, Wanger had only ten minutes of usable ompleted film and none of it had any scenes of Elizabeth. Rouben Mamoulian was asking to resign as the director. Skouras called Joe Mankiewicz in the Bahamas, where he was staying with the Hume Cronyns, and begged him to take over Mamoulian's job.

Now Elizabeth refused to do any work until she knew who was oing to be her director. Mankiewicz came to New York, met Skouras for dinner at The Colony and finally agreed to take over the *Cleopatra* assignment after Skouras said he'd be willing to spend hree million dollars buying him out of a previous commitment to lirect Lawrence Durrell's *Justine* for Figaro Films.

Flying to London in February to replace Mamoulian, Mankiewicz ound the *Cleopatra* script "unreadable and unshootable" and the en minutes of completed film "unusable." "As for the sets they were using," he added, "they were a disaster."

He wanted a completely different story line, which would have Antony following desperately behind Caesar, on the battlefield and n Cleopatra's bed, trying to triumph over his old leader. Antony ucceeds in surpassing Caesar only in his conquest of Cleopatra. But then Antony realizes that he himself has actually been conquered by Cleopatra, and this leads him to self-destruction. The original script depicted Cleopatra as a virginal character who could be loved only by a godlike conqueror whom she adored. Wanger warmly endorsed Mankiewicz's proposed changes in the story and approved bringing in new writers. Mankiewicz also wanted to recast new actors in several leading roles and to start production again from scratch.

113

But in February, before Mankiewicz was able to get the *Cleopatr*
script revised and the cast reorganized, Eddie Fisher had an appen
dectomy and Elizabeth came down with an attack of Asian flu.
doctor was called, and for "safety's sake" he ordered an oxygen ter
for Elizabeth. Around-the-clock nurses watched over the famou
patient, and early on the morning of March 4, the nurse on duty a
Elizabeth's bedside in her suite at the Dorchester saw that her fac
was turning blue and that she was having trouble breathing. Th
nurse immediately called the desk in the lobby and asked for
doctor. The desk clerk remembered that a physician named J
Middleton Price, a noted British anesthesiologist, was in the hotel a
a reception. Dr. Price rushed to Elizabeth's room. "There had been
sudden collapse," he said afterward. "Miss Taylor was unconsciou
extremely blue and gasping for breath." In a desperate effort t
clear her breathing passage, which was almost closed by inflamma
tion, he took a thin plastic tube from his bag, pushed it into he
mouth, down her throat and into the trachea. Then, from a portabl
oxygen tank, he pumped air directly into her lungs. After takin
oxygen from the tube, Elizabeth regained consciousness. "I read
later she had been given an hour to live," Dr. Price said. "I'd say i
was worse; she didn't have fifteen minutes."

Dr. Price saw that a tracheotomy, cutting an opening in her throa
and inserting a tube into the trachea to get air to the lungs, would b
necessary to keep her alive. Even though moving her to a hospital
where the emergency treatment had to be performed, was extreme
ly risky, he decided to take the chance. With Eddie Fisher following
his face pale and obviously in anguish, Elizabeth was rushed to
London Clinic, the private hospital where she had been treated for
meningism the previous October. There Dr. Terence Cawthorne
drew a scalpel across the soft part of her throat directly above the
breastbone, placed a silver tube into the opening and connected it to
a respirator. At the hospital, her illness was diagnosed as acute
staphylococcus pneumonia, which is often fatal. (She still bears
a small scar from the tracheotomy, often covered by a piece of
jewelry, though sometimes she leaves it bare, as a wound worn
proudly.)

The next day, a Barnet Ventilator, an electronically operated iron
lung named after the hospital north of London where it was de
veloped, was wheeled to her bedside. The instrument monitors
respiration and supplies the precise amount of oxygen required to
maintain it at a normal level.

114

Elizabeth was still gravely ill, though. Seven physicians, including Lord Evans, were at her bedside; some believed she could not survive, for along with the pneumonia it was found she was suffering from anemia. She was given blood transfusions, intravenous feedings and doses of antibiotics through an incision in her ankle. Three days later she was removed from the ventilator, and a drug, staphylococcal bacteriophage lysate, was administered. It was very difficult to get, and Milton Blackstone, Eddie Fisher's agent, had flown to London with it.

Catherine Morgan was one of the nurses. She said, "I've been around patients for seventeen years and during that time I've seen some who died in several days, several hours, several minutes. But in comparison to Miss Taylor, they all looked in bonny health—she was the most lifeless individual I've ever seen. I still get goose pimples when I think of it."

Elizabeth's close brush with death made headlines all over the world. Nightly, huge crowds gathered around the London Clinic, and hundreds of thousands of letters arrived from all over the world.

On March 10, six days after she was taken to the hospital, her doctors issued a statement announcing that she had made a "very rare recovery."

A number of persons who had "died" and been brought back to life have described their experiences as painless, even beautiful. Elizabeth found her encounter with death "horrifying."

A month later, recalling those terrible days in the hospital, she said, "There's a saying that when you're drowning, you see your whole life come before you. It wasn't that way with me, even though I was suffocating. I dimly knew that I had had some kind of an operation and that I couldn't make a noise in my throat, and I knew I was dying. When I would come out of unconsciousness, the only question I wanted to ask was whether I was dying and when I would die, but I couldn't make myself heard. I just heard myself screaming to God for help. I was frightened. I was angry. I was *fierce*. I didn't want to die.

"I stopped breathing four times. I died four times. You feel yourself going, falling into a horrible black pit. You hear a screaming, jet noise. Your skin is falling off. But even when I was unconscious, I had my fists clenched, the doctor told me later. He said the reason I'm alive is because I fought so hard to live."

115

SKOURAS AND WANGER DECIDED TO CANCEL ALL PLANS TO FILM *Cleopatra* in England. It was announced that the project would be halted, $600,000 worth of sets at the Pinewood studios were to be scrapped and the filming would be resumed six months later, in September, at Rome after Elizabeth recuperated. Even though almost no usable film had been made, the Fox officials reminded each other that Elizabeth's dramatic recovery had given the picture many millions of dollars' worth of publicity.

On March 27, with Eddie Fisher and her parents, she left the hospital to fly back to America. Wearing a sable coat with a white scarf covering the incision in her neck, she was mobbed in her wheelchair by the crowd of photographers and fans who pressed in on her police escort when she was taken to her waiting limousine. At London Airport, more police had to hold back a huge crowd of admirers while she was lifted on a canvas blanket into the waiting plane.

And so the "wrecker" of Debbie Reynolds's marriage returned as a heroine to attend the Academy Awards presentations on April 18. Elizabeth won an Oscar because of her "outstanding acting in *Butterfield 8*."

"Liz nearly had to die to wrest the prize from her reluctant peers," wrote *Life* magazine.

She agreed with Shirley MacLaine, another contender, who was said to have remarked later, "I was beaten by a tracheotomy." In her memoirs Elizabeth wrote, "I was filled with profound gratitude at being considered by the industry as an actress and not a movie star. My eyes were wet and my throat awfully tight. But I knew my performance had not deserved it, that it was a sympathy award."

That summer, Wanger and Mankiewicz persuaded Spyros Skouras to hire Richard Burton for the Mark Antony role, even though it would cost $50,000 to buy Burton out of *Camelot*. Though Burton is, of course, one of the most precise-speaking actors using the English language, Skouras, who disliked him personally, argued that nobody could understand his dialogue lines and told him so at one meeting. Burton glanced at Skouras, who has a Greek accent, and said, "Like I can't understand you?" Burton agreed to play Mark Antony for three months for $250,000, plus overtime pay. Overtime earnings later ran his pay up to around $500,000.

Mankiewicz managed to sign up Rex Harrison for the part of Julius Caesar without showing him a script, an unusual feat in dealing with an actor of Harrison's quality. Burton had hesitated about agreeing to play Antony without reading that character's scenes and dialogue.

"I took the part of Caesar only because Joe Mankiewicz was directing the film," Harrison said. "There's only one other director whom I would take on professional trust like that—Carol Reed."

Under the terms of Harrison's agreement, he was to be provided with a chauffeur-driven Cadillac for the duration of his stay with the *Cleopatra* company. One morning, emerging from his house on the Via Antiqua to go to work, he found the chauffeur waiting with a Mercedes-Benz.

"Where's the Cadillac?" Harrison asked.

"They say it's too expensive," the chauffeur said.

When Harrison arrived on the set where Elizabeth Taylor was waiting to appear in a scene with him, he said in a loud voice, "Where's the money man?"

A manager in charge of transportation appeared and said, when Harrison inquired about his Cadillac, "We felt that perhaps you wouldn't mind a Mercedes. It's a little cheaper."

"Rex went stark, staring mad," Elizabeth reported later. He said, 'I want my Cadillac and I want it now. And I will not appear on the set until my Cadillac is back. And what's more, I understand that Elizabeth Taylor's chauffeur is paid far more than my chauffeur. I insist that my chauffeur gets the same pay as Elizabeth Taylor's chauffeur. Why the hell should Elizabeth Taylor's chauffeur get more than my chauffeur just because she's got a bigger chest?"

Among the other players in the huge cast were Hume Cronyn, Roddy McDowall, who had become friendly with Burton while they were playing together in *Camelot*, Pamela Brown, and Carroll O'Connor, later to become famous as Archie Bunker in television's *All in the Family*. When work started at Cinecitta, the movie studio in Rome, early in September, Hermes Pan, the dance director, had already been rehearsing hundreds of dancing girls for the scene showing Cleopatra's triumphant entrance into ancient Rome.

One of them, Frances DeLuca, recalled: "I was so busy ogling Richard Burton that sometimes I would forget to lift my feet. Once he walked by so close I could touch him—he looked so handsome. I was going to ask him for his autograph when Pan shouted, 'Frances,' and I suddenly remembered what I was supposed to be doing."

In other parts of the lot, a black ballet troupe was planning another scene, chariot drivers were rehearsing a race, and archers and swordsmen were engaging in battle maneuvers. The wardrobe department was assembling 26,000 costumes at a cost of $475,000. That figure did not cover the 65 costumes for Elizabeth herself, designed by Irene Sharaff, which cost another $130,000. One item alone, a 15-pound ceremonial dress of gold which Cleopatra wears on entering Rome, cost $6,500. In Rome, not far from the ancient Forum, the company was building a larger one where Caesar would welcome Cleopatra. At Anzio, where the American forces made a landing during World War II, the Fox organization rented a privately owned beach from Prince Borghese for $150,000 as the scene for the Actium naval battle. Then it was learned that the beach was still planted with wartime mines.

Two huge barges were constructed, based on descriptions by the Greek biographer and essayist Plutarch. They ended up almost 250 feet long, with masts 100 feet high, covered with gold-colored linoleum and fitted with purple sails and oars of silver. For Cleopatra's triumphant entry into Rome, a sphinx 65 feet long and 35 feet high was built. A procession of snake dancers, white horses bearing trumpeters, bowmen, charioteers, elephants with acrobats whirling on their backs and other attendants would follow her—all costing hundreds of thousands to hire and outfit.

Sparing no expense to keep their star happy, Fox rented a whole house on the studio lot for Elizabeth's dressing-room quarters. It had an office for Eddie, a large salon for relaxation and receiving visitors, a special room for her wigs, a dressing room and a makeup room with a bath and shower. Even the luxury-loving star was taken aback when she first looked at the five-room building. "Isn't it a bit much?" she asked.

Elizabeth and Eddie needed their $3,000-a-week living allowance to maintain the entourage that stayed with them at the Villa Pappa on the Appian Way in Rome during the filming of *Cleopatra*. The villa was a 14-room garden-surrounded mansion with a swimming pool and a tennis court. The couple brought with them to Rome Elizabeth's three children, Michael Wilding, Jr., Christopher Wilding and Liza Todd, and her Hollywood physician, Dr. Rexford Kennamer, who stayed for six weeks for a fee of $25,000 plus expenses. The hired help included sixteen persons; among them were a children's governess, a general handyman, a butler, three male and four female servants, a cook and kitchen helper, a laundress, and a woman who came in four days a week to do the pressing and ironing. There was also a chauffeur, Lucky, who drove Elizabeth's Cadillac, and Eddie's chauffeur, Carlo, who drove his Rolls Royce. Two other cars were available for shopping trips.

During the fall months, while Elizabeth was working with Harrison on the first part of the film, she seldom saw Burton, who did not do his scenes with her until the end of the year. When Elizabeth had met Burton many years earlier at the social gathering in Stewart Granger's house in Hollywood, he had not affected her favorably. "My first impression was that he was rather full of himself," she said later in her memoirs. "He never stopped talking and I had given him the cold fish eye."

Meeting Burton again on the *Cleopatra* set in Rome, she was still unimpressed at first. "There was a lot of hemming and hawing, and he said hello to Joe Mankiewicz and everyone," she says. "And then he sort of sidled over to me and said, 'Has anybody ever told you that you're a very pretty girl?' And I said to myself, *Oy gevaldt*, here's the great lover, the great wit, the great intellectual of Wales, and he comes out with a line like that. I couldn't believe it. I couldn't wait to go back to the dressing room where all the girls were and tell them."

But her early disdain for Burton soon changed. The first day that they worked together, he was suffering from a bad hangover, his hands shaking so badly he was unable to lift his coffee cup to his lips. Elizabeth had to assist him. "My heart just went out to him," she recalled later. That day, Walter Wanger, the producer of *Cleopatra*, watched his two stars doing one of their first scenes together on the

119

set. "You could almost feel the electricity between Liz and Burton," he said.

Elizabeth and Eddie Fisher began to go out for dinner with Burton and his wife, Sybil, and Elizabeth's close friend, Roddy McDowall. During their previous months in Rome, the Fishers had very seldom gone out in the evening. Eddie, who seemed to be more of a manager than a husband, had been keeping Elizabeth at home in their villa, allowing her only one glass of wine and seeing to it that she went to bed early.

In her memoirs, Elizabeth recalls one of those first nights out with the Burtons when Eddie was saying, at nine-thirty, that it was time to go home.

"And I kept saying, 'Please let's stay a little longer,' " she wrote. "Richard evidently saw the expression on my face. I was keyed up and having a marvelous time and I really didn't want to go. So Richard, talking very busily to distract Eddie, kept taking my empty glass and exchanging it with his full one. I thought, 'I absolutely adore this man.' "

Her adoration of Burton was still not widely known when Joe Mankiewicz, the director, who spent most of every day with them on the set, talked the situation over with Walter Wanger. "I've been sitting on a volcano all alone for too long, and I want to give you some facts you ought to know," Mankiewicz said to the producer. "Liz and Burton are not just *playing* Antony and Cleopatra."

Then people in the *Cleopatra* company began to notice that she was no longer wearing Mike Todd's wedding ring. The ring, twisted and charred, was found on Todd's finger in the burned wreckage of his plane in 1958. Elizabeth had been wearing it ever since, before and during the three years of her later marriage to Eddie Fisher. When she was unable to wear it on her finger during the filming of a movie scene, she pinned the ring to her underclothing. Now the ring was put away, along with the many pictures of Todd that were taken down from the walls of the Villa Pappa house. Elizabeth had often said that she had been attracted to Fisher by their mutual devotion to the memory of Todd, Eddie's idol and mentor. When Burton replaced Todd, Eddie Fisher's days as "Queen" Elizabeth's consort became numbered.

Thus began the most publicized morality drama, next to the Watergate disclosures, of modern times. After a year of restless respectability, Elizabeth Taylor was plunging into notoriety again.

120

Early in the year, when Elizabeth and Richard were beginning to notice each other, it was announced that another occupant had moved into the Villa Pappa. In Germany, Elizabeth had adopted a baby girl named Maria, who had been born with a crippling hip defect. The arrival of Maria kept Elizabeth from dropping Eddie sooner than she did. She was afraid that the rising public scandal about the breakup of her marriage and her affair with Burton might force the German adoption authorities to take Maria away from her.

Not far from Villa Pappa, Richard and Sybil Burton were sharing a smaller house with Roddy McDowall. The Burtons' two young daughters, Kate and Jessica, were often in Rome with them until the scandal broke. Sybil, who gave her moody husband no trouble during the fifteen years of their marriage, maintained a dignified composure during the uproar of the *Cleopatra* episode.

As Elizabeth herself said later about her affair with Burton, Eddie Fisher couldn't have mattered less to her, but she and Richard were both upset and worried about Sybil. "We didn't want it to happen because of Sybil and their children," she said.

The two older men whom Burton admired most—his foster father Philip Burton and Emlyn Williams—were both outraged when they heard that Richard was breaking up his marriage. Williams hurried to Rome, visited Burton and blasted him for hurting Sybil. While he was shouting at Burton, Elizabeth herself walked into the room. Williams pointed at her and said to Burton, "Look at her—she's just a third-rate chorus girl." Williams told a British journalist later that when he returned to his home in England and told his wife what he had said, Mrs. Williams became indignant.

"Emlyn!" she said. "When you met me, *I* was a third-rate chorus girl!"

In February, Elizabeth began to visit the *Cleopatra* set on days when she wasn't working there, and sat talking and giggling with Burton between his scenes. Then Fisher left Rome on a business trip and she and Burton went out on the town alone, dining and dancing. That started a big outbreak of Taylor-Burton romance stories in gossip columns all over the world.

Mankiewicz told Wanger about a disturbing new development. Fisher had telephoned Sybil Burton, complaining that her husband was having an affair with his wife. Wanger talked to Burton, who promised the producer that he would put an end to the gossip. That

121

evening Burton was to fly to France to spend a few days there redoing some of his scenes in his previous film, *The Longest Day*. Before leaving Rome, he went to see Elizabeth and told her that they would have to break off their romance. She became angry and hysterical. There was a report in the next morning's newspapers that she had to be restrained from leaping through a glass door to chase after Burton when he was leaving the house. Dick Hanley, her secretary, called Wanger later in the evening and told him nervously that Elizabeth would be unable to work on the set the next day.

The following morning Wanger went to the Villa Pappa to find out what was going on. He learned that Elizabeth was in her bedroom being treated by a physician, but Hanley assured him that she was feeling well and would be downstairs shortly. About an hour later she appeared and said to the producer, "I feel dreadful. Sybil is such a wonderful woman."

Wanger made a remark about how hard it is sometimes to swim against the tides of life.

"Funny you should say that," Elizabeth said. "Richard calls me Ocean."

Midway in the conversation, Elizabeth excused herself and went upstairs to rest while Wanger joined Roddy McDowall, Dick Hanley and Elizabeth's hairdresser, Vivian Zavits, in the reception room. After a while Wanger went upstairs to see how Elizabeth was feeling. She was in bed, sleepy, and said that she had taken some pills. Wanger suggested something to eat and went downstairs to see about it.

An employee who was told to bring Elizabeth sandwiches and milk saw that she had fallen into a deep sleep. She looked at her closely and cried, "Miss Taylor's taken pills!"

Downstairs, somebody panicked and called for an ambulance. A spy in the household telephoned a newspaper. When the ambulance carrying Elizabeth arrived at the Salvator Mundi Hospital, a horde of *paparazzi*, Rome's prowling freelance photographers, were waiting to snap pictures.

Now the Taylor-Burton affair came out of the gossip columns and flashed into page-one headlines all over the world: LIZ POISONED IN ROME.

The *Cleopatra* press agent gave out a story about "a bad bowl of chili" and Wanger said something about "bad beef." But the news stories were filled with reports about the Burton-Taylor romance,

122

about a rumored suicide attempt, a throat hemorrhage, a nervous breakdown, a Seconal overdose. The previous day, after her unpleasant phone call from Eddie Fisher, Sybil Burton had left Rome to visit her foster father-in-law, Philip Burton, who was ill in New York. Now it was reported that she had left Richard and was about to file divorce proceedings.

Eddie Fisher, "looking as gaunt as a secondhand scarecrow" according to one reporter, hurried back to Rome to be at Elizabeth's bedside. He sat in the waiting room at the hospital for seven hours before she agreed to see him. Then, after visiting his wife, he came out of her room grim and unsmiling and told reporters, "I've got nothing to say."

Richard Burton came back from his work on *The Longest Day* in France and was enraged when he learned that his press agent had issued a statement in his name. It said, "For the past several days, uncontrolled rumors have been growing about Elizabeth and myself. Statements attributed to me have been distorted out of proportion and a series of coincidences has lent plausibility to a situation which has become dangerous to Elizabeth. . . . In answer to these rumors, my normal inclination would be simply to say no comment. But I feel that in this case things should be explained to protect Elizabeth."

Burton said later that he was upset by the release because he did not like the way it had been written. "It was a terribly worded statement," Burton said. "Horrendous. I never authorized it." He called all the rumors of a "true" romance "bloody nonsense."

Wanger then wrote in his *Cleopatra* journal, "The romance is a front page story all over the world. Reporters are flocking like vultures to Rome from all over the continent. Burton on the set today—very gay, cocky, with a glass of beer in hand. We talked a few moments and I realized a strange thing has happened to this canny Welshman. When he came to this picture some months ago, he was a well-known star but not famous; his salary was good but not huge. Suddenly his name has become a household word. His salary for his next movie has skyrocketed. The romance has changed his life, but I don't think he realizes how deeply involved he is."

That week's *Time* magazine reported, "Burton, according to gossip, has made more than his mark as Antony. Taylor, according to gossip, is merely using the Burton rumors to shield the real truth: she is mad, mad, mad for her personable director, Joseph L. Mankiewicz, 53, who, however, is very busy shooting all day and scripting all night. The total cost of the picture will probably run to $25 million, making it the most expensive motion picture ever made. As far as most of the studio executives are concerned, Taylor could have an affair with Mao Tse-tung—provided she stays on the job in Rome. The trade freely predicts that Twentieth Century-Fox may never become Twenty-First Century-Fox if Taylor should bug out of the film now."

The rumor about Taylor and Mankiewicz was reported by the director himself with his tongue firmly planted in his cheek. The absurd level to which the entire situation had fallen is indicated by the fact that the Mankiewicz quip was actually taken seriously by some.

Now came a new complication to add to Wanger's headaches. A very beautiful and young ex-Copacabana show girl, Pat Tunder, with whom Burton had carried on a close friendship in New York while he was appearing in *Camelot*, turned up in Rome. Burton brought her with him to his dressing room at seven o'clock one morning and did not show up for work on the set until ten.

Elizabeth said to him angrily, "You've kept us waiting."

"That's a switch," Burton said to her. "It's about time somebody kept *you* waiting for a change."

Rex Harrison quickly interrupted. "Let's rehearse, everyone," he said.

Much to Elizabeth's annoyance, Pat hung around the set, staring at the acting for a few days. Wanger finally told Burton to get rid of her.

Louella Parsons, in her widely syndicated Hollywood column, wrote a story that was headlined ROW OVER ACTOR ENDS LIZ, EDDIE MARRIAGE. "It is difficult to appraise how the world will react to another scandal involving Elizabeth," Louella said. A few years earlier, in commenting on such a scandal, Louella would not have hesitated to condemn Elizabeth with no reservations. Now maybe Elizabeth Taylor had reached a peak as a colorful celebrity where her escapades only made her more colorful and interesting.

"Our offices in New York and Hollywood are hysterical over the publicity the 'romance' has been getting," Wanger noted in his diary. "They refer to it as a cancer and say it will destroy us all."

Spyros Skouras, accompanied by Otto Koegel, Fox's chief legal counsel, arrived in Rome to straighten out the situation personally. Skouras blasted Wanger for insisting on hiring Burton, who, he said, was responsible for "all the trouble." Wanger said that Burton would be a much bigger star after *Cleopatra* was released.

"He will never be a big box-office star!" Skouras shouted.

The next day, however, Skouras watched two hours and forty minutes of the *Cleopatra* film and was enthusiastic about the performances of Taylor, Burton and Harrison. He had lunch with Burton and offered him two more pictures.

Skouras decided to send letters to Elizabeth and to Richard, demanding that they clean up their private lives and behave themselves. He first had a letter delivered to Burton, who went berserk with rage. Elizabeth sent word to Skouras through Wanger, warning him that if she received such a letter, she would quit working on *Cleopatra* immediately. Skouras decided not to send her a letter.

On March 19, Eddie Fisher left Rome and went to New York, supposedly for recording sessions. Now came the final downfall of Eddie as Elizabeth's husband. In New York, Eddie talked too much about the romance between his wife and Burton. He told friends, who promptly relayed the story to Earl Wilson, the *New York Post* columnist, that Burton said to him in Rome, in the presence of Elizabeth, "I'm in love with your wife." And Elizabeth, according to Eddie, "beamed with joy." Wilson's story continued:

" 'How do you like him saying a thing like that to me?' Eddie exclaimed in bafflement.

" 'Why didn't you punch him?' he was asked.

"Eddie shrugged."

In New York, Eddie went into Gracie Square Hospital, reportedly suffering from a nervous breakdown. On March 30, he called a press conference at the Hotel Pierre to discuss his marital situation and scoffed at the widespread reports that his marriage was on the rocks.

Dressed in a plaid sport jacket and gray slacks, Fisher looked rested. He labeled the reports "preposterous, ridiculous, absolutely false." He said, "The only romance between Elizabeth and Richard Burton is Mark Antony and Cleopatra." He also ridiculed reports that he had entered the hospital because of a breakdown.

"How did this gossip start?" a reporter wanted to know.

"I don't know," Eddie replied. "Maybe some press agent."

One journalist asked if Elizabeth would issue a statement denying the rumors of an affair with Burton and a breakup of her marriage with Eddie.

"I think she will—yes," Fisher replied.

"Will you get her on the phone right now and ask her to deny the reports?" another reporter wanted to know.

"Yes, I will," Eddie said.

That was a grave mistake.

Fisher went to a telephone and reached Elizabeth in Rome. She reported their conversation later in her memoirs.

"He told me that he'd called a press conference," Elizabeth wrote. "He said he wanted me to tell them there was no foundation for the stories coming out of Rome. And I said, 'Well, Eddie, I can't do that because there is some truth in the story. I just can't do that.' And he said, 'Wait a minute, what do you mean you won't do that?' And I said, 'I can't do that because it's true. There is a foundation to the story.' And he said, 'Thanks a lot!' And then he hung up. Eddie and I never did live together again."

Fisher came back to the press conference and told the reporters sheepishly, "You know you can ask a woman to do something, but she doesn't always do it."

The next morning's headlines: LIZ TURNS DOWN EDDIE'S OCEAN PHONE CALL LOVE PLEA.

In Rome, Elizabeth was meeting Richard on the Via Veneto, as private a rendezvous area as Times Square, Hollywood and Vine, or Piccadilly Circus. Rome's elegant restaurants, nightclubs and specialty shops are clustered along the famed thoroughfare. Here the *paparazzi* clicked away and pictures of the couple appeared all over the world.

A Washington, D.C., newspaper termed the affair "a tasteless, tedious charade." So much was being written about the pair that *Corriere della Sera*, a Milan newspaper, made a promise to its readers not to publish a word about Elizabeth "for 24 hours." It barely made it.

Rome's *Il Tempo* was harsh, pointing to her as "this vamp who destroys families and shucks husbands like a praying mantis."

The Vatican radio, mentioning no names but not needing to, declared that the publicity given to marital scandals and divorces is not only "an insult to the seriousness of marriage" but endangers the "moral health of society." A commentator said, "To many, marriage seems to be a game which they start and interrupt with the whimsical fantasy of children."

Then, much to the consternation of Spyros Skouras and the movie industry in general, the influential *L'Osservatore della Dominica*, published weekly in Vatican City, ran a letter castigating Elizabeth.

"When some time ago," it read, "you said that your marriage (your fourth) would last for your whole life, there were some who shook their heads in a rather skeptical way. We, always willing to believe the best, kept our heads steadily on our shoulders and did not say a word. Then, when you reached the point of adopting a baby girl, as if to make more stable this marriage which had no natural children, for a moment we really believed that things had changed. But children—whether they are natural or adopted—count little for illustrious ladies like you when there is nothing to hold them together. It appears that you had the bad taste to state: 'My marriage is dead and extra dead!' And what of the 'whole life' you had declared it would last three years ago? Does your whole life mean only three years? And if your marriage is dead, we must say according to Roman usage, it was killed dead. The trouble is, my dear lady, you are killing too many. . . . Where will you finish? In erotic vagrancy?

"And your poor children, those who are your true children and the one who was taken from an honest institution. Don't these institutions think before handing children to somebody? Don't they request moral references? Was it not better to entrust this girl to an honest bricklayer and a modest housewife rather than to you, my dear lady, and to your fourth ex-husband? The housewife and the bricklayer would have worked harder and would have seriously made sacrifices for their child. You, instead, have other things to do."

The attack was presented as an anonymous letter and not as an official denunciation from the Vatican, but it could not have been published in the Vatican newspaper without the approval of Pope John himself. It made headlines all over the United States, and all over the world, and became the subject of the week for editorial writers and television and radio news commentators everywhere. Spyros Skouras sent Walter Wanger a six-page letter complaining about the wave of bad publicity stirred up by the Vatican's blast.

A few hours after the letter was published in the Rome newspapers, Elizabeth made a public appearance with Burton in the dining

127

room of the Grand Hotel, looking radiant in a black faille toque ha and a tight-fitting black silk bodiced gown with a flaring ballerina skirt. After a dinner of cheese soufflé and steak, she and Richard went off to meet Mike Nichols in a Via Veneto nightclub. People on the street shouted at her, "Home wrecker! Unfit mother!" She tried to seem casual and gay, but late in the evening she broke down in tears and sobbed uncontrollably. She rushed home alone in her car hounded by the *paparazzi*. Burton left alone a few minutes later.

Elizabeth was "gobbling sedatives" for her twanging nerves as the barrage continued unabated. Yet, incredibly, she continued to perform on the set and even took time to greet and play hostess to an old friend—no celebrity, but the daughter of a prop man who had worked for many years on the MGM lot where Elizabeth had starred.

It is a story worth telling, for it illustrates an aspect of Elizabeth's character that has been hidden beneath the thick overlay of scandal and tragedy that has bedeviled her life.

Ethel Cammarata, who is the same age as Elizabeth, met the young actress on the set of her first movie, *There's One Born Every Minute*, when each was nine years old. Ethel slipped and started to cry. Elizabeth put her arm around her and comforted her. Ethel then shared a box of Malomar cookies with the young actress, who bolted them down furtively because she had been forbidden to eat desserts.

Their paths crossed infrequently after that. Many years later, during the filming of *Cleopatra*, Ethel was in Rome on vacation with her husband, an industrial designer, and their two small daughters, ages four and six. She decided to visit the set, hoping Elizabeth would remember.

Elizabeth did. She ordered the heavy guards at the entrance to admit the visitors at once, emerging from her palatial dressing house herself to greet them.

Mrs. Cammarata: "She kissed me, kissed the girls and my husband, remembered my father and was so sorry when I told her he had died. I could tell she was genuinely sorry. Then she took the time to show the girls through her dressing room.

"My oldest daughter is named after her. Elizabeth was ecstatic when I told her. She took a gold-colored belt from one of her costumes and gave it to her, and gave my youngest daughter, Josie, some antique buttons.

"Then she introduced us to Richard Burton, proudly telling him that one of the girls was named after her. He promptly gave my Elizabeth a present too, a wrist plate from one of his costumes.

"Then Elizabeth Taylor did something I thought was so human, so understanding—and so wonderful. She saw at once that little Josie was crestfallen. She whispered to Burton, who immediately gave the other wrist plate to Josie. Her face lit up as she saw the joy in Josie's face. Then she had to appear in a scene, so we said our goodbyes and left."

The sky was falling in around Elizabeth. She was undergoing the most frightening times of her life. And yet she gave the time, and had the emotional equilibrium, to play out this warm, almost domestic scene.

The day after the Vatican's attack on Elizabeth, she went to the Forum set to appear in one of the most spectacularly staged and dramatic mob scenes in the history of film making. The scene was to show Cleopatra, seated on a huge sphinx as high as a three-story building with her son by Julius Caesar at her side, making her first entrance into ancient Rome. The sphinx on which she is seated, draped in a gown of 24-karat-gold-beaded fabric, is mounted on wheels and pulled by 300 gold-draped slaves, following a procession of dancing girls, trumpeters on white horses, charioteers driving black horses, elephants, and an elite guard on sorrel horses. As she makes her grand entrance into the city, Cleopatra is closely surrounded by a crowd of more than 6,000 Romans who are seeing her for the first time, some fascinated and others skeptical and antagonistic.

Cleopatra's future life and happiness depend completely on how she is received by the Roman people on this first visit to their city. If the Romans accept her and acknowledge her son Caesarion as Julius Caesar's only child and heir, the Roman and Egyptian empires will merge and she will be the most powerful woman in the world. If the crowd turns against her, she will be ruined.

The similarity between Cleopatra's situation in that day's scene and Elizabeth Taylor's situation in real life when she arrived on the set to play the scene was amazing. She was to be closely exposed to a huge crowd of modern Roman Catholics who were likely to have been aroused emotionally by the Vatican's attack on her the day

129

before. Several bomb threats had been telephoned to the studio tha morning. Police detectives, dressed as extras in Roman togas, wer to be scattered through the mob.

Her costume designer, Irene Sharaff, said that Elizabeth ha never been as nervous at any time in her career as she was gettin dressed that day. In a crowd of thousands of extras, she asked, how could they possibly find the one with the bomb?

Elizabeth panicked. Clutching Richard, she told him she would b unable to go through with the scene. He promised her all would g well, that she would be well guarded, not only by him but by platoon of police. Somewhat, but not entirely, reassured, she got into he heavy costume with its yard-high headdress and emerged from he dressing room, feeling trembly but determined. Slowly she climbe atop the three-story sphinx.

The scene called for the sphinx, with Cleopatra seated on the top of it, to be pulled through a high archway into the Forum, where the 6,000 Romans were waiting to see her. Cleopatra's appearance wa to set off an immediate outburst of emotional ovation, and the mob was to run toward her, shouting happily, "Cleopatra! Cleopatra!"

When the directors called, "Action!" Elizabeth, high on he throne on the sphinx, saw the huge mob running toward her and wondered for a moment if she was to be knocked to the ground.

Then she saw that the crowd were smiling and waving to her. Instead of shouting "Cleopatra!" all of them were screaming, "Leez! Leez! *Baci! Baci!*" *Baci* is the Italian word for kisses. The extras were throwing kisses to her as they cheered and shouted.

Long after Mankiewicz stopped the camera and declared the scene completed, the cheering and the throwing of the kisses went on and on. Elizabeth looked at the crowd gratefully, with tears running down her cheeks. Somebody handed her a microphone and she said in Italian, "Thank you very much."

Like Cleopatra in the script, Elizabeth Taylor had won the hearts of the Romans. "Again I thought, watching the scene, the parallel between the life of Cleopatra and the life of Elizabeth Taylor is incredible," Walter Wanger said.

The bewildered Hedda Hopper, conservative spokeswoman for the Hollywood establishment of that time, wrote later about the Taylor-Burton affair, "In the old days, the scandal would have killed her professionally. In these changed times, it seems only to help her reputation."

130

Elizabeth and Eddie agreed to a divorce, but working out a financial settlement to Eddie's satisfaction took another two years, which did not bother her. "I was in no big hurry to marry Richard," she said later. "I just wanted to love him." When the divorce agreement was finally announced, the Flamingo Hotel in Las Vegas promptly announced that Eddie would soon be staying there while he divorced Elizabeth. The management of the rival Thunderbird Hotel, without hearing a word from Elizabeth, quickly announced that she would be staying at the Thunderbird while she was divorcing Eddie.

Meanwhile, Burton scoffed at reports that he would seek a divorce from Sybil. On May 3, he sat for an interview with Sheila Graham, the Hollywood columnist, which began with a quote from him, "Am I going to marry Elizabeth Taylor?" And then, Miss Graham continued, "he gave a resounding one-word answer, 'NO!' "

To elude the press, Miss Graham said, Burton wore dark glasses when he met her for the interview at the Grand Hotel in Rome. "He was casual and unconcerned about it in his debonair British way," Miss Graham wrote, "admitting frankly that he is enjoying the publicity." Burton told her that "a famous actor," whose name he would not reveal, had cabled him, "Make up your mind, dear heart, do you wish to be a household word, or a great actor?" He spoke the words in his perfect imitation of his close friend, Sir Laurence Olivier. Burton said his answer to the cable was, "Both."

Miss Graham reported he shrugged off her suggestion that the "over-publicized antics" would hurt Elizabeth's career. "It will be a nine-day wonder," Burton said, "and by the time the picture is released at the end of this year, everyone will have forgotten—unless something new happens, like me announcing I am divorcing my wife to marry Elizabeth. But darling, there's no chance of that." To Sheila Graham's observation that Elizabeth was very much in love with him and that "she usually has her way with a man," Burton just laughed and shook his head.

"He seemed to be holding the situation well in hand," Miss Graham wrote, though he had a twinge of conscience when she told him the publicity over the relationship with Elizabeth had made him a great star. "What a shameful way to become a star," Burton said.

After Elizabeth survived the blast from the Vatican, she and Richard promised Wanger they would make a determined effort to stay out of the newspapers, but that seemed impossible even whe they tried to slip off secretively to an isolated spot. Over the Easte weekend, on April 21, they drove to a hotel located on a promontor some five miles from a luxury seaside resort 100 miles north o Rome.

Elizabeth left her children in Rome with her mother and th servants. No mention was made of their destination. The resort, ir Porto Santo Stefano, is connected to the mainland by a narrow strip of land and is presumably inaccessible to outsiders. It had, in recen years, become an exclusive refuge for wealthy Italians and for eigners, including members of the Dutch royal family.

But bad luck dogged her again. Elizabeth showed up in Rome the next day, an eye black and her nose bruised. Once again the gossips went on a spree. Was it a suicide attempt. Did Burton sock the face that launched a thousand headlines? Elizabeth spent twenty hours in the Salvator Mundi Hospital in Rome and then followed the officia explanation: She had injured her nose and eye when her chauffeur had to halt the car suddenly on the drive home.

The *paparazzi* besieged the Taylor and Burton homes day and night. One of Elizabeth's maids was found to be wearing a camera on top of her head under an elaborately high-piled hairdo. A pho tographer came to the house one day disguised as a priest seeking contributions to foreign missions. Another day a photographer, posing as a roofer, climbed a ladder on the outside of the villa and tried to shoot a picture through a bedroom window. The children often turned a garden hose on the lurking *paparazzi*.

One day Elizabeth and Richard were sailing with friends on a yacht in the Mediterranean off Naples. During lunch, Elizabeth had the feeling that she was being photographed. Burton said that she was getting paranoid. Elizabeth asked a waiter to throw back a curtain between the dining area and the ship's galley. Sure enough, a photographer and a newsreel cameraman were behind the curtain.

Still, there were many peaceful days when Elizabeth and Burton managed to escape from the photographers. "Richard and I had some of our happiest times in Italy in a really crummy one-room apartment on a beach," she said. "We would go there to be together even though we had my huge Roman villa with a cook and servants. We'd spend weekends there. I'd barbecue. There was a crummy old shower, and the sheets were always damp. We loved it—absolutely adored it."

Elizabeth's work in *Cleopatra* in Italy was not concluded until June 3 when she appeared in a scene of Cleopatra's barge arriving at Tarsus, filmed at a cost of $500,000. The barge alone cost $277,000. Seventy-five swimmers in the water beside the barge dived for coins tossed to them by thirty-five handmaids sitting on the prow. Another forty handmaids scattered flower petals on the water. Clouds of incense rose from burners on the deck. The rigging on the masts was garlanded with flowers.

The entire stupendous project—and never did a movie more truly deserve that overworked press-agent adjective—at last ended in early March 1963, almost five years after Skouras assigned the task to Walter Wanger. Few undertakings in any business had been so grossly underestimated in terms of the time and money involved. Skouras, for example, had figured at the start that the film might take about fifteen weeks to complete!

Mankiewicz managed to cut the completed film from twenty-six hours down to a little more than eight. Then he took out three more hours and pleaded in vain with Zanuck to divide the film into two movies, each running two hours and twenty minutes, one entitled *Caesar and Cleopatra* and the other *Antony and Cleopatra*, which seemed a sensible solution. But Zanuck demanded that the whole thing had to be condensed into one four-hour film. The only way that Mankiewicz could compress the long film into four hours, without cutting most of the best scenes, was to compress and eliminate most of Burton's role in the second part of the picture. As Elizabeth Taylor pointed out, Burton's role as he originally played it, showed a strong man with a character flaw who gradually disintegrates. "But they cut the film so that all you see is him drunk and shouting all the time," she says, "and you never know what in his character led up to that. He just looks like a drunken sot."

Elizabeth was in London when *Cleopatra* was first shown there. She had been determined not to see it but was persuaded to escort a group of dancers from the Bolshoi Ballet to a screening of the picture. When she saw how much it had been cut, she was so upset that she became physically ill. "When it was over," she said, "I raced back to the Dorchester Hotel and just made it into the downstairs lavatory before I vomited."

Not all critics were that nauseated by *Cleopatra*. Many of them admired the film as "a gorgeous spectacle of cinema art" but complained about the chopped-up story line. Rex Harrison was hailed for his masterly performance as the young Cleopatra's fatherly love in the first half of the picture. Elizabeth and Burton were both panned. The *Time* magazine critic wrote:

"In the big love scenes 'the ne'er-lust-wearied Antony' seem strangely bored—as if perhaps he had rehearsed too much. As fo Taylor, to look at, she is every inch 'a morsel for a monarch.' Bu when she plays Cleopatra as a political animal, she screeches like ward heeler's wife at a block party."

One pleasant surprise, however, was the review of the usually hard-to-please critic of *The New Yorker*, Brendan Gill, who wa carried away by both the spectacular picture and by Elizabeth' performance in it. *Cleopatra*, Gill felt, looked as if it had cost twice a much as forty million dollars. He hailed Taylor as "less an actres than a great natural wonder, like Niagara or the Alps, and it wa right of the director to deal with her as the thing she has become— the most famous woman of her time, and probably of all time, who perfectly made up, her nakedness picked out in cloth of gold (and the camera never failing, from scene to scene, to make obeisance to that justly celebrated bosom), is set pacing from bed to bath and from Caesar to Mark Antony not as the embodiment of a dead ancient queen but as, quite literally, a living doll, at once so sexy and so modest that her historical predecessor, seeing her, might easily have died not from the sting of an asp but from the sting of envy."

The film ended up costing Twentieth Century-Fox $62 million, including distribution costs, by far the most expensive film ever made in the Western world and probably in the whole world. (The Soviet Union claims that it spent $96 million on its seven-and-a-half-hour version of *War and Peace*.)

Cleopatra finally got out of the red and into the black, not in the movie theaters but when Fox sold the television rights to the American Broadcasting Company's network for a large but undisclosed sum. Then the picture got into a tangle of lawsuits. Wanger sued Skouras, Zanuck and the Fox company for $2,660,000, charging a breach of his contract, and settled for $100,000. Taylor sued Fox, claiming that she had not been paid her proper share of the gross receipts. Fox sued Elizabeth and Richard for $50 million, claiming that the picture had been hurt by their scandalous public conduct. The company also brought a legal charge against Elizabeth because she had made public statements saying that she hated the film.

"It was like a disease," she said later about *Cleopatra*. "An illness one had a very difficult time recuperating from."

After Elizabeth finished her work on *Cleopatra* in Italy, she went with her children to her home at Gstaad in Switzerland and decided there that she would never see Richard Burton again. She wrote a long letter to him, telling him that they had to break up their affair because it was destroying his life with his wife and their two daughters. Burton agreed with her feelings and joined his family at their Swiss home near Geneva, about seventy miles away from Elizabeth's place in the Bernese Alps.

It was the first time in many years that she had tried to live without a husband and she found her loneliness hard to endure. "I was dying inside and trying to hide it from the children with all kinds of frenzied activity—games, picnics," she wrote later. One day her son Christopher said to her, "I prayed to God last night that you and Richard would be married."

After a few months of solitude, broken only by occasional visits with her mother and father, who were staying across a valley near her home, Elizabeth received a telephone call from Burton. He said that he was worried about her and he wanted her to meet him for lunch, and suggested the Chateau de Chillon on Lake Geneva, about midway between their homes. Elizabeth found herself too excited by his call to turn down his invitation.

Her father and mother drove with her to the appointed meeting place and they arrived there at the same time that Burton was getting out of his car. "Oh, I don't know what to do," she said to her parents. "I'm scared!" Her father gave her a push and she finally managed to get out of the car and shake hands with Richard. Her parents drove away.

"We stood there looking at each other," Elizabeth says. "It was like my first date when I was sixteen, and it was as though he had never seen a girl before. At last we began to relax and we had lunch at a place overlooking the lake. Then he drove me home. We didn't even kiss."

Elizabeth and Richard began to see each other, usually for lunch, every few weeks. She had come to a decision which she says was the most mature and unpopular decision of her life—she would be waiting for him whenever he called her.

135

She realized that they could not stay away from each other, but she did not want to marry him because she did not want him or Sybil to be unhappy. She decided to settle for seeing him occasionally and talking with him now and then on the telephone.

Then they found themselves working together again in Paris on the additional scenes of *Cleopatra* that finally brought the filming of the picture to a close. Richard told her about a role that he had been offered opposite Sophia Loren in *The VIP's*, a movie that Metro-Goldwyn-Mayer was planning about a group of important people stranded at an airport in London by a dense fog. "Why don't I do it?" Elizabeth said. "Let Sophia stay in Rome." MGM, smelling more Taylor-Burton publicity, signed her up immediately.

So their romance bloomed again in London. Elizabeth and Richard were seen together everywhere, drinking in pubs, going to rugby matches and occupying nearby suites at the Dorchester Hotel. Sybil and the Burton children moved back from Switzerland to England to spend some time with Richard. It was then, for the first time, that Burton asked Elizabeth to marry him. She gave him a quick answer. "I wanted to be his wife more than anything else in the world."

Sybil agreed to a legal separation until a divorce could be arranged and flew to New York with her two daughters to spend Easter with Philip Burton. When Sybil landed at Idlewild Airport, a reporter asked her, "Are you going to date Eddie Fisher while you're in America, Mrs. Burton?"

Elizabeth and Richard spent a happy and busy summer together in London. She appeared for the first time in a television documentary show, *Elizabeth Taylor in London*, acting as the commentator during a filmed tour of the city. The show was seen later in America on the CBS network. She gave her own reminiscences of London and quoted from essays about the city by Shakespeare, Keats, Churchill, Queen Victoria and Elizabeth Barrett Browning. For her performance, which was acclaimed by critics, she was paid $250,000, the highest fee ever given to anyone for a single show in the history of television up to that time.

"We just called her up cold and asked her," the producer of the documentary said. "She said nobody had ever asked her before to be on television."

Meanwhile Burton was playing the saintly title role in the filmed version of Jean Anouilh's *Becket*, with Peter O'Toole as the bawdy King Henry II, and John Gielgud as the King of France.

During their work on *Becket*, Burton and O'Toole often ate lunch at a nearby pub called The King's Head, where Elizabeth would join them. She was fond of the proprietor, a genial man named Archie, who addressed Burton as "master." Fergus Cashin, Burton's journalist friend, was with the group one day at The King's Head when a local character named Len arrived and asked Archie if he could get Elizabeth and Richard to autograph some sports equipment that would be raffled off at a charity bazaar. Archie directed Len to the back bar where Richard and Elizabeth were sitting with Cashin and O'Toole.

As Cashin reported later, Burton came out to Archie afterwards and said to him, "A bloke has just come in and asked Elizabeth if she would please be kind enough to give him her signature. 'You want my autograph?' said Elizabeth. 'I will be delighted.' Then she was just about to sign a menu when this bloke said, 'No, no, no. I don't want you to write it on paper. I want you to sign my balls.' And Elizabeth said, 'That's going to be a bit difficult, isn't it?' Then this fellow says, 'No, no. I've left a bit of space between Bobby Moore and John Lennon.' Now, Archie, tell me. Just what in the name of God is going on?"

Archie said, "Oh, he's a nice chap. No harm in him at all. Just tell Elizabeth to sign with a ballpoint—it's the easiest thing for signing his balls. By the way, master, he forgot to take them in with him." He reached behind the bar and handed Richard two soccer balls.

In September, Elizabeth and Richard flew, with her daughter Liza, from England to Mexico where they spent three pleasant months at Puerto Vallarta while Burton was starring in the Tennessee Williams screen drama *The Night of the Iguana* under the direction of John Huston. Burton had three notable leading ladies in the production, Ava Gardner, Deborah Kerr and the then 17-year-old Sue Lyon, fresh from her triumph as the sexy nymph in *Lolita*.

Michael Wilding, Elizabeth's second husband and the father of her two sons, spent some time with her and Richard in Puerto Vallarta. He had given up acting to start a new career as a Hollywood agent, and Burton had signed up as one of his first clients. Wilding arranged for Elizabeth to rent a handsome white stucco, four-story villa on a cliff in Puerto Vallarta, which Burton later bought for $40,000. The star-studded cast worked smoothly under the shrewd and entertaining direction of John Huston, who presented each of the four stars, Elizabeth and producer Ray Stark with a gunbox containing a gold-plated pistol and five gold-plated bullets. Each bullet was engraved with the name of one of the other five recipients.

Early in December, just before the completion of *The Night of the Iguana*, Burton received word that Sybil had been granted a Mexican divorce *in absentia* on charges of abandonment and cruel and inhuman treatment. Her laywer had noted among other things, that her husband had been "in the constant company of another woman." *Newsweek* called that "the throwaway line of the decade." Sybil was given custody of the two Burton daughters, Katharine and Jessica, with Richard being given totally free visitation rights. She was also given the Burton home in Geneva, and it was reported unofficially that she was receiving one million dollars, plus another half million to be paid over the following years.

Eddie Fisher, protesting publicly that he was anxious to help Elizabeth get a divorce, was privately giving her lawyers a lot of trouble. Her attorneys, Aaron Frosch in New York and Milton Rudin in Hollywood, claimed that Fisher was demanding one million dollars from Elizabeth in return for a divorce, "the sum of $750,000 tax free, and the use of an additional sum of $250,000 for ten years." The lawyers said that Elizabeth had been willing earlier to give Eddie half of the stock in her MCL Films, the company that controlled her interest in *Cleopatra*, but she had refused to give him the cash that he was demanding. Fisher had been denying her charges in lengthy and sarcastic statements.

"I'm supposed to be standing in the way of this lovely young couple who have been going together for so long," Fisher said in Las Vegas as 1963 ended. "They're acting like a couple of kids in a playpen. They've been in their playpen long enough. They can wait a few days." He wasn't objecting to giving up anything, he said. "The one thing I'd like to give up is my marriage certificate. I'm willing for her to be happy with Richard the Lionhearted as soon as possible." He wouldn't stand "in the way of this earth-shattering, world-shaking romance for anything in the world."

Some kind of a private settlement may have been reached. When Elizabeth filed a divorce petition in Puerto Vallarta on January 14, 1964, claiming abandonment, the judge gave Fisher twenty-one

138

days to reply. He did not go to Mexico to contest the petition, saying that he was sick of the whole proceedings.

Elizabeth and Burton flew to Toronto where he appeared on the stage in a production of *Hamlet* under the direction of Sir John Gielgud. When Elizabeth came to the theater to see his performance, she created so much confusion in the audience during the intermissions that the stage manager found it difficult to raise the curtain and resume the play. "Ladies would come to her seat and stare at her through lorgnettes and say to each other, 'Her eyes are blue, not violet,' " Burton complained. On March 5, Elizabeth was granted a divorce in Puerto Vallarta because Fisher had failed to answer her charges. She and Richard celebrated with a bottle of champagne in his dressing room.

Four

The Frantic Years

Two stars keep not their motion in one sphere.
—*HENRY IV, PART ONE*

1. Marriage, Burton Style

N TORONTO, RICHARD TELEPHONED HUGH FRENCH, THEN HIS PERSONAL agent, and suggested dinner at a small out-of-the-way restaurant. French arrived at nine but Burton was uncharacteristically late. Forty minutes later he arrived with Elizabeth. To French, both seemed apprehensive. "There were just the three of us," French recalls. "Richard took a deep breath and then paused. I waited. Finally, he spoke, 'Hugh, it's really good news that I'm about to tell you. We hope you will be pleased with it. We've decided to get married!'

" 'That's wonderful,' I replied. 'Calls for a bottle of champagne.'

"Richard turned to Elizabeth. 'That's the bloody English for you,' he said. 'They act properly in all situations—nothing riles them.'

"Richard and Elizabeth knew I was very fond of Sybil, Richard's first wife. Neither of them ever want to hurt other people if they can help it. I'll wager that all of Elizabeth's former husbands—those she divorced—never thought very poorly of her. Sybil still thinks well of Richard."

The couple flew to Montreal in a chartered airliner which also bore ten guests. They had no license to wed but needed none because in the province of Quebec, all marriages are religious ones and can be performed by clergymen who need only be convinced that the couple is legally marriageable.

On March 15, 1964, in the Ritz Carlton Hotel, Richard and Elizabeth were married by the Reverend Leonard Mason, pastor of the local Unitarian Church of the Messiah. Elizabeth was wearing a yellow chiffon daffodil-styled dress, created by Irene Sharaff, the designer of her gowns in *Cleopatra*. She wore a clip of emeralds and diamonds, the first piece of jewelry given to her by Burton when they were first going together in Rome. It had cost him $93,000.

"There weren't many of us in attendance," French recalls. "Elizabeth's mother and father were there. Richard and Elizabeth were a wee bit nervous. Certainly, Richard was. The minister began by saying, 'You both have suffered because of your love.' I could tell that they were agreeing and thinking it was well worth it.

"When the minister pronounced them man and wife, the loveliest smiles appeared on both of their faces. It was so very apparent that they were thrilled and took the vows very seriously. Under other circumstances—normal circumstances—Elizabeth and Richard Jenkins would be a very happy and compatible couple."

Elizabeth was unattended. Best man for Richard was Bob Wilson, who had been his wardrobe man during the Broadway run of *Camelot*. It was a single-ring ceremony. That night, the couple remained at the Ritz Carlton, talking, laughing, weeping, until the sun came up.

Although the Burtons were extraordinary celebrities, they were hardly as powerful or influential as the Kennedys or Eleanor Roosevelt or some great industrialist or muscle-wielding senator, yet they attracted more attention than any of these. They were not thought-changers or idea-molders, save for the role they played in altering moral standards; nor, and this may astonish many, did either set any styles in fashions. Few women have wanted to dress like Taylor though many emulated Jacqueline Kennedy Onassis, from the shoes she wore to her hairdos.

Richard set no fashion trends, either. When Clark Gable, in a movie, was seen putting on a shirt over a bare chest, manufacturers of undershirts trembled because they knew men would similarly shuck the undergarment. Hat manufacturers pleaded with the usually hatless John Kennedy to appear in public with a fedora once in a while to prevent a downdip in business. No reports have come in from anywhere about Burton's influence in haberdashery.

Yet they caught the imagination of the world and were treated like royalty wherever they went. And they traveled like royalty, often with no fewer than 140 pieces of luggage, two nannies, four children, four dogs, a brace of secretaries, a parakeet, a turtle and—believe this—a wildcat they once had as a pet. Stewards, porters, airline stewardesses and hotel managers raced around them like

144

water bugs, anxious to do anything that would make their journeying just a little easier. Customs inspectors in almost any foreign country would smile happily, kiss Elizabeth's hand and wave her on through. Restaurants, even the world's most exclusive, where reservations are demanded months in advance, would suddenly find a vacant table if they arrived unheralded.

Once they stopped for dinner at a multistarred Guide Michelin eating place en route to the Cote d'Azur. Two of their quartet of dogs leaped from their car and scuttered up the steps, angering the proprietor. He emerged scowling, but the moment he saw Elizabeth, his anger faded and the Burtons were ushered to a choice table. They served the Burtons soup, skewered quenelles, and Napoleons for dessert, charging them $100, which Burton thought was a little much, even though they threw in food for the dogs.

They were never free of the *paparazzi*, one of whom once doubled Elizabeth over with a quick punch to the midsection so that he could obtain a photograph unique enough to sell. That they annoyed other travelers is understating the facts. The number of passengers who missed trains and flights because they could not get through the throngs has never been documented but it must have been impressive.

The acerbic Rex Harrison was vastly annoyed one time when the Burtons checked into their favorite Paris hotel, the small but very swank Lancaster on the Rue de Berri, a few steps from the Champs Elysées. The Lancaster's garden is one of the most beautiful in the city, its suites large and elegantly decorated. Harrison was there, too, and found himself unable to squeeze past the Burtons' vast luggage pile in the corridor. "Why," he groused, "do the Burtons have to be so filthily ostentatious?" Later, at the bar, Richard explained that only two of the dozens of bags were his and Harrison mellowed.

The marriage was surreal, a drama so loaded with absurdity, love, tears, rage of jealous mates and near tragedy that no movie audience would ever swallow it. They flared up at one another and then staged passionate reconciliations. Halfway through the marriage, Paul Askew, an international banker and close friend of the couple, remarked, "Sometimes I doubt that they could ever be happy without the constant turmoil. I think they each need that sort of chaos to keep things exciting."

Exciting it was. Several years after they were wed, Elizabeth became incensed because her husband had flirted, or so she thought, with a pretty girl in a Los Angeles club. She left in a fury, fumed all night, and the next day, still angry, went looking for him. She found him drinking with pals at the Polo Lounge of the posh Beverly Hills Hotel. In full view of the movie celebrities who gather there daily, she drew back her right clenched fist and delivered a roundhouse squarely to Burton's jaw. Then, her anger finally released, she kissed him tenderly.

"Sometimes, of course, that amount of high-powered emotion can get out of hand," Askew said. "Not all their fights are easily solved. I've known Elizabeth to be furious for days at a time. They run to extremes. All it means is that they care for each other a great deal, maybe even too much, if such a thing is possible."

(It wasn't the first time Burton got socked in the jaw in public by a wife. When Sybil was still married to him, she attended a New Year's Eve party with her husband in Hollywood. At the stroke of midnight, she saw him take an actress in his arms and kiss her fervently. Sybil marched up to Burton and delivered a thirteenth stroke, her own, a sharp slap across his face which left a reddened imprint of every finger. Then she wheeled, left the room and went home.)

Elizabeth throws an excellent punch; ironically, it was Richard who showed her how. Once in the early years of their marriage, relaxing in a hotel suite, they talked about the art of boxing. Elizabeth, a total novice, wondered what sports writers meant when they talked about prizefighters "throwing a right." Richard, no stranger to the art, replied, "Get up and I'll show you."

They squared off on the carpet. He taught her where to place her feet, left one forward, to turn the left side of her body toward him in a slight crouch, to stretch out the left arm and hold the right back, protecting the body and poised to deliver a blow. "Keep that left out straight," he said. "Fine, that's it. Now move onto the other foot and come in with the right with all your weight behind it. Got it?" She got it.

Several years ago in a Mexican bar Richard boasted to Elizabeth that he could split a one-inch piece of wood with a single punch. "It's all in the proper leverage," he said as he rolled up his sleeve. "Now watch me closely!"

He punched, but nothing happened. He punched a second time and still the stick remained in one piece. In quick succession he

146

unched again and again—nothing. In disgust he ordered a double martini.

A very slight bartender brought the drink over and asked, "Is this what you're trying to do?" Then with one punch he promptly split the wood in two.

"Buster, perhaps I should take lessons from him?" Elizabeth said sweetly.

Gloves-off battling was a way of life with them. "We have different personalities," he said just before their second divorce.

Elizabeth doubtless agrees with Dr. Evelyn Millis Duvall, a respected sociologist, that "the marriage in which there is never any conflict should be investigated." Says Elizabeth, "Fighting is very healthy. It clears the air. I think there's nothing worse than one partner sulking, especially if the other person wants to get the problem out into the open and cleared away."

She told Charles Collingwood of CBS that she and Richard enjoyed their battles. "Fighting with somebody you love and are really sure of—and if you're really sure of yourself in your love—having an out-and-out outrageous, ridiculous fight is one of the greatest exercises in marital togetherness," she said.

And so, they proceeded to show him, on national television:

COLLINGWOOD: In a sense, both of you identify with young people. Those symbols that you're wearing around your neck. Isn't that a peace or love symbol?

BURTON: It seems to work because we haven't quarreled for at least forty-eight hours.

TAYLOR: Stick around. . . .

COLLINGWOOD: Do you think he dominates you?

TAYLOR: You must be joking.

COLLINGWOOD: In your real life?

TAYLOR: Charles, you've got to be kidding. He sure does.

COLLINGWOOD: Richard, do you think you dominate Elizabeth?

BURTON: No, I don't. I would say offhand, when the bludgeon is out, which Elizabeth employs with remarkable efficacy, that I'm afraid that I have to withdraw. I think that if there is a henpecked one around the place, it's me.

TAYLOR: Oh, mama mia!

Back in 1961, when Elizabeth was married to Eddie Fisher, she confessed that she was "an impetuous person," adding, "A lot of discomfort could have been avoided if I had stopped to think or count to ten. This has been the story of my life; I very rarely count to ten. But at times," she continued, "I enjoy losing my temper. But that can lead to a childish tantrum and I must learn not to indulge it."

Apparently she did not learn well, because almost ten years later she was still admitting that she had "quite a temper" and proving it by calling Burton such names as Schmuck Face (a Yiddish obscenity meaning one has a face like a penis), Ratfink, Boozy and Obscenity Lips. Buster, which she employed often, was the mildest of the lot.

Their public battles were high decibel and always good for head-lines. In January 1970, she had a nationally publicized fight with him in front of Bumbles, a Hollywood discotheque. After the usual name-calling, she left him at curbside and spent the night with Edith Goetz, a close friend. An unconfirmed report about the affray was that Burton took another right to his celebrated nose.

They would even fight about Elizabeth's Jewishness. Once he told a newsman that he was more Jewish than his wife. "My great-grandfather," he said, "was a Polish Jew named Jan Ysar, and that was the family name until they changed it to Jenkins. It's true. I'm one-eighth Jewish. Elizabeth hasn't a drop of Jewish blood in her. I've told her so. Makes her furious."

"You don't become a Jew by going to a hospital and having a little piece of something cut off," he told her. "You have to be born Jewish. You have to feel Jewish blood in your veins. You're not Jewish at all. If there's any Jew in the family, it's me!"

Elizabeth replied furiously, "I'm Jewish! And you can fuck off!"

Once she was asked if Burton's role as a "professional Welshman" doesn't sometimes irritate her. "Well," she replied, "I'm a professional Jew, so you know, it's a good contest. I mean, after all, we do have Jesus Christ, don't we? He doesn't. He's claimed it, but he hasn't convinced me yet."

Burton, needle poised, interjected, "Jesus Christ was unquestionably Welsh."

Another time, for no reason he could explain except the perverse-ness of the Welsh, he began talking about Blacks in the South. "I don't like Negroes," he said. Elizabeth promptly clipped him on the ear.

"I said, 'I don't like Jews, either.' Another clip. 'Nor Russians'—clip. 'Italians'—clip.

" 'The only people I do like are the Welsh'—clip. 'And of them I only like the miners—clip. 'The only miners I like are my family'—clip. 'And I don't like all of them'—*bang*!"

Interviewed by David Frost on the latter's TV talk show, Burton insisted that "we have a rule always to fight in public, never to fight when we're alone."

That was the way their aides and servants saw it. There were plenty of times when tempers were unleashed before audiences no larger than, say, Elizabeth's private secretary, Raymond Vignale, or some maids and butlers. Indeed, Vignale has even timed their private eruptions, estimating they would last an average of one hour each.

Vignale also revealed that Burton had small studio refuges built in their homes to which he could retreat until Elizabeth's anger would sputter out. Richard had an enormous sign placed on the door of his sanctuary in Gstaad: PLEASE DO NOT DISTURB. But Elizabeth would pay no heed. "The beautiful Elizabeth would not stop banging on the door," Vignale says.

During one outburst at home, Elizabeth was self-composed while Burton flew into a rage. It happened during the run of *Hamlet* in 1964 in New York. On May 6 (a day Burton has never forgotten), a man in the balcony booed loudly as Burton declaimed, "The play's the thing wherein I'll catch the conscience of the King!" Aghast, Burton wouldn't believe it was really a boo; New York theatergoers seldom boo, and nobody, but nobody, had ever booed Richard Burton. Yet it was a boo, lusty as a foghorn at sea. Burton stepped forward. "We have been playing this production in public for over eighty performances," he told the audience. "Some have liked it, some have not. But I can assure you, we have never before been booed!"

Through the applause that followed, the boo came once more, low-throated, sonorous, filling the theater. Burton stomped home to their eight-room, $135-a-day suite at the Regency Hotel on Park Avenue. Elizabeth was watching a television show. Still amazed, Richard burst out, "I was booed tonight!"

Elizabeth, eyes on the screen, replied, "So what?"

Burton angrily asked her to switch off the set. "Do you understand that I played Hamlet tonight and *I* was booed!"

Elizabeth still refused to turn off the show. Whereupon Burton blacked it out for her—by shattering the picture tube with a mighty

kick. Unfortunately, he had removed his shoes and cut his foot s
badly a doctor had to be summoned to stitch up the wound. H
played the next few performances with a decided limp.

One reason for their many quarrels, says Hugh French, Burton'
former agent who was the first to know of their impending marriag
in 1964, could have been their divergent attitudes toward punctuali
ty. "Richard is a man who is always on time," French points ou
"while Elizabeth, poor darling, finds it very difficult to be prompt
I'm sure it was the source of much irritation."

Richard would nag her about her constant lateness. She woul
nag him about his habit of using long words, which she consider
stuffy. At a London dinner party, Burton came out with ramenta
ceous, sporiferous and melonium in two sentences. Then, in th
third, he used the word excrement. Elizabeth had enough. Sh
shouted to all the other guests, "Don't you think shit is a much bette
word?"

On location in California's Big Sur region for the film *The Sand
piper*, a dreadful movie which nevertheless grossed $14,000,00
because of its stars, Burton missed several lines. Elizabeth giggled

"I'm so henpecked," Burton sighed, "I don't know why I bother t
act."

"You don't, dear," Elizabeth swiftly replied.

He glared. "I can get a divorce on the grounds of that."

Once he told Merv Griffin, the talk-show host, that Elizabeth tol
him what to wear, even suggested the stories he should tell. "How
long will you take it, Richard?" Griffin asked. Richard answered
quickly, "Oh, I suppose forever."

Burton, an omniverous reader, prides himself on not having t
resort to swear words. Elizabeth, however, can curse like a
longshoreman. For years, he tried to cure her of using four-letter
words. One day, Elizabeth proudly told an acquaintance as Richard
looked on, "You know, he *has* finally succeeded in making me stop
using four-letter words."

Said Richard, "She's quite right. I've cured her of that terrible
habit."

Said Elizabeth, "You bet your ass."

Burton sighed. "Well, anyway, that was a three-letter word."

Between battling and needling, there were hilarious times during
the frantic years of their marriage, much laughter and joking, many

merry parties and numerous pranks one might not expect from two superstars of their magnitude.

In London, they maintained a suite at the Dorchester, one of the city's poshest hotels, which the management boasts is as English as the Tower of London. It is located in Mayfair on swank Park Lane, and world-famous celebrities (and rich tourists) stop there. Yet one day, a large paper bag filled with water came hurtling down from a high floor and burst upon the pavement.

It was a prank a prep-school freshman might pull. A former maid, meeting for tea at Brown's Hotel not far away, said many on the staff were darkly suspicious that the culprit was none other than Richard Burton. "But we never could prove it," she said.

"I must say, though," said the maid, who looked as though she could walk into any episode of *Upstairs, Downstairs* and be at home, "that Mrs. Burton used towels to beat the band. I sometimes think she used one for each of her ten fingers."

One evening, Elizabeth ordered some soda sent to their suite. When the room-service waiter delivered it, Burton opened the door and took the tray. "Now," he said, "watch me balance it on my head." He placed it carefully, then as though walking a tightrope, he inched his way across the living room.

Says the waiter who related the story, "The door shut behind him as he walked, and I couldn't see the continuation of the performance. But a moment later I heard Mrs. Burton titter and then a loud crash. There was a moment's silence and then Mr. Burton said in that wonderful, melodious voice, 'Damn! If it hadn't been for that bloody wrinkle in the rug I'd have made it.' "

The waiter remained outside to eavesdrop on the epilogue. Elizabeth laughed again and said, "Richard, sometimes you are absurd, but at all times so dear. There's nobody else quite like you."

Another time, as they got off the elevator and headed for their suite, Richard grabbed Elizabeth around the waist, said he'd always cherished a hidden wish to dance like Fred Astaire and whirled her down the corridor. "You're Ginger Rogers," he told her, "so dance." She giggled, fell in with his mood and danced to the door and into their suite, finally collapsing in laughter on the sofa.

A brilliant mimic (her Mae West and Marilyn Monroe imitations are uncannily accurate), she once did an impersonation of Richard at a backstage party that convulsed the actors and stage crew. During the run of *Hamlet* in New York, the cast gave her a birthday party which featured an enormous cake that had taken days to prepare and had been lugged backstage at the Lunt-Fontanne Theatre by a small platoon of men who took great care lest a sliver of icing fall out of place.

In a climactic scene, Richard, as Hamlet, raises his massive sword above his head in his right hand and, left arm outstretched, roars his lines, fury in his face and voice. The production, directed by Sir John Gielgud, was performed as a final run-through, with the actors in rehearsal clothes. Burton wore black slacks and a black V-neck sweater.

After the curtain calls, Elizabeth came backstage, dressed in an identical costume. After the toasts and the "happy birthdays," she was handed the sword to cut the cake. She grasped it and suddenly she duplicated Burton's rousingly dramatic pose, one arm out, the other brandishing the sword, the dark fury in her face. Just as suddenly, she brought the sword down, smack in the middle of that lovely confectionary, smashing it into a mess of cream, crumbs and icing.

For their tenth anniversary, Richard ordered a Hollywood florist, at stupendous cost, to fill their Mexican home at Puerto Vallarta with Elizabeth's favorite bloom, orchids. A truckload came down. Orchids were placed in each of the twelve rooms, including the kitchen and the bathrooms.

Unhappily, retakes were needed for the film they were currently working on in Hollywood. By the time they arrived in Mexico, they opened the door to a houseful of withered flowers. Elizabeth laughed for hours at the stricken look on Richard's face.

"I enjoy giving her things," he once said. "Elizabeth is a most luscious receiver."

Richard was enormously proud of her. Happily, he brought her to Pontrhydyfen and introduced her to the gnarled Welshmen at the Miner's Arms.

A dart board, a staple in all pubs of the British Isles, hung on one wall, across the room from the bar. Young Burton had been an expert at the game. After introducing Elizabeth to the townsfolk, he told her proudly of his skill.

"How do you do it?" she asked, picking up a dart. "Like this?" She tossed it and struck the bull's-eye dead center. The entire pub rocked with applause, Burton leading.

"See," he howled above the tumult, "didn't I pick myself a talented wife?" Then, as everyone watched, he kissed her full on the lips. Elizabeth blushed and Richard ordered drinks for the house.

A woman patron who was there recalled, "That's Richie for you. A good lad. I remember him when he spoke only Welsh, not a word of English. Aye, and he's still a good lad and married such a fine, fine lady."

Fine lady or no, Burton would not take her part when a Welsh miner pinched her backside. He knew his countrymen and their weaknesses, and if his wife happened to be a victim, that was her tough luck and no blame on him.

In one of the Welsh pubs to which he took her, she was surrounded by the burly miners. One reached out and put his fingers into her mouth, peeling her lips from her teeth. The others crowded around, peering into the opened cavity. "Oh dom," they said, marveling. "Oh dom, look at all the white teeth!"

Elizabeth, recalling the incident, shudders and says, "Just like they were looking at a horse they had bought."

It got worse. "Then this big miner grabs me by the elbows and lifts me straight up and holds me there and they all look at me. 'Oh dom, look at her but she's handsome.' " Richard watched gleefully from the bar.

It got still worse. The following day, she went with Richard to a football match and afterward visited another pub. She was wearing tight white ski pants, apparently irresistible to one miner. He reached out and grabbed a slice of her. Elizabeth slapped his face, but afterward Richard defended the miner. "It wasn't his fault, my love, you wearing those white ski pants. Practically asking for it." Women's libbers would unquestionably be appalled at the position he was seeking to defend.

"I was not!"

"Well, what do you expect—here's a coal miner sitting there, and here's this girl passing by and he says to himself, 'Well, what's this? I think I'll take a reach of that.' He meant no harm by it. He just took a reach. We Welshmen are an independent lot."

Despite Richard's claim—or perhaps because of it—Elizabeth watched over him constantly. Besides acting as stand-in, she would trail him on a set, carrying props for him. She would, on occasion, heat a can of soup for him on a portable hot plate and make him sit down and eat.

When they were not battling or acting, their home life was surprisingly ordinary.

Elizabeth said in 1970, "Our most precious commodity is being alone—no servants, no anybody—just us. How we cherish it and look forward to it! Sunday is the best day of the week because it often offers that privacy. There are no servants hovering around, or very few. Last Sunday was one of those blissful days. We got up at ten o'clock; the newspapers had been delivered and Richard fetched them. Then we both read parts of the paper.

"There was a story about President Johnson and we discussed it. That was a tragedy when Kennedy was assassinated, but I suppose Johnson is trying to do a proper job. His civil rights program. His domestic program. They're not bad. But his foreign policy can be a nightmare.

"Then I prepared some bacon and eggs just for the two of us. Richard said it was very tasty and he wasn't lying. If I say so myself, he's very accurate—about my cooking. Then we finished reading the newspapers. More discussions. The telephone rang about six or seven times, but we refused to answer it. We listened to some music, read some books, straightened pictures. Just lazed around.

"Now isn't that a cozy, domestic scene? All that was missing was a pipe and a fire in the fireplace—but it was hot and Richard doesn't smoke a pipe. Despite the missing items, it sure was blissful."

Meanwhile, Richard said in 1970, "Elizabeth loves to cook, but she just can't stop when she's ahead. She hears about some new dish and tries to improve on it—the results are staggering. Just staggers the human imagination! We don't eat out much, but if I had to subsist on Elizabeth's cooking, I'd be on a perpetual diet. Fortunately, we have an excellent cook. You can tell when Elizabeth does the honors—not just by the content, but by the aftermath. Invariably, she leaves a mess!

"She likes to read and that's a strong plus. Elizabeth is a well-read person. We make it a practice to talk about the contents of the article or book we read. Sometimes we even read aloud. My, this sounds lovey-dovey.

"Despite what you may have been told, Elizabeth joins me in shunning fancy clothes. Blue jeans would be her constant attire if she had her way. But custom and society deem otherwise and so she puts on the fancy clothes. That's fine until she insists that I do the same⟩

154

The Burtons in Who's Afraid of Virginia Woolf?, *1966.*

Members of the Burton family dine out in Rome during the filming of The Taming of the Shrew. *The children are, from left, Liza Todd; Maria, adopted daughter of Elizabeth and Richard; and Michael and Christopher Wilding.* (UPI)

At a UNICEF gala, Elizabeth displays her new emeralds. (Sygma)

Richard displays the diamond pendant inscribed "Eternal Love till Death," which he gave his wife on her fortieth birthday. (Keystone)

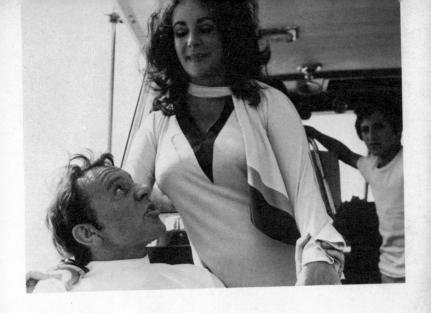

Aboard the Burton yacht. (Sygma)

Richard and Sophia Loren, his co-star in The Journey, *1973. (Sygma)*

Richard and his new friend, Princess Elizabeth of Yugoslavia, with his adopted daughter, Maria, in Switzerland, 1974. (Sygma)

Elizabeth leaves a London hospital where she spent ten days in April 1975. She is accompanied by her friend Henry Wynberg. (Sygma)

Newlyweds again, October 1975, in South Africa. (Sygma)

Richard in a scene from the play Equus, *in which he made a triump*
return to the stage, 1976.

Susan Hunt, the new Mrs. Richard Burton, former wife of British racing car driver James Hunt. (UPI)

Elizabeth and John Warner, who became her seventh husband, with some of their children in Austria. From left, Michael Wilding, Jr., Liza Todd, Mary Warner, Naomi Wilding (daughter of Michael, Jr., and his wife, Jo),

"She fancies herself an interior decorator. Often the results are very good. But other times—oh, where, oh, where has taste fled to? She insisted on hanging that hideous picture. But for all her shortcomings, I tap her!"

Like many husbands, he tended to forget birthdays and anniversaries, but only at the very beginning. Elizabeth let him know forthrightly that these occasions were to be remembered.

Once, taxi driver Basil Ward, driving Burton alone one night, confessed he had forgotten his own wedding anniversary. Burton told him, "You should know that you can never understand a woman—they're real mysterious, but we can't do without 'em. If I ever forgot my anniversary, Elizabeth would throw the piano at me."

At their Gstaad home, Richard was always first to rise but would return to bed, where they would often spend the entire day. None of the servants would dare knock until summoned. Richard would make his own tea and take their little Pekingeses, E'en So and O Fie, for a stroll, no matter the weather. They would always take the same route through the village, a lovely spot in the Saane Valley surrounded by forests, mountains, glaciers and lakes. When he returned, Elizabeth would still be in her nightgown, hair uncombed. Richard would brew another cup of tea or mix a drink and both would read the newspapers.

Richard and Elizabeth have often said they never read what has been written about them. Perhaps not deliberately. But avoiding text and photos about the Burtons in the days of their marriage would not have been possible unless they refused to read all newspapers and magazines. Elizabeth did read the papers, always turning first to the *Peanuts* comic strip, twirling a braid of hair around her finger as she read. Richard would become truly angry when his eye caught photos that did not show his wife at her best. She would be equally furious.

Aware that one bad picture could sour her day, Raymond Vignale became a self-appointed censor, glancing hurriedly through the newspapers and magazines and throwing out those that displayed Elizabeth unflatteringly. He did not always get there first.

Once, in a British newspaper, Elizabeth spotted a photograph of herself taken on the beach at Capri. She was sitting on the sand, with rubber-tire folds around her middle clearly (and to her, painfully) evident. She erupted. Vignale pointed out that even the most slender woman, pictured in that position, could not possibly display a flawless abdomen, but Elizabeth was unconsoled. "Why," she demanded, "do these bastards show things like this?"

There were times when Elizabeth couldn't look slender even though she was photographed through the wrong end of a telescope. She was always aware of this fact and so was Richard. "Where," he would demand, "is that fat Jewish wife of mine?" She loves to eat. "My taste buds get in an uproar and I get a lusty, sensual thing out of eating," she says. Her favorite of favorites is hardly calculated to keep her weight down—it's mashed potatoes! She is also extremely fond of cheesecake (300 calories per small piece), drinks great quantities of milk and will often spread peanut butter and mayonnaise on huge slices of bread as a postmidnight snack. Disliking scheduled meals, she eats at odd hours, another eating habit to be avoided by those who would keep streamlined figures.

At the same time, she is a complete professional who can, if she must for a film, lose fifteen pounds within two weeks. Her secret employed now for more than twenty-five years: "I do it by starving. I have coffee for breakfast, scrambled eggs for lunch and steak for dinner—with pink grapefruit coming out of my ears." When she craves something sweet during her dieting weeks, she places a forkful of chocolate cake or other much missed dish in her mouth and keeps it there for minutes, tasting the flavor. Then she removes the mass without swallowing.

Most of the Burtons' fan mail would be sent directly to the studio, but more than fifty letters a day would still arrive at their home. They would be divided in the usual proportion received by movie stars. Most were requests for photographs, about ten percent pleas for money, and a few, the unsigned ones, sexual. All letters were burned because, as Vignale explains, "tourists would go through their garbage."

The Burtons lived well. Richard once admitted they often outspent the legendary Aristotle Onassis, the late multimillionaire husband of Jacqueline Kennedy Onassis. The couple's combined wealth gave them an incomparable life-style. Let's move in for a closeup look.

2. All That Wealth

WHEN THEY WERE RIDING HIGHEST AS SUPERSTARS AND WORLD celebrities, the coal miner's son once observed, a measure of awe in his voice, "They say we generate more business activity than one of the smaller African nations."

Mind-boggling though it may sound, they actually did! Consider: Between the end of *Cleopatra* and 1966, they starred in five films together, and Elizabeth made one without him (*Reflections in a Golden Eye*). These seven pictures are estimated to have grossed a total of $200,000,000 in the United States and throughout the world from all sources.

In comparison, in a recent year the gross national product (all the goods and services produced) of Angola was only $3.8 million; Equatorial Guinea, $36 million; Brazzaville or Republic of the Congo, $56 million; and Lesotho, $86 million. Play with some more figures: At their height, the Burtons' annual business activities exceeded the exports of Chad, which ran to some $30 million in a recent year; Brazzaville, $31 million; Mila, $35 million; and Niger $32 million. Clearly, the pair caused a great deal of money to be spread around.

When Richard and Elizabeth were man and wife, their combined wealth was tremendous. Her fortune was estimated at more than $20 million, his at about $10 million, although some sources have put Elizabeth's as high as $75 million and Richard's at $50 million. The couple never revealed their total wealth, and perhaps they never even knew their actual worth. It is not uncommon for the very affluent to be vague about the extent of their holdings; they accumulate riches every day.

In the final years of their marriage, the Burtons' joint annual income was more than $3 million. Expenditures, however, often surpassed that staggering sum, and despite their opulence, they often found themselves short of cash.

"Seventy-five percent of our income goes before we see it," Richard complained. "We need so many people to help us and they need to be paid. For example, we need four guards to watch the villa or someone will try to crawl over the wall to photograph us in the lavatory."

Despite his wealth, Burton has always mocked superaffluence. "All capitalists," he once remarked, "should be forced to pay taxes. Everyone—except actors—Welsh actors!"

About Elizabeth's wealth, he said, "She's richer than I am. But then she's more parsimonious. Seriously, Elizabeth has one of the kindest hearts imaginable. She has given away millions to worthy causes, but most of the time in great secrecy, as she regards donating her private affair."

Annually, the Burtons contributed more than $1,000,000 to charities—and not all tax exempt. A great many contributions were made in Great Britain where tax write-offs are difficult to come by, but this didn't discourage the couple's philanthropy. While accountants ranted and pounded the table, Elizabeth said sweetly, "Donations give me such a warm glow in my private parts, so why stop to worry about deductions?"

A great part of Elizabeth's wealth—about $8 million of it, according to one estimate—lies in her red leather jewel boxes. Most, of course, are real, though she owns some semiprecious brooches and bracelets which she describes as junk jewelry. Among these, she counts an enamel cameo bracelet which Empress Josephine owned when she was married to Napoleon, and an Iranian caftan with silver and gold embroidery, each worth thousands.

She acquired a taste for huge precious stones after Mike Todd, who presented her with a gift each day, came up with a 27-carat sparkler that made her gasp. Once she would wear a good part of her collection wherever she went, even on the beach in a bathing suit, scorning all criticism with the observation that "them who has 'em, wears 'em." Now she is more careful and the gems are heavily guarded.

Her crown jewel is the Cartier-Burton diamond. An inch thick and weighing 69.42 carats, it had been put up for auction in New York in 1969. Elizabeth desperately wanted it and sent an agent to offer bids. He dropped out at $1,000,000, and Cartier's, which went to $1,050,000, acquired it. Next day, Richard telephoned from London and bought the gem for Elizabeth at a markup, of course, which has remained undisclosed.

As part of the deal, he agreed to allow Cartier's to put it on public display. The diamond drew throngs and a quick roasting from *The New York Times*, which editorialized about the "peasants" who came to "gawk." *The Times* wrote, "As somebody said, it would have been nice to wear in the tumbril on the way to the guillotine. . . . It won't seem out of place on the yachts parked in the Bahamas or in the Mediterranean where the Beautiful People spend much time, not to mention money, impressing others.

"In this Age of Vulgarity marked by such minor matters as war and poverty, it gets harder every day to scale the heights of true vulgarity. But given some loose millions, it can be done—and worse, be admired."

Elizabeth's second-best diamond is the Krupp, weighing 33 carats and appraised at $305,000. (In comparison, the famous blue Hope diamond, bought by Edward B. McLean in 1911 and later worn with flair by the late Evalyn Walsh McLean, is 44-1/2 carats. The Koh-i-noor, the central diamond in the Queen of England's state crown, is 106 1/16 carats.) The Krupp came from the estate of Vera Krupp, former wife of the German munitions magnate. Elizabeth, so fond of the gem that she shampoos it daily, said with neat irony, "I think it's charming and fitting that a little Jewish girl like me ended up with Baron Krupp's rock."

Once Elizabeth proudly displayed it to Princess Margaret of England at a London affair. Margaret sniffed and called it "the most vulgar thing I've ever seen." Said Elizabeth, "Want to try it on?" Margaret allowed that she might. She put it on and her eyes were riveted to the stone, which she turned, twisted and held up to the light. "See," Elizabeth said, "it's not so vulgar now."

The ring has been on other than royal fingers. A former maid at the Dorchester said, "Miss Elizabeth let me try it on." Virtually everyone who has admired it has been allowed a try-on, too.

On Elizabeth's fortieth birthday, Richard gave her a heart-shaped pendant that once belonged to Shah Jehan, who built the Taj Mahal. It is valued at $100,000 and is inscribed, "Eternal love till death." Another Burton present was the La Peregrina Pearl, once owned by King Philip II of Spain. He gave it to his bride, Mary I of England

("Bloody Mary"), on their marriage in 1554. A rare pink 25-carat diamond in a 16-1/2-carat setting was also a gift from Burton. His florid presentation speech contained: "This may be considered rare, but far rarer are you, my love."

Elizabeth will sometimes encircle her blue jeans with a belt encrusted with diamonds. Her collection also includes a ruby and diamond piece, many pairs of earrings set in diamonds and emeralds, a square-cut diamond and emerald necklace—and a tiny diamond weighing less than a quarter of a carat, worth about $35, but treasured. Richard bought it for her with earnings he won in a Ping Pong game.

Another prize gem is her 40-carat sapphire brooch, a beautiful blue in a Tiffany setting, which reportedly was once owned privately by the British Royal Family. Purchased by Richard from Collingwood Jewelers in London, it was reportedly worth $65,000 at 1969 prices.

Besides gems, the couple possessed literally fabulous means of locomotion. Aircraft, for example. Ironically, neither cares much for flying, preferring train travel. But when they had problems getting from remote places to world capitals, the solution seemed quite natural.

Why, Burton reasoned, charter a jet from Sardinia, where they were on location for a film, to fly to a masked ball in Venice or to get to Paris for the European premiere of *The Taming of the Shrew* or to get to Oxford for the opening of *Dr. Faustus*? "So," he said, "I decided we might as well buy it. Now we can hop over to Nice for lunch."

Nice is only a couple of hundred miles from Sardinia, handy to reach when one owns a jet. He added, "Besides, luv, I'm convinced the world is going up in blazes in five or ten years, so we might as well go down in a jet." Had the gloomy prediction materialized, they would have gone down in ultracomfort.

The ten-passenger twin-jet de Havilland, costing $1 million, had a modern kitchen, lounge, bar and built-in movie projector and screen. It was named, of course, *The Elizabeth*.

Their lavish gifts to one another would have made an Arabian oil potentate gape. Elizabeth once explained, "We get such great pleasure out of spending money. So why not enjoy it?"

They spent, and they must have enjoyed hugely. Burton gave his wife a white hand-built Panther car, costing $25,000, as a Christmas present in 1975. Her gift to him was a $50,000 helicopter.

They sailed in their own 110-foot, ocean-going yacht, the *Kalizma*, valued at $850,000, which costs $150,000 a year just to leave idle. The *Kalizma*, named for daughters Kate, Liza and Maria, has seven bedrooms, three baths, the latest in radar equipment, Chippendale mirrors, Louis XIV chairs, Empire sofas and many priceless antiques. It sleeps fourteen. "A larger number makes it almost impossible to spend sufficient time with your guests," Elizabeth once observed.

Each sleeping chamber has all Continental hotel comforts, including a highly polished brass bed warmer and the services of a valet who fetches and polishes shoes when placed outside the cabin door. The master bedroom, however, is the vessel's true showplace. A huge, hand-carved mahogany bed dominates the room. "Luv, no bunks for us," Richard ordered.

A brocaded Empire sofa is set casually on a thick carpet. (Duplicates of the sofa and the carpet are to be found in the Louvre Museum.) The adjoining bathroom is done in pale pink with matching toilet facilities, including a low seventeenth-century teakwood table to hold Elizabeth's wigs.

All Burton bedrooms contain bookcases, and this one is no exception. There are several filled with his well-thumbed volumes. The clerk at the Dorchester book stall said, "Before Mr. Burton would depart on his yacht he'd sweep up several dozen books. Mostly history and biography. That man has an insatiable appetite for the printed word."

The Burtons also spent much time in their chalet in Gstaad, Switzerland—because of favorable tax laws, their lawyers listed them as permanent Swiss residents—and owned 685 acres on Tenerife in the Canary Islands, where they grew bananas; ten acres of land and a farmhouse in County Wicklow, Ireland, where they bred horses; and Casa Kimberley, a villa in Puerta Vallarta on the western coast of Mexico.

Casa Kimberley is a large white stucco Spanish-style hacienda, set squarely in the middle of the village, but with a magnificent view of Banderas Bay. It is actually two houses joined by what the Burtons called their "bridge of love." One home originally belonged to Richard, and later the couple built the bridge over a cobblestone

169

street. The main house, on three levels, has no windows—a visitor has the feeling of walking into a lovely garden. There are six guest bedrooms and a huge living-dining room and terrace. Pre-Columbian relics are everywhere, presented to Elizabeth and Richard by a grateful Mexican government for giving them so much favorable publicity.

In addition, the couple had investments in theater chains, hotels, television stations, transportation corporations. They owned a thriving boutique in Paris.

Their estate also included dozens of original paintings by masters —Van Gogh, Monet, Renoir, Roualt, Utrillo, Pissaro, Degas, Modigliani.

Richard once declared that his paintings are on the pound notes he gives to his family. All his immediate relations have received equal sums from Burton, and he has helped them to purchase their own homes. He has also given each of them an automobile and issued pensions to all of retiring age. The contributions have run into the hundreds of thousands of dollars.

A heavy-set man in Pontrhydyfen's Blue Scar Welfare Club, a gathering place for many of the locals, said, "I know Richie from childhood on, and devoted, he is. The family is a big one, but he gives equally to all. A lovely person, he is. Many is the time I wished he was related to me. I've always been poor. Why, when I was a lad we slept three in a bed. Maybe if I tell him that his dada worked side by side with me in the pits, Richie will adopt me. That's fair play, isn't it? The next time he comes round I shall ask him!"

Richard and Elizabeth have said repeatedly that money may provide material comforts but can never bring the happiness one gets from children. "They are true wealth," Elizabeth remarked. She and Richard have tried hard to be good parents, often succeeding, but at times failing. Between them, they have six children.

Nineteen-year-old Kate Burton (whose mother is Sybil) is a bright, attractive sophomore at Brown University in Providence, Rhode Island. She has light brown hair, a round face and bears a strong resemblance to her father. She's five foot four, slender, and possesses the brightest blue eyes.

According to schoolmates, "She is very much into the theater." At Brown, she is a member of the school's Production Workshop, a student-run dramatic group which puts on plays twice a month, ranging from the classics to Noel Coward. Says a friend, "Kate is very committed to that and eventually wants to go into the theater."

Kate was extremely excited when her father came to New York to star in *Equus*. She would slip into the city and, unnoticed by the audience, watch the play. She saw the play several times before her father assumed the leading role and told friends she thought he was better in the part than Anthony Perkins, who had played it before Burton.

At Brown, the students take no special notice of Kate. There have been no interviews in the college newspaper. Says another student, "Celebrity kids are not afforded any special status here unless they prove themselves—and that's how Kate herself wants it."

Kate, who lives with her mother, stepfather and eight-year-old half sister, on Central Park West in New York City, was educated at the United Nations International School in Flushing, Queens.

Jessica Burton, the younger daughter of Richard and Sybil, is seventeen years old and has been retarded since birth. She lives in Pennsylvania in a special school for the mentally handicapped. Like her mother and father, she is very attractive. Sybil and Richard visit her often.

Twenty-four-year-old Michael Wilding, Jr., son of Elizabeth and Michael Wilding, has presented some problems. Seven years ago, at age seventeen, he announced that he was marrying keypunch operator Beth Clutter, who was several years older. He wore gold earrings and a dark red caftan when he was married in London's Caxton Hall Registry. The Burtons gave the couple a London townhouse, but young Wilding preferred a commune in the English countryside. His wife objected and they were divorced. Wilding moved to another commune, this one in Wales not far from Richard's birthplace, called *Ffyon We*, Welsh for White Springs. Home is a large farmhouse near the village of Ystumtuen, set in a valley where sheep graze and small creeks run. Nearby is an unused lead mine, now in ruins. Michael lives with twenty-four-year-old Johanna Lykke-Dahn and their daughter, Naomi, and a number of other young people. Several of them, including Michael, who plays guitar, flute and trumpet, are part of a rock group called "Solar Ben."

"I try not to interfere in his life-style," Richard said during his

171

second marriage to Elizabeth. "But sometimes I get Goddamned mad when I think what it took to climb out. . . . I made it up and the boy's trying to make it down."

In London, Geoffrey Lansing, a twenty-five-year-old youth who spent some time in the commune, said, "Imagine being heir to all that money and wanting to live in a rather depressing commune. I was told that Michael was the son of actress Elizabeth Taylor, but frankly I didn't believe it. However, when Michael and Johanna had a daughter (Michael's second child), Elizabeth Taylor came to the commune for a visit. There's no mistaking that face, and come to think of it, Michael does resemble her a great deal.

"She sang to the infant as she held it in her arms. I'd venture to say that she actually liked being a grandmother. She brought along a galaxy of toys that must have cost hundreds. That baby will have few money worries. With all Elizabeth's wealth, I'm sure that she will always come through."

Christopher Wilding, Michael's younger brother, is a handsome and charming twenty-two-year-old who had been seriously considered for the role of Jesus in Franco Zeffirelli's television play *Life of Christ*. He was turned down because the casting director thought he was too young. But there was agreement that "the lad possessed tremendous talent."

Until recently, Christopher expressed interest in an acting career but decided to shelve it until he completed his studies at the University of Hawaii. He lives on the island with Elizabeth's brother, Howard, who is a professor of oceanography.

Christopher consistently gets good grades, and his fellow students regard him as a "very level-headed, sweet guy." Said one schoolmate, "He's the sort you select to be the referee, because you know you'll be sure to get a fair shake."

Elizabeth agrees. Shortly after Christopher's fifteenth birthday she said, "I don't know if he will ever get to be President or Prime Minister, but if he doesn't, the people will be the poorer. He's the fairest person I know."

When Liza Todd was born, Mike Todd said, "Thank God she doesn't have my mug. She looks exactly like her mother!" Elizabeth added, "And Heaven be praised that she's got her father's personality!"

At age nineteen, Liza still possesses both characteristics. She studies sculpture at Middlesex Polytechnic School in London. Her mother has Liza's creations all over her Mexican and Swiss houses. Liza has told friends that she would like to be a sculptress and doesn't want a movie career. But many in the movie world agreed with Donna Quinn, Elizabeth's former West Coast press representative, that "with her heritage, she'll have a difficult time avoiding one."

Sixteen-year-old Maria Burton is the youngest child. After giving birth to Liza, Elizabeth was warned by doctors that she faced a grave risk if she attempted to have another baby. When she was married to Eddie Fisher, she decided to adopt one. She chose a tiny German infant who had a badly dislocated hip, the daughter of a mother too poor to feed the child. A doctor said the baby was suffering from one of the worst cases of malnutrition he had ever seen. But with much "tender, loving care" and a series of complicated operations, the youngster has developed into a pretty and active teenager. She attends the International School in Geneva, Switzerland, and often goes skiing.

Richard has legally adopted Maria, who now bears his name. "It's become difficult to keep up with Maria," he says. "I fancy myself as a fairly active man, but that child leaves me in the lurch!"

Elizabeth frequently admitted her dearest wish would have been to be the mother of Richard's baby. She once told reporters, "If we had our way, we would have at least a dozen children."

Richard added, "Elizabeth has a splendid idea. That way we would be assured of being provided for in our old age. Why, twenty-five dollars a month from a dozen children would amount to . . ."

Richard and Elizabeth had some strange attitudes concerning money. They would happily toss away thousands of dollars but carefully count the small change. Shortly before their last divorce they bought some fish and chips from a London street vendor. Richard rarely carries any money with him and borrowed some cash from the driver of their Rolls Royce. Then he paid the merchant, making sure he received the shilling due him. After pocketing the coin, he gave the man a five-pound tip.

"I just don't want to be gypped," Burton explained.

3. Crackup

IN THE HARSH WORLD OF REALITY, WHERE THE WAR IN VIETNAM WA
causing the bitterest division since the American Civil War, where
assassinations were sending the nation reeling into shock, where
students were occupying college buildings, where crime was rising
inflation soaring and the economy dipping, the Burtons offered :
measure of relief. They were among the last survivors of a glittering
age, thriving, performing outrageous things for our delectation
and a great many of us loved it all.

We might pretend not to care, but few actually wished to see the
performance end. It was such great escapist entertainment. But i
did end—as explosively as it began.

In the spring of 1973, the Burtons parted for seventeen days, then
reconciled with much kissing and expressions of mutual love. Kaij-
iro Hayami, a Japanese professor of psychology, who was visiting
California, took some candid photographs of the couple embracing.
The first picture shows Richard and Elizabeth in an all-consuming
kiss. There is a picnic table and a white ironstone pitcher in the
background. In the second shot, the two lovers are still ardently
kissing but are a bit nearer the table and pitcher. The third, fourth
and fifth photographs show the couple finally unhinged, but apparently wishing to cool off after the torrid kiss, they are pouring the
water in the pitcher over each other's heads. It was that kind of a
reconciliation.

Unfortunately, it lasted only one month.

In June came an explosion. Burton, by his own admission to
Sophia Loren, "blew my top." He almost literally threw Elizabeth
out, telling her to leave within twenty minutes. What had happened?

We both burst apart virtually at the same moment," he confided later to Sophia. "It got to the state when I was running around like a lunatic, behaving a bit madly, boozing of course."

Elizabeth, shaken, flew to California where she visited her mother and old friends. At the home of the late British actor Laurence Harvey she watched a private showing of the movie *Night Watch* she had made a year before. A frequent escort was actor Peter Lawford, who had been divorced in 1966 from Patricia Kennedy, a sister of the late President, and married in 1972 to Mary Rowan, the twenty-two-year-old daughter of comedian Dan Rowan. Elizabeth and Peter were seen around town a great deal, and the inevitable gossip began.

Not only was Elizabeth linked romantically by press reports to Lawford, but some rumors were actually published that she had fallen in love with his son, Christopher. Chris, identified as handsome and twenty-four years old, was actually barely eighteen. "We laughed a lot and we talked about old times," Lawford says.

Burton had gone to an isolated summer home in Quogue on Long Island's south shore, a tranquil place owned by the couple's close friend and attorney, Aaron R. Frosch, where he and Elizabeth had spent many weekends. The clamming is good at Quogue, and one can sit for hours on the scrub grass looking out at the sand and Shinnecock Bay. Burton read the news from Hollywood and could no longer be tranquilized by the peaceful setting. He telephoned Elizabeth at the Beverly Hills Hotel and roared into the mouthpiece in that great voice with which Hotspur exhorts the troops into battle in the famous St. Crispin's Day speech:

"Get your ass back here or you won't have an ass to sit on."

Elizabeth boarded a plane. Burton met her at Kennedy Airport in a limousine and together they drove to Quogue. It was a tender meeting. But before they had gone halfway, they began to argue. The quarreling became so bitter that Elizabeth returned to New York and checked into the Regency Hotel on Park Avenue.

"She didn't do anything," recalled a maid. "Just sat there and stared in space."

A statement issued by their public-relations office was a marvel of nonspeak: "The only thing I can say is that nobody else is involved if there is a split temporarily or otherwise and I'm not admitting there is."

On July 3, Elizabeth wrote her own statement to the press. Th one was, like Elizabeth herself, a clear and straightforward expre sion of her feelings, intentions and hopes:

"I am convinced," she stated, "it would be a good and constructiv idea if Richard and I are separated for a while. Maybe we have love each other too much (not that I ever believed such a thing wa possible) but we have been in each other's pockets constantly, neve being apart except for matters of life and death, and I believe th has caused a temporary breakdown in communications. . . ."

She said she would return to California in a few days to see "m mother and old and true friends." Touchingly, she added, "An friends are to help each other, aren't they? Isn't that what it's a supposed to be about?"

"And if anyone reads anything lascivious into that last statemen all I can say is, it must be in the mind of the readers—not mine, or m friends' or my husband's."

She said that she hoped with all her heart that the separatio would "ultimately bring us back to where we should be—and that i together.

"Wish us well, please," she concluded, "during this most difficul time."

Elizabeth flew to California the next day in a private jet afte pushing through a dense throng of newsmen and TV camera which virtually barricaded all entrances and exits to the hotel.

One reporter said, "I know she isn't a giant, only five-four, but sh seemed to hunch close to the ground. She looked so emaciated—lik the tiniest and skinniest pygmy. One of the guys who weighs abou three hundred pounds called out with black humor, 'Liz, if that kin of love affects you that way, I've got to give it a try. Maybe then I car lose some weight.'

"Despite herself, I saw the corner of Liz's lips suddenly turn up as if she was about to break out in a smile, but she controlled hersel and soon it disappeared."

Burton read about the flight and the statement in the newspapers in his Quogue hideaway. Next morning, though it was barely 10 A.M., he poured a hefty quantity of vodka in a large glass, topped it with orange juice, and sadly told a British reporter, "I cannot imagine life without her. But if Elizabeth really wants a separation, so be it."

Nonetheless, he wasn't accepting it as final. From Quogue, he called California countless times, trying to get Elizabeth to change her mind. Then, a few days later, he left for Rome, where he was scheduled to co-star with Sophia Loren in *The Voyage*, to be directed by Vittorio De Sica and produced by Sophia's husband, Carlo Ponti. He stayed with the Pontis at their lovely and secluded seventeenth-century villa on the city's outskirts.

On his arrival, he looked terrible. His eyes were red, his face pale; he seemed ill. Sophia, a close friend and a kind, generous woman, walked with him along the shaded paths, listening as he poured out his troubles, talking soothingly, comfortingly, as a mother would to a heartbroken son whose girl had just left him. And as an adolescent who might have worried out loud in his insecurity, Burton said to her, "You know, Sophia, the trouble with me is that women don't like me any more." What can a "mother" reply to that, but to say, as Sophia did, "Don't be silly, Richard. You are a most brilliant and fascinating man."

Sophia Loren's encouragement apparently provided the psychological stimulation he needed. He said he felt somewhat better and thought he could now win his wife back.

In California, Elizabeth was staying at the Mexican-style Beverly Hills home of Edith Head, the Oscar-winning costume designer who was a friend and confidante. Saddened and confused, Elizabeth had by no means given up on the marriage. "She loves him very much," Miss Head insisted, "and she has every intention of returning to him."

A sagacious woman, Miss Head was born in Searchlight, Nevada, just south of Las Vegas, and she had learned that one never bets on a supposed sure thing. Everyone but her, she said, was counting the marriage out. "I would bet you 100 to 1," she said, "that this is a very temporary separation, and that they'll be back together. They're just taking a breather from being together too much. I've been with Richard and Elizabeth all over Europe, and I can tell you I have never seen two people who are so absolutely and completely compatible. It's much more than being in love. They complement each other, they need each other. But they're just taking a little vacation."

Elizabeth would have preferred to remain in seclusion, but friends prevailed upon her to go out to dinner, attend parties for diversion. She was escorted around town by Roddy McDowall, Dr. Rex Kennamer and Peter Lawford. It was Lawford who introduced her to Henry Wynberg, who had made millions in the used-car business. He met Elizabeth on July 6, 1973, a Friday evening, at a private club called the Candy Store in Beverly Hills, much favored by the film set.

Wynberg had known Lawford for about two years. "He had been recuperating from a serious illness," Wynberg says, "and was having marital troubles. I tried to make his life a little more bearable. So his introducing me to Elizabeth was perfectly natural."

Next day, Lawford, chatting with Wynberg on the phone, said he was escorting Elizabeth to a party that evening. Wynberg invited them to his home in Beverly Hills for cocktails. Lawford accepted and they came. Elizabeth was entranced by an eight-foot-long aquarium, with its darting, rainbow-hued fish, in the foyer of the house on Beverly Estates Drive.

The following day, Elizabeth and Wynberg talked on the telephone. She asked if she could take her children to see Wynberg's aquarium. "Of course," he replied. "I'd love to meet them." Later that day, she arrived with Christopher, Maria and Liza, who glued their faces to the glass for a long time while Wynberg told them about the occupants.

A friendship began. From then on, Wynberg was to play a significant role in her life, but the relationship would not blossom until later—for Burton was on the phone from Rome, insisting that she join him. And she agreed. Edith Head knew what she had been talking about.

Burton announced he was "bored" with the interminable stories of their separation. Elizabeth's press aides were sending out similarly optimistic statements, and it seemed that everything was indeed patched up.

On July 23, 1973, Elizabeth flew to Rome in a private jet, after switching planes in London. Burton, in dark glasses which fooled nobody, sat in his Rolls Royce in a parking lot, waiting. So were one hundred newsmen and photographers, and platoons of police, all of whom watched and waited as though an empress was arriving. Elizabeth, looking out a window, saw them and quailed. She knew she had to run the gauntlet but waited twenty minutes before she could get up the courage. Finally she emerged in form-fitting embroidered blue jeans and blouse, and another familiar, yet scary, scene ensued. The police tried vainly to block the newsmen who came at her in waves, squawking questions, thrusting microphones into her face, snapping hundreds of photographs. Fights broke out among the journalists as Elizabeth swept across the airport into the waiting Rolls Royce.

Inside the car, through the smoked windows, they were seen embracing, clutching one another, kissing warmly. In each other's arms, they drove off to Sophia and Carlo Ponti's villa, whose tranquility was instantly shattered by their presence. Later, Donald Zec, Sophia's biographer, who was there at the time, wrote, "It is my personal, and admittedly crudely expressed view, that Sophia and Carlo Ponti needed that invasion of their villa by the Burtons like a hole in the head."

Zec may have been right. For one thing, newsmen now surrounded the Villa Ponti, a fact which Ponti and Sophia abhorred and had sought, not always successfully, to avoid. For another, both Ponti and producer Franco Rossellini had millions invested in the two stars. Ponti, about to start work with Burton on *The Journey*, needed an emotionally stable actor. And Elizabeth was scheduled to go before the cameras in *The Driver's Seat*, a dramatization of the Muriel Spark novel which Rossellini would produce. With Elizabeth and Richard together, and given their volatility and past performances, who could tell when another explosion would occur?

Nothing happened—for a while. Richard and Elizabeth began work on the films, and since the Villa Ponti had sixty rooms, they could have all the privacy they wished. In her free time, Elizabeth would come to the set to watch Burton and Loren. It seemed like old times, the insults flying, but delivered with smiles. He would poke Elizabeth in the stomach and tease her about her fleshiness there; she would call him a pain in the back of her stomach. Once in his dressing room, he extended a hand and pinched her breasts as though they were old-fashioned automobile horns, making the accompanying sound: *Honk! Honk!*

The summer passed, but not idyllically. The warmth of the July reconciliation cooled and the Burton quarrels resumed. Once Richard and Elizabeth separated.

"What she needs is comfort and lots of it," Henry Wynberg told the press after the latest breakup was reported. He offered some to Elizabeth and she gratefully accepted.

Burton had to go to Naples with co-star Sophia Loren for the filming of *The Journey*. Matters were not helped by the sparks which Sophia and Richard set ablaze on camera while making the movie.

179

The Italian magazine *Oggi* published photographs of Burton nip ping his co-star's ear; the caption hinted at love scenes between th two that went above and beyond the call of the script or the director Gossip swelled; nor did it abate when Sophia went aboard Burton yacht for a weekend cruise. Her children were with her, and Carl Ponti had driven her to the dock and bade her a fond *adieu*, but th tongues wagged nonetheless.

In November, Elizabeth suffered severe abdominal cramps and with Wynberg at her side, was flown to California for diagnosis and ultimately, another operation. In December, she entered the Medi cal Center at the University of California in Los Angeles, wher surgeons removed an ovary upon which a cyst had developed.

She wanted Burton, asked for him. And he came, flying to Lon don from Rome, then taking the exhausting eleven-hour fligh across the Arctic Circle to Los Angeles. Pale, quivering with weari ness, he rushed into the hospital and stayed at her bedside, leaving only to purchase a get-well gift at a Beverly Hills jeweler—a diamond pendant.

In mid-December, the couple returned to Italy to complete their films, then went to their Gstaad home for Christmas, seemingly happy. "Mr. Burton waited on her hand and foot," a servant recalls. "But as she got stronger, so did his voice. And soon they were fighting once more."

Four months later, on April 26, 1974, the couple announced in Los Angeles that their new reconciliation had ended in failure and they would seek a divorce in Berne. "I'm afraid," said a spokesman for the couple, "the breakup is final."

On June 26, 1974, Elizabeth, prim in a short white dress, dark glasses covering her eyes, sat in a courthouse near Gstaad, listening to lawyers present the case of Taylor vs. Burton. She sat silently, stone-faced, throughout the fifteen-minute proceedings. And when they ended, the judge awarded her a divorce on the grounds of incompatibility, and the almost legendary marriage had ended—for the time being.

Richard and Elizabeth renounced appeal rights. Lawyers for both told the judge a month earlier that the couple had arrived at a friendly settlement. Elizabeth received custody of their adopted daughter, and rights to their yacht *Kalizma* and her fabled collection of gems, then valued at about $5,000,000.

Burton was in seclusion in New York, having presented a doctor's ertificate through his attorney that he was too ill to travel to Switzerland.

The remarkable part of all this was the extent to which the world was caught up in the imbroglio. Gossip columns and fan magazines were filled with chatter about what would come next; the large-circulation publications ran thoughtful articles by marriage experts; *McCall's* magazine had the distinguished Max Lerner do a lengthy piece analyzing "what happens now?"; the *Ladies' Home Journal* persuaded Richard to write an article called *Life Without Elizabeth* and used the Burtons as subjects in its long-running series *Can This Marriage Be Saved? Good Housekeeping* had an article on Elizabeth's "endless ordeal," and even astrologers looked into the heavens to see what was in store.

"It was almost inevitable," said Mary Wildcliffe, a popular British astrologer. Writing in a London newspaper, she told her readers, "Miss Taylor, born under the sign of Pisces, has an unusual dual personality which violently came to the forefront. Astrological interpretations reveal that she doesn't want Richard Burton when she feels certain that she can have him. And Burton, born under the eighth sign of the zodiac, Scorpio, is a very proud man and explodes easily. He refused to make any necessary changes. So for the time being the marriage is over. Tomorrow, however, should prove to be a completely different story as both realize that for them life without each other is meaningless."

4. Why?

ACTOR PETER USTINOV BELIEVES THE BURTONS WERE DRIVEN APART "BY the pressure of being the Burtons." It is a perceptive analysis of a close friend—the need to live up to an image can produce a force destructive enough to wreck any personality, to say nothing of a marriage. There was, over the years, too much stress to live up to for the Burtons, to be on display as the world's great superromantics whether they felt superromantic at the moment or not, to act, in short, the parts the public was paying them to perform.

Allied to this was high-intensity togetherness when there should have been some benign neglect of each other. Family "togetherness," coined in the 1950s to sell magazines, was a clever concept, but unfortunately unsound; too much often causes irritations that ultimately send a couple to the divorce court more rapidly than some healthy apartness. Elizabeth herself was totally aware that they were "Dick-n-Liz" far too much. "We were living too much out of each other's pockets," she remarked, "never being apart except for matters of life and death."

In 1969, although Twentieth Century-Fox originally planned to film *The Only Game in Town* in Las Vegas, Elizabeth insisted that screening be shifted to Paris so that she could be near Richard who was then busy making *Staircase* with Rex Harrison. Producer Fred Kohlmar was forced to construct the Las Vegas settings in Paris studios while another group of photographers shot background material in the United States.

At noon, the two stars would leave their respective movie lots and rendezvous midway, where they would have a hand-holding lunch. This practice occurred on most of their films, causing Elizabeth to say, "Buster, where I goest, thou goest!"

182

And he replied, "At your side forever, except when I traverse to he men's room!"

Sociologist Evelyn Millis Duvall has written, "Marriage isn't a state of bondage. . . . It requires no shackling of personality if it is a good marriage. It releases rather than imprisons if it is well built." Spaces, she says, must be provided in the togetherness. Overcloseness, like overprotection and overpossessiveness, can be overpowering and ultimately stifling.

Diversity of background may have been another factor. Although both ended up rich, one partner rose from near poverty, and the other from the upper middle class. Attitudes formed early in life by backgrounds are layered thickly upon the personality and form character traits that may never be eliminated.

Rivalry may also have played an important role. Psychiatrists have become aware that with the growing participation of women in all occupations, competition between mates is rapidly becoming one of the most serious threats to modern unions. Declares Dr. Phillip Polatin, professor emeritus of clinical psychiatry at the College of Physicians and Surgeons, Columbia University, "More marriages are destroyed, in spirit if not in actual fact, by the rivalry of mates than is ever realized."

Dr. Polatin cites the case of a doctor, married to another doctor, who found that his wife was playing a game of one-upmanship in the production of scientific papers. As quickly as he published one, she would write two. "There was a grim contest between husband and wife for honors and reputation which left no room for home life or love," he said.

Could Elizabeth and Richard, the superstars, actually have been engaged in a similarly grim contest for acting honors and reputation? Could their outbursts at one another, their admitted clash of temperaments, their highly charged personalities be manifestations of an unconscious rivalry? Did one feel that he or she must outdo the other? Note this:

In late 1962, Margaret Rutherford, the venerable British actress, appeared with Richard and Elizabeth in MGM's *The VIP's*, a movie the studio hoped would capitalize on all of the *Cleopatra* publicity. Shortly before she died, the octogenarian performer, who received an Oscar for her supporting role in the film, (and incidentally stole the movie from the stars) said:

"It's no secret that they both can act beautifully. But at times it became a 'who-is-the-better?' contest. Elizabeth would play a scene to the very hilt and make it the zenith of perfection. Richard would come along and try to top it with his own brand of dynamism. They would then ask someone to select the winner. When they appointed me the judge, I had to plead prejudice and declare Richard the victor. After all, he oozes such charm. If I were only a bit younger I'd definitely single him out romantically."

Still another reason may have loomed large. Where Richard Burton was raised, the traditional attitude in mining families toward wives was that the man was the breadwinner, the woman the homemaker. Elizabeth, in an interview some years ago, stated that Richard did indeed hold to the view that a wife should remain at home. Dr. Floyd M. Martinson, a sociologist well versed in marital problems, has said, "Many husbands are unprepared emotionally to accept the wife as an occupational equal, or even to accept the wife in a supportive part-time occupational role."

Then there was the rootlessness. A marriage that has no home base is handicapped from the beginning. For Richard and Elizabeth, their many lavish houses and apartments did not add up to a true home, a refuge from their world and their craft and their retinue. Most of their time, in fact, was spent not in their own homes at all but in hotel suites.

A maid who worked at the Dorchester Hotel during many of the couple's visits to London, said, "Miss Taylor always came loaded down with baggage—more than several dozen suitcases and huge trunks. Even if her stay was only for a fortnight or less, she'd take most of them along. Once she saw me eying them. 'I suppose they are a bit much,' she said, 'but their contents do make me feel more at home. Don't you feel that way, too?'

"I replied that I didn't travel much except to my sister's place in Kent. 'Most of the time,' I told Miss Taylor, 'I remain right at home.' That's when she said, oh so sadly, 'I do envy you so very much to have a home that you rarely leave. Because of our work we are never in one place for very long. I so wish we could spend all of our time in Mexico. That's where Richard and I can kick off our shoes and run around without much clothes on.' "

Elizabeth felt that being surrounded by her pets would also provide a touch of home life. Domestic animals, however, had to remain in quarantine for six weeks before being permitted into the country.

On one trip to London, the Burtons were away for seven weeks, which meant they had the dogs for only one week.

It was always life on the run. The room service was perfect, and instant; the restaurant food was superb; every wish was granted and with not even the need to rub Aladdin's lamp. Yet it was a nomadic existence, unstabilized, with no real center for family living and growth.

A side effect of their status as entertainment royalty has been immaturity, and this, too, may have been a factor in the collapse of their marriage, for, as Clark W. Blackburn, former director of the Family Service Association of America, points out, "Marriage is for grownups." Though in middle years, Richard and Elizabeth behaved at times—many times—as children not quite grown, throwing temper tantrums, wanting their own way, competing and aggressing as children will do. All of their screaming and loving, quarreling and kissing, invectives and endearments performed before the world audience are childish traits.

One prominent New York psychiatrist put it this way: "Time and again, Elizabeths and Richards—they are far more common types than most people imagine—sit in my consultation room and tell me about their shattered marriages. They don't have the stars' glamour or status, but they have their problem. They have not grown up. They are like children who play with a toy, love it and then get bored with it and throw it aside. Maybe, they tell themselves, one day they will return to it when it interests them again.

"Children, you see, are egocentric; they have to be the center of their own universe. As a child grows older, he will throw off this egocentricity and join the world, interacting with it, adjusting to its harsh realities and to other people. They learn, in short, to compromise with the world and each other.

"But the Elizabeths and Richards both want to be the center of their universe, and unfortunately, you cannot have two centers in one place. People like them will split up unless they come to terms with themselves. Basically, the Burtons had a powerful emotional attraction for each other, which may explain why they have catapulted apart after disagreements and darted back together as though drawn by magnets."

All these circumstances probably played a significant role in pushing the couple to the breaking point, but beyond them all was one overriding problem, one that has wrecked—and will continue to destroy—marriages of far less celebrated persons. *Elizabeth had lost the feeling of protection, of emotional security, that she needed and wanted from Richard Burton.*

"Happy marriages are no accident," says Dr. Polatin. "They are made by people who are suited to each other. Nor do suitable people find each other by accident, either consciously or unconsciously. *They are guided in their choice by a recognition of their own emotional needs.*" (Our italics.)

Elizabeth has articulated her own vulnerability. "I have the emotions of a child in the body of a woman," she once said. Thus, she was not unlike millions of other women who have not attained full emotional maturity, who need strength and support for their vulnerability.

She had developed, of course, an outer crust. She could be direct, frank, earthy in her language, tough in her financial demands because she knew her value in terms of the box office. Inwardly, though, she is not so bold. "Until Richard," she has admitted, "I needed marriage because of my basic insecurity, my basic fear."

With Richard, she found not only security, but a deep and satisfying love, a perfect combination for a woman such as Elizabeth. The union could have lasted forever—as it does for women with her emotional needs—had both elements remained.

One did. The other, tragically, did not. "The problem is most often a female one," says a psychiatrist who teaches at the Harvard Medical School. "When a woman loses the support of a man upon whom she relies to protect her against a hostile world, she feels frightened, alone, helpless. She may leave him to seek other protection. Or she may leave him to shock him into awareness."

What was about to happen could have come as no great surprise to Burton, for he had known all along he was poor husband material. He admits that one of Elizabeth's close friends had urged her to forget the whole idea of marriage to him. The friend, Richard says, told Elizabeth, "I love you, darling, and I beg you not to go through with it. You'll never understand the Welsh. You never know what they're going to do next. I know. I married a Welsh girl."

"Basically," Richard says, "I don't like Richard Burton very much. I think I'm a fairly easy man to get along with, but not easy to be

186

married to. I'm a creature of high temperament. I soar from highs to lows. With me, there's very few middles."

He would get what he calls "black belts of melancholy," the Welsh *hiraeth*. "The nearest translation," he says in discussing it, "is a longing for unnamable things." When the mood would come upon him, he would become uncharacteristically morose and untalkative—extraordinary for Richard. Elizabeth and the children came to recognize the signs, calling it the "Welsh hour" or the "death." And they would leave him alone until the gloom lifted.

Elizabeth thought she had neatly solved all existing problems. Two, however, defied all solutions and contributed heavily to the downfall. The overriding reasons why Elizabeth was losing the bulwark she needed to protect her against her own weakened sense of self-worth lay in a whisky bottle and in a tube of lipstick.

5. Liquor and King Flirt

EVER SINCE HIS YOUTH, RICHARD BURTON WAS AN AWESOME TIPPLER. He would drink vodka and tonic, whisky and soda, champagne. Frequently, he would drink all day long. He would have a glass in his hand from the time he rose to the time he went to bed, drinking at home, on the movie set, at parties, after parties. That was on weekdays. "On weekends," he says, "I would double my liquor consumption." "I am just not civilized with drink," he has admitted. "It is all or nothing with me."

He was capable, he once admitted, of "knocking off three bottles a day of vodka or whisky." He added, "I had to keep away from the rum because I then fancied I could take on Muhammad Ali or George Foreman. Or, on a heavy day, both."

He had one of his first heavy days while still in his teens at Oxford. He was cast in the role of Lord Angelo in an open-air production of *Measure for Measure* produced by the university's dramatic society. Philip Burton, his proud foster father, went up for the weekend and, after the evening dress rehearsal, worked most of the night with Richard, preparing for the opening. The boy was superb; the elder Burton returned to his lodgings at Exeter College, awaiting Richard's arrival. But the young actor was celebrating with the other members of the cast. In the early morning, Richard finally came to the room, looking terrible. He had passed out from the drinks, and in attempting to climb a fence to reenter the college, which forbade students from leaving the campus area, he had torn his clothes and skin. "It was a grisly dawn for both of us," the elder Burton recalled.

Most of the time, Richard was a happy, song-singing, back-slapping, fun-to-be-with drinker. After having had a few, for example, Burton would boast to companions that he could spell, quickly and correctly, the longest place name in the world—a village on the island of Anglesey off the coast of North Wales. He'd draw a deep breath and rattle off: Llanfairpwllgwyngyllgogery-chwyrndrobwillllantysuliogogogoch.

Few can say it, much less spell it, while sober.

Once in Wales, he challenged an entire team of Welsh rugby players, tough men who can drink as hard as they play, to a drink-down. Richard had twenty boilermakers and was among the last to quit. Another time, at the Oceana Bar in Puerto Vallarta, Mexico, he told a writer-friend to keep count. When the score was toted up, the friend, no mean drinker himself, gasped: Burton had downed twenty-three straight shots of tequila.

When a former employee died of lung cancer in London, Elizabeth and Richard mourned his passing and extended their sympathies to the bereaved family. The deceased had had a fondness for martinis, and Richard felt it would be appropriate to conduct a memorial service in a pub.

The Burtons went off to the bar and toasted their departed employee. Both were in tears. Said Richard, martini glass in hand, "May his bier be as dry as this martini."

Burton has always been ready to help friends who were problem drinkers. In London, veteran British actor Bernard Lee, who plays the part of 007's boss in the James Bond films, said:

"One time I had had only two weeks' work in two years when I met Richard in a pub. We had worked together some years before in *The Spy Who Came in from the Cold*. He asked me why I looked so forlorn. He got the truth out of me. My wife had died not long before in a fire which destroyed our home, a shattering blow after thirty-five years of happy marriage. I'd hit the bottle and I was up to my eyes in debt to the tax man.

"To cap it all, a few weeks after my wife's death, I'd been mugged, had two teeth knocked out and was put in the hospital.

"Richard told me everybody had a bad patch sometimes and they just had to hide it. Then, before he left the pub, he slipped a letter in my pocket. In my state, I almost forgot it, but when I opened it later, there was a check for 3,000 pounds.

"I got my drink problem well under control and resumed my career. Since then, I've had more than a bit of good luck—and all because of him."

A good time to hit Burton for a loan is on St. David's Day, the national Welsh festival celebrated on March 1. Richard is supergenerous at that time as Welshmen pay St. David the same homage Irishmen reserve for St. Patrick. St. David, who died about the year 600, was primate of South Wales, founded many churches there and was canonized about 1120. Ever since, his day has been marked by rejoicing by all Welshmen, and the rejoicing is marked by twenty-four hours of heavy drinking. Burton, as loyal a Welshman as ever emerged from its rugged mountains and deep valleys, always rejoiced too, wherever he was.

On one St. David's Day early in his career, an unrehearsed incident occurred onstage. Richard was in Stratford, England, playing Prince Hal in *King Henry*. He had begun celebrating with boilermakers exactly one minute past midnight and continued throughout the day, arriving at the theater still upright. Before donning his costume, however, he had neglected to empty his bladder, a mistake in view of the costume he had to wear. As Hal, he buckled on a heavy suit of chain-mail armor which usually took at least thirty minutes and almost as long to remove, considerably longer than it would take to unzip a fly when urgency demanded.

King Henry is a lengthy play, more than three hours in the acting, and by Act Four, Richard was beginning to suffer. He was speaking with legs tightly closed and veins bulging on his forehead. And then, during a sword fight with Hotspur, the accumulated boilermakers gushed out. "Noah's Ark could have floated," he later told David Frost in a TV interview. Fortunately, the spreading stain was not too apparent against the gray metal of the chain armor. Michael Redgrave, who was playing Hotspur, was not aware of the consequences of Burton's all-day rejoicing until Richard apologized after the curtain. "Oh," Redgrave said, "was that it? I thought you were sweating rather more than usual."

A remarkable Burton drinking story comes from a setting far from a theater or Hollywood film lot.

In 1960, Richard was in Alaska with Jim Backus, the late Robert Ryan and a Warner Brothers company, filming Edna Ferber's *Ice Palace*. They were on location in Petersburg, a tiny town flanking the shores of Wrangell Narrows. The best drinking place, seven miles from the town center, was a combination bar, dance hall and whorehouse. But for its juke box and chrome tables, it could have come straight out of a Jack London tale of the Klondike. Fishermen

190

ame here to drink hard after a hard day's work—tough, bearded
men in Levis and furlined Windbreakers who rarely went to the
movies and knew little of Burton and his formidable reputation as a
prince of players.

Richard called the place the Knocking Shop. If it had another
name, he has long since forgotten it. (In British slang, a Knocking
shop is a brothel.) There was a small room on the ground level which
contained a bar, tended by one of the three female owners, several
tables and an elaborate neon-lit juke box. Every other room in the
place was a bedroom, all of them actively occupied from 8:00 P.M.,
when the men began trooping in, to closing time which was
indefinite.

Burton, Backus and Ryan would come here often after a day's
filming because, as Backus says, "It was the only game in town. We'd
sit, drink and talk."

One evening, after a particularly hard day in the windswept
wilderness the three men, in faded jeans and Windbreakers, arrived
at the Knocking Shop and began ordering drinks. The juke box, at
full volume, was filling the place with incomprehensible sound. The
fishermen were dancing with the girls, clutching them closely, rub-
bing bodies as they moved. The dancing never ceased; as some
dancers disappeared into the bedrooms, others took their places.
And nothing stopped the juke box.

Jim Backus: "It was three-thirty in the morning, but the sun was
shining. The days up there had no nights. Outside, very close, we
heard wolves howling even above the din of that damned juke box.
We were sitting near the bar, drinking scotch. Ryan asked Richard
how he played Hamlet. Ryan was going east after the filming to do
some Shakespeare with Katharine Hepburn and was intensely interested in Burton's interpretation. Ryan asked him, did he play
Hamlet as a homosexual? Was Hamlet in love with his mother?
Burton tried to explain this and other points, but the juke box was
drowning him out.

"Finally, Richard had enough of the noise. He walked over to the
box and yanked the cord from the socket with the toe of his shoe.
There were forty fishermen in the room, most of them dancing.
Most hadn't shaved in days. Men with beards. Men with ugly scars.
They saw what Richard had done and they were plenty angry. From
all directions, they charged in Richard's direction. It was like some
kind of weird surrealistic ballet.

"Burton took no notice of them. He walked back to his table an pulled out a chair. He put one foot on the seat and, facing the angr fishermen but not glancing at them, began the soliloquy: 'To be o not to be . . .'

"Those fishermen froze where they stood. I looked at their face and could see they had no idea what in the world Richard was saying but somehow they knew they were in the presence of greatness Something was happening and it stopped them cold. The entir room fell silent. The lady bartender stopped pouring drinks. All yo could hear was Richard's rich voice, speaking those noble lines.

"When he finished, his face seemed to have changed. He was no Richard Burton, drinking in a bar and whorehouse in a remot Alaskan fishing village. He was Hamlet, the prince of Denmark.

"Then I wondered, 'What about the men? Were they planning t kill him now?' Their faces bore the oddest expression. They wer silent for a long, long minute, and then they burst into applause an whistles. The girls, the female bartender, everybody applauded whistled and cheered until the place shook.

"Richard bowed low, then sat down, his back to the fishermen That soliloquy, in that dreary place, was the greatest I ever heard and I never hope to hear it equaled. It was one of those rar moments in a man's life when he knows he is in the presence of tru genius."

It was a virtuoso performance few actors would have attempted much less carried off successfully.

In 1962, after Richard's farewell performance in *Camelot*, Moss Hart, the late playwright and director, said, "Actors like Richard Burton are born once in fifty years." He offered this advice to Burton, "Don't waste your gift. The next five years may decide whether or not you'll become the leading actor of the English-speaking stage."

Hart was prophetic. Burton's star arched high in the next two years, then turned sharply downward.

In 1964, the year he married Elizabeth Taylor, he played *Hamlet* in New York and received rave notices for his theatrical vitality, glorious voice and immense power and authority.

Walter Kerr wrote in the New York *Herald Tribune*, "Richard Burton is one of the most magnificently equipped actors living, and in John Gielgud's rehearsal clothes production of *Hamlet* he places

n open display, not only all of his own reverberating resources—a
ace that is illuminated in repose, a voice that seems to prove that
ound spirals outward, an intelligence that hears wit when wit is
rying to steal by tiptoe—but also all of the myriad qualities which the
nan Hamlet requires."

Howard Taubman of *The New York Times* was hardly less ecstatic.
"Richard Burton dominates the drama," he wrote next morning, "as
Hamlet should. For his is a performance of electrical power and
sweeping virility. . . . I do not recall a Hamlet of such tempestuous
manliness. Mr. Burton's Hamlet is full of pride and wit and mettle.
He is warm and forthright with Horatio. Mr. Burton's voice is not
mellifluous like those of a few highly cultivated classic actors. It has a
hearty ring and a rough edge, attributes that suit his interpretation.
He has a fine sense of rhythm. It is very much his own, with a flair for
accenting words and phrases in unexpected ways."

The New York *Post*'s Richard Watts, Jr., called Richard's Hamlet
"forceful, direct, unpretentiously eloquent, more thoughtfully in-
trospective than darkly melancholy, with the glint of ironic
humor. . . . The vitality and imagination of the whole production
and Mr. Burton's distinguished performance provide a notable
theatrical event."

And Norman Nadel of the New York *World-Telegram & Sun* was
even more enthusiastic: "Last night . . . Richard Burton swept mind
and memory clean of all other Hamlets, in a performance so lucid
and sensible that people will speak of it for years. What a problem he
has posed for Hamlets to come."

Early in Burton's career, R. C. Worsley, a British critic had written, "The mantle of Olivier will surely fall upon him. If he works at
his art long and humbly, he has every chance of becoming a great
actor by the age of forty."

The forecast seemed uncannily accurate, for those glowing reviews of his Hamlet were written when Richard was just seven
months short of his fortieth birthday. The official number of performances, excluding previews, set a new record, and the play closed
while still drawing full houses. Burton had exceeded Barrymore's
101 performances, which had topped Edwin Booth's famous 100.
He played it 133 times. It had been the most profitable Shakespearean play ever presented. A total of 204,000 persons had paid
$1,718,862 during the 17 week run. The play was also recorded by
Columbia Records and filmed for showing in 1,000 movie houses.

But Burton blew it.

The critics had measured him for the mantle of greatness, but h[e] only got to try it on. He returned to films, where they were payin[g] him $500,000 for each picture, a fancy price that was to get fancie[r] very soon. After the middle sixties, his fee per film doubled t[o] $1,000,000 and then rose to $1,250,000. Later, he and Elizabet[h] were to give up their huge guarantees for each movie and accep[t] percentages of the gross, an arrangement that was even mor[e] profitable.

From one picture, he estimated that under the percentage deal he would earn the price of a new Rolls Royce every week. Since Roll[s] Royces cost between $30,000 and $40,000, and even more, the reader can do his own arithmetic. The film, incidentally, was *Villain* in which Burton played the part of a London crime overlord and about which *The New York Times* wrote, "It's an awful movie, really."

The offers and the money poured in, so much that he lost count o[f] both. After *Cleopatra*, he made eight films with Elizabeth, a few o[f] them excellent, others dismal, and a batch on his own.

He received high praise for his work in *Who's Afraid of Virgini[a] Woolf*, and an Academy Award nomination for his Henry VIII in *Anne of the Thousand Days*. *The Spy Who Came in from the Cold* was richly decorated with prizes in the United States and England. But at the same time, critics grimaced at many of the films for which he earned such incredible sums.

Burton could hardly have enjoyed such notices in *The Times* as these: About *The Sandpiper*: "The same old Hollywood stuff." About *Villain*: "In its title role, Richard Burton, grown somewhat fat and soft, like a potato that's been left too long, reads his lines well while keeping himself at a safe remove from them, as if he didn't want to be identified with the part." About *Raid on Rommel*: "Sluggish, tedious and absurd." About *Dr. Faustus*: "It is of an awfulness that bends the mind. . . . At moments, one has the feeling that *Faustus* was shot mainly as a home movie for them [the Burtons] to enjoy at home." About *Boom*: "A fuzzy unconsummated work." About *Bluebeard*, in which his co-stars were such beauties as Joey Heatherton, Virna Lisi, Nathalie Delon and Raquel Welch: "There is a lot of decorous titillation, on the level, say, of a *Playboy* center spread . . . the real distinction of the movie is that before it ends, just about everybody gets undressed—except for Burton and Miss Welch." About *Massacre in Rome*: "A curiously bloodless film."

By 1965, his fortieth year, the year he could have become what the British critics had predicted, Burton was aware that the theater world was accusing him of throwing away a brilliant classical career. But he was assuming a defensive posture and defending his life-style.

"My brother sent me a cutting saying that Dylan Thomas and I were both typically Welsh," he said in July of that year, "and we'd both sold out our talents, him for booze and me for Elizabeth. I don't see it that way. I'm doing what I know to the best of my ability. I have a wonderful life and I manage to make a few pennies. Show me a man who has any more."

Despite these brave words, Burton had a great ache for the stage. He talked about the excitement of live audiences, and perhaps he might like to do something by the existentialist Jean-Paul Sartre, who wrote *The Flies, No Exit, The Respectful Prostitute*. He would discuss stage acting and its challenges and talk about the bad audiences that can destroy an actor inside. "Sometimes," he'd say, "they're as heavy as mashed potatoes, not at all interested in you, not responding to what's taking place on the stage. That's when you must do your damnedest. You have to pull them out of their lethargy. . . . But when an audience is tensely with you, it's very, very exciting."

The years went on, however, and Burton apparently was not pulled out of his gilded cocoon in Hollywood. He was overpaid and he knew it. "It's quite indecent," he said of the sums he got. Nonetheless, he would do as they asked, so long as the cash kept flowing. Once Vincente Minnelli, directing him in *The Sandpiper* on location in the Big Sur country of California, placed a large, fat pillow behind his back to improve the camera angle. Burton, angered, exclaimed, "Don't give me this rubbish that it looks all right. I know perfectly well it doesn't look all right. However, for the money, we will dance."

Later, Max Lerner, the author, educator and columnist, was to call Burton's slide "a deterioration story, much like the hero of F. Scott Fitzgerald in *Tender Is the Night*."

By 1971, Richard Findlater, a theatrical historian, said, "If Burton had spent twenty years on the stage, he might perhaps have achieved true greatness. If he comes back, perhaps he could still do it." And then Findlater wrote Burton's theatrical obituary, "Meanwhile, he must be regretfully written off as another loss to the theater."

Said Lerner, "In terms of his acting, the decade of marriage now looks like a lost decade. At the start of it he seemed to many to offer the promise of becoming another Laurence Olivier. Whether because of too much drink, too much money or too much Elizabeth, he has not fulfilled it."

Dr. Bernard Grebanier, a teacher of Shakespeare for fifty years, professor emeritus of English at Brooklyn College, author of many books on drama and literature, wrote a work on the theater in 1975 called *Then Came Each Actor*. He had thought Burton, he said, "the lucky possessor of that inner glow which I have spoken of as so invaluable to an actor, and additionally endowed with a beautiful speaking voice. But it would seem that if one must be born with that special illumination, one can lose it too. Burton has more or less lost his. My own explanation is that with the years, ever since his romance with Elizabeth Taylor . . . he has chosen to live his private life screamingly and vulgarly in public, and that this wallowing in public vulgarity has debased his acting. Another factor might be mentioned—his willingness to take part in so many worthless films; as for his films, I make two great exceptions in which his old magic resulted in great performances: in *Becket* and *Who's Afraid of Virginia Woolf?* he was superior to the actors who had performed the roles on the stage."

In 1974, Burton himself made a brief but telling self-appraisal. In an article for *The Ladies' Home Journal*, he wrote, "Have spent all night in bed with Elizabeth for real and all day in bed with Sophia [Loren] for unreal. Not bad when you come from the bowels of the earth." Sophia, Burton said, treated him as though he were a "clown prince." "So she should; I am both."

"I look upon him," writes Dr. Grebanier in a devastating conclusion, "as having debased himself, as did John Barrymore, though in a somewhat different way. There is something unfortunate in the waste of such a remarkable talent."

Others too were also seeing the Barrymore shadow across Burton's path: Joe Pilcher in the New York *Sunday News* found a "startling parallel" to the youngest member of the royal family of the theater, who died in 1942 at the age of sixty, "his greatness lost in the swamp of alcoholism." Two years before, *Variety*, the foremost publication of the entertainment industry, reviewed *Hammersmith Is Out*, which starred Burton and Taylor: "Burton goes through the film with a single bored expression. . . . It's getting uncomfortably ifficult to watch Richard Burton now without thinking of John arrymore in his last days, parading the bleary remnants of a considerable talent through material at once third-rate and elf-parodying."

Barrymore became a national joke in the late 1930s. Unable to remember lines, he ordered them printed in huge letters beyond camera range. He became a drink-sodden wreck, was forced into bankruptcy, and at the end, made a fool of himself onstage almost every night during performances of a play called *My Dear Children*. Brooks Atkinson, the only drama critic to have a Broadway theater named for him, wrote of Barrymore in *Broadway*: "When he finished *Hamlet*, he abdicated from Broadway and devoted the rest of his mercurial life to making films—and huge sums of money. He spent the money recklessly, drank excessively, and destroyed himself wildly."

A cameraman on the set of the television drama special that Richard made with Elizabeth, *Divorce, His; Divorce, Hers*, in 1972 said, "We used to constantly joke about the three B's—Burton, Barrymore and Booze!"

Looking back upon those bleak days, Burton does not spare himself or make excuses. He is able to stand apart from himself and evaluate his actions with a painful honesty. "For about five years," he says, "I drank hopelessly. I drank and drank. Booze was taking its toll. I was the not so innocent victim of the perpetual hangover.

"You can't drink seriously and hope to remain an actor who receives rave notices. Sadly, very sadly, I discovered that alcohol and acting can never mix. I was regarded as a very physical actor. But alcohol reduces that quality. You become sluggish. Your lines slur. Your timing is off. You forget. . . ."

It is interesting to note that this was said in the spring of 1976. Almost exactly ten years before, he had known this. "Some actors," he said then, "can take a drink before going on and one during the intermission and be fine. But heavy drinking? No, it's very dangerous. You're out there in this great glow and you think you're just wonderful, and you're doing everything so slowly that the audience is yawning. Those ten-minute pauses between words, you certainly know."

(Most actors like to think of themselves as high-capacity imbibers who can rip off memorable performances though stoned to the eyebrows. It is "the actor's favorite fantasy," as William Redfield said. "The boring and Spartan fact," he wrote in his recollections of the *Hamlet* production, "is that few actors can ingest so much as a single jigger of alcohol before a theater performance. If they do they trip over sandbags and forget their lines. Those who *can* drink usually limit their intake to two at the most." And then, he says, they nap for a couple of hours before curtain time.)

Why did he drink? Answers from both Elizabeth and Richard will probably dent, if not shatter, the extrovert image he has projected over the years. He has what Elizabeth has called a "terrible shyness," and "nobody knows the death throes that he goes through." To become the extrovert Burton, she says, "he really has to have a couple of drinks."

Burton points to still other reasons: One, he says, was sheer boredom, the boredom of the long delays between filming scenes and especially the boredom that followed the discovery that he had landed in stultifying, totally uninteresting films. There were plenty of these in recent years. "It becomes very dangerous," he said, "if you find a congenial actor who likes to drink too."

Another reason: "Alcohol cured me from facing the sheer idiocy of a weird world I was forced to live in."

He admits his friends were deeply concerned. "They worried about my drinking," he declares, "and urged me to cut down or quit. But I paid little attention to their nagging, and drank some more.

"During the years, I was oblivious to the slightest happening. I'd forget the names of longtime friends. Streets and place names became a blur. I'm told that on one occasion I introduced a Miss Fish as Miss Carp, and a Miss Goode as a Miss Terrible. An actor can get away with a large amount of incorrectness, but he must never mess around with names.

"I was really off the mark."

The realization that he was blowing it all must have rocked the proud Welshman to his back teeth—because early on he exploded almost defiantly to the career gods: "By heaven, I'm going to be the greatest actor, or what's the point of acting?"

Elizabeth knew time was running out. She was seeing that Richard Burton was losing his sense of purpose, destroying his magnificent gifts through disuse and perhaps even destroying himself as a human being.

She saw the steady, almost day-by-day deterioration, and she

198

pleaded with him to stop. He had been offered a post as an Oxford don. She urged him to accept, but he did not. She encouraged him to continue with his writing. Often he would appear on a movie set at an early hour and peck away furiously at a typewriter. But he did not stop drinking for long.

Raymond Vignale says, "The love that Burton bears for the bottle has always taken pity from the widow of Mike Todd. A hundred times she has threatened to leave him if he did not put a limit to his drinking. Twenty-four times fifteen they have reconciled and their reunions always result in close embraces."

Eight years after their stormy marriage, Elizabeth Taylor admitted she could not sleep when Richard was not with her, couldn't even read a book. "We can't bear to be apart, even for a matter of hours," she said. "When I'm alone, I can't concentrate on anything."

But at the same time, she could not bear to see what was happening, especially since another element was in the picture too—the "other woman" problem.

Burton has complained many times that his reputation as a lover was a Hollywood-inspired publicity device, yet he has done little to dispel it and would, in fact, feed the gossip. *Example*: Jestingly, he once said that the only leading lady he had not taken to bed was his *Camelot* co-star Julie Andrews. In mock anger, Miss Andrews retorted, "How dare he say such an awful thing about me!"

Wisecracks like this, plus being seen often in the company of beautiful women, helped fix his reputation as a great lover. Gossip about his amatory exploits has been as exciting a parlor game in show-business circles as whispers about the lusty, vigorous Kennedy males. Scores of women claimed to have shared beds with Richard; just as many "confessed" to intimacies with one or another of the Kennedy brothers—and this because some women believe that affairs with men like Burton and the Kennedys endow them with a certain cachet. (One woman in Washington boasts that she slept with all three Kennedy brothers, a claim she still uses as a conversation stopper at parties.)

Richard Burton has been scandal-prone all his professional life. Like the Kennedy men, gossip has followed him everywhere; and, like them, his attitude and actions have tended to thicken rather than dispel the rumors. Burton is not circumspect. He is an uninhibited, charming and at times outrageous flirt. Indeed, in 1976, the

199

Chicago Tribune enthroned him as *King Flirt*, which the dictionary defines as "playing at courtship."

The distinction is not unimportant. Many of the Burtons' marital problems could be traced to Richard's inability to resist girls. While making *The Klansman*, a pretty, dark-haired waitress stopped at his table in a restaurant, pad and pencil poised. "God, you're pretty," Burton said to her. "Come to Paradise Valley with me." She did not go, nor did he expect her to. But he boasted to a companion, "She wanted to. They all do."

He is warmly attentive to beautiful actresses in the casts of his films. The late Fredric March, who played Richard's father in *Alexander the Great*, said, "Burton has a terrific way with women. I don't think he's missed more than half a dozen."

These comments and attentions, duly recorded in the press, may have been ballyhooed out of proportion and interpreted as unrelenting girl-chasing. Burton himself says that no human male could possibly have the potency, let alone the time, to have done all he has been reputed to do.

One widely known Hollywood correspondent reports, however, that he has tried. James Bacon, who covered the film capital for the Associated Press for eighteen years and who now writes a syndicated column, wrote in his book, *Hollywood Is a Four Letter Town*, that Richard had once boasted of having "batted a thousand" with his leading ladies. "From observation," said Mr. Bacon, "I would say that was a little high, but maybe .900. On *Ice Palace* he jumped everything that moved, including one fifty-year-old production assistant who is still eternally grateful."

When he was separated from Elizabeth because of film commitments, he would take a number of young women to dinner, yet he prided himself on never demanding what has euphemistically been called sexual favors, although according to close friends, "they were freely offered."

A number of his dates were interviewed, and while this may surprise readers who have been led to expect swingier stories, the following account is typical:

On the set of one of his movies, Richard stopped to watch a young actress we will call Marcia Morgin do a scene and, when it ended, he complimented her on a good job. Several days later, he came to her and said, "I didn't have the pleasure of seeing your performance today, but I'm sure it rivaled the one you gave the other day. I'm sure you were superb."

Marcia Morgin: "That's when he asked me if I'd like to join him for dinner. Naturally, I accepted. Who wouldn't? He said he knew a nice place that wasn't too far away. At the restaurant, we had drinks before dinner. A woman came over to our table. She was a real snob who said she wanted an autograph for her five-year-old grandchild. 'Not for myself, of course, you know.'

"Richard grabbed the paper and signed it. She took it back, read it, and said, 'But you wrote *Julius Butwinick*. You're Richard Burton—aren't you?'

"And he replied with a straight face, 'Julius Butwinick the plumber, at your service. Madam, do you leak?' She almost ran away and Richard burst out laughing.

"He ordered champagne, three bottles, and drank all of it. He said that he had just read a book about Julius Caesar and started to discuss it. He was full of stories and sang some Welsh songs. He has a real good voice. I had heard him in *Camelot*, but in person and up real close, he sounds even better. Then he filled up his glass for about the hundredth time.

"I commented on his drinking and he said, 'I drink when I'm happy and I'm happy right now.' He told me some more stories and sang some more Welsh songs. He talked about Elizabeth's command of dialects. 'She can make you think she's Welsh or French or Italian! Perfect imitations. She can do Marilyn Monroe or Mae West. Her Welsh dialect is the best.'

"He spoke some lines in Welsh. I didn't know what they were, but from the look on his face, I felt they had something to do with Elizabeth. I said, 'I bet they are some kind of love messages to her.'

"He took me out to dinner simply because he was lonely and bored and wanted some company. Believe that or not, but it's true!"

Consider another incident that received wide publicity. Two days after Elizabeth won her divorce, Burton boarded the transatlantic liner *France* for Europe. His traveling companions were a pet Pekingese called E'en So (Shakespearean for "even so") and a young woman named Ellen Rossen.

The press set up a hullabaloo about Ellen's presence, with leering references to a "grieving" Burton mending his broken heart. The suggestion of an affair between the two was untrue. Actually, he had known Ellen since she was a child. She was the daughter of an old friend, the late director Robert Rossen. An affair with Ellen, Burton told friends, would be practically incest. Undeviously, he had asked Ellen along just for company. It was as simple as that.

"King Flirt" displayed his art on national television the day he sailed. When he was asked by a pretty TV reporter if he would marry again, he replied, "Who knows what fabulous creature might suddenly appear and light up my eyes and dazzle me with her brilliance?" Then, roguishly, he added, "You're not bad yourself."

The strength of the Burton libido, the extent to which he exercised it, and the range of his roving eye properly should have been nobody's business but Elizabeth's. To her, it all mattered enormously and revealed the depth of her own vulnerability.

While Elizabeth knew flirting was as natural to Richard as breathing, the habit irritated and at times infuriated her. More than once she berated him, and at least once battered him for it. "Buster, you better watch your step," she would warn.

When he insisted that since their marriage he had not "done anything" with other women, she told him bluntly that he couldn't help flirting and that "anything beyond that, and you'd be singing soprano by now."

Once at the Dorchester in London her resentment overflowed upon him, literally. The couple was having a late supper in the hotel's dining room. A close friend who was with them related what happened:

"Richard had become involved in a flirtation with two pretty, young girls seated at the table behind us. He kept looking over his shoulder to talk to them. Elizabeth was steaming because it was all so obvious. Richard kept turning on the charm, and finally he asked the girls if they'd like a bottle of champagne. At that point, Elizabeth really lost her temper. 'Why not give them *this* one?' she said as she poured the contents of her own champagne bottle right in Richard's lap!

"Then she walked out, leaving Richard drenched. He muttered a few curses as he tried to mop up the mess in his lap. I felt so terribly tense, I thought I was going to have a heart attack. Richard's such a forceful, explosive man. I didn't know what to expect from his temper. Then, as he was tossing soaked linen napkins onto the table, he suddenly broke into a great big smile and looked at me with an

202

almost boyish quality about himself. 'Isn't she wonderful!' he laughed. Then he bounded away—only a bit embarrassed—and saying that when he got upstairs to the hotel suite, he was going 'to paddle Elizabeth's ass.' At this point, he was already laughing out loud about what she'd done to him."

Aware, too, as newsman Robert Musel once wrote, that "fidelity involves constant vigilance," Elizabeth took as few chances as possible. At Bavaria Studios in Munich, Germany, where they co-starred in *Divorce, His; Divorce, Hers* for General Continental Productions in association with Harlech TV, a beautiful German girl was assigned as Elizabeth's stand-in while the lighting was adjusted. Director Waris Hussein instructed her to lie down on a carpet, her body pressed against Burton's, her arms around his waist. Elizabeth approached from the outer edges of the set. Her eyes, Musel noted, were like laser beams. "Why can't I do that?" she asked.

She could and she did. The young actress unwound herself from Richard, and Elizabeth, half-clad in a short nightie, took her place, warmly embracing her husband as the lighting crew went to work and the onlookers stared. Baffled, director Hussein wondered why a star so luminous would act as a stand-in. Musel, an old-time reporter who has chronicled the goings-on of world celebrities since before World War II, dryly responded, "If she wants to stay married as much as Elizabeth Taylor does, she does."

Rarely a season passed without some new "revelation" about Richard and some beauty or other—in a movie magazine, gossip column or even the news sections of the world press, hungry for another paper-selling story like the *Cleopatra* scandal.

In the spring and early summer of 1968, newspapers and fan magazines made a great to-do about Burton and a 25-year-old Brazilian actress named Florinda Bolkan. On July 21, 1968, the New York *Sunday News* published a three-page, profusely illustrated article in its feature section bearing the inch-high headline SHE'S GOT LIZ IN A TIZ. A smaller headline read, "If you had Liz Taylor at home and millions in the bank, would you go chasing after some chick hardly half your age? Sadly, maybe Richard Burton would. . . . Here, then, are the known facts about Flo, the luscious Latin who just might shoot down the highest-flying marriage of our day."

The "known facts," according to the reporter were that Burton had met Flo while they were both appearing in the film *Candy*. Richard Burton, said the reporter, had "taken a helpful interest" in Flo's career. Later, in London, Burton reportedly invited Flo to a party to celebrate the English opening of *Dr. Faustus*, in which he played the title role and Elizabeth co-starred as Helen of Troy. Quoting an Italian magazine, *Bella*, the article went on to say that Burton flew under an assumed name to Rome "for a romantic rendezvous" with Flo. When he was spotted having dinner with the actress at a posh Roman restaurant, *Bella* went on, he received a peremptory summons by telephone from Elizabeth to return home. "Maybe," the story said, "she was remembering those romantic Roman restaurants and her own late candlelit suppers, or maybe had a professional interest about who was to get top billing."

Burton came home. Again, headlines in the world press took up the story, making much of the fact that it was all happening in Rome, where it all began. After the boiling gossip-pot had simmered down, Flo told writer Liz Smith, "I could die of embarrassment over the dumb things they've made up which I'm supposed to have said. Why, I barely know Richard, though he is very nice."

Hardly had this furor ended when a new one arose over Burton's alleged romance with Lesley Patterson, an actress who was then seventeen years old. Or consider the incident played out on the Budapest-Rome axis in 1972. Elizabeth had accompanied Richard to the Hungarian capital where he began filming *Bluebeard*, one of his long line of failures. The cast included such sex-bombs as Raquel Welch, Virna Lisi, Joey Heatherton and Nathalie Delon. Rumors that Richard was reportedly involved with one or another of his leading ladies reached Elizabeth, and the stories did little to ease her mind.

What does a glamorous movie queen do in a situation such as this? What would most wives do? One of two things. Either get her husband alone, put her hands on her hips and say, "Now look here . . ." Or get away from the tension-producing atmosphere for a while.

Elizabeth got away. She went to Rome for a week.

But Elizabeth could no more escape headlines than Burton could resist turning on the charm when a pretty girl hove into sight. In Rome, she was escorted to dinner by Aristotle Onassis, already ill of myasthenia gravis, the neuromuscular disease which would take his life two years later. The gnomelike multimillionaire's marriage to Jacqueline Kennedy was reportedly less than idyllic at that point. In January, London newspapers had reported that Jackie and Ari had had a flaming row at Heathrow Airport. An Onassis-Taylor dinner was a good story, and newsmen and *paparazzi* made the most of it. They trailed the pair to the famed Hostaria Dell'Orso on the Via Monte Brianzo, a luxurious restaurant in a historic building dating back to the fourteenth century. Here, in a popular nightclub called La Cabala on the top floor, flashbulbs popped faster than champagne corks.

Headlines, plus undignified photos of Elizabeth trying to hide under a table, reached Burton. On her return to Budapest a few days later, Elizabeth got what-for from her enraged husband.

If Richard's drinking and the "other woman" problem were causing Elizabeth to lose the feeling of protection she needed from her husband, it may surprise many that Richard did not take reports of other men in Elizabeth's life casually.

He cared more than he allowed the world to know.

When reports circulated that Elizabeth was having a secret romance in Switzerland with a Maltese advertising executive named Peter Darmanin, Burton turned to one of his wife's bodyguards and said bitterly, "Do you want to be her lover this week?" The remark was intended to wound and probably did. It revealed only too clearly the jealous pain Burton had been feeling. As a Columbia University psychiatrist explained, "Burton's jealousy was probably an instinctive reaction, like fear and anger. There was a threat, real or fancied, to his happiness, self-esteem and security. Faced with this threat, an individual often lashes out at a loved one."

Most revealing of all was the comment made by Vittorio De Sica, the late great Italian film maker who directed Burton in Naples and Rome the summer the marriage shattered. Burton, De Sica said, was shaken by the breakup.

"Richard," he said, "was a man ready to die. A man killing himself. He drank, he came onto the set shaking, in a daze. It broke my heart to see him, because he has pride and you knew he didn't want it that way."

Five

Curtain Descending

Last scene of all,
That ends this strange eventful history.

—AS YOU LIKE IT

1. "Booze, No Me"

THE YEAR FOLLOWING THE MID-1974 DIVORCE WAS AN UNHAPPY TIME for Elizabeth. It was worse for Burton.

Elizabeth was in Hollywood; soon she left for Leningrad to begin work on the Maurice Maeterlinck classic *The Blue Bird*, the first American-Soviet co-produced motion picture. Richard telephoned her frequently, often several times daily, from New York or wherever he traveled, but she remained adamant about a reconciliation. She put it bluntly, "Booze, no me. No booze, me."

Close friends and employees reported that Elizabeth was still deeply in love with her husband, and that this was precisely why she left him and proceeded with the divorce. She hoped that the shock would give Richard the strength he needed to straighten out his own life.

But Richard was not yet ready. His reaction seemed to be, "Well, I'll show her."

He began dating other girls. One was a twenty-four-year-old fashion designer, a tall beauty with large eyes. One day he took his daughter Kate to the Russian Tea Room in New York. Nearby sat a lovely girl with long dark hair. He walked over, introduced himself, and she joined Kate and him for lunch. Afterward, the three drove off in Burton's chauffeured limousine. She was, he said, "intelligent, understanding and a good companion." Another girl he dated was a German stewardess.

Earlier, before the divorce became final, the Italian press had made a great to-do over his supposed courtship of a twenty-year-old Sicilian schoolgirl named Carmela Basile, who, the magazine *Novella 2000* solemnly declared, had "broken the heart of sentimentalist Richard Burton." On her way to school one day, Carmela, known as

Lina, and a friend stopped to watch the filming of a scene for *The Journey* near the town square of the port city of Noto. Burton spotted her, goggle-eyed, in front of the throng and asked her to lunch. Next day he visited her school, Lina said, and "gave lots of my friends autographs. In the afternoon, he came to see me at home. We had a late lunch in a restaurant in Noto and went home." Afterward, Lina told a journalist for *Novella*, he would send his Mercedes to wait for her outside the school and take her to the set four miles away. When the film company moved on to Palermo, Lina remained behind in her native village of Avola, with memories.

In the fall, a new Elizabeth came into Richard's life, the 38-year-old Princess Elizabeth of Yugoslavia. On October 17, with the princess at his side, he announced, "We are going to get married as soon as it is possible." The princess was married to Neil Balfour, a thirty-year-old British banker. She was the daughter of Prince Paul and Princess Olga of Yugoslavia, who fled their country following World War II, and was a second cousin to the heir to the British throne, Prince Charles. After the announcement of the engagement, Elizabeth Taylor telephoned Burton from Hollywood to give him her good wishes. A friend said "She was being brave; she wished truly for his happiness. But friends said she took some delight in an article published in England about Burton which contained the sentence 'After being deposed by a Queen, Burton is lucky to find a princess who would be bloody foolish enough to marry him.'"

Princess Elizabeth didn't. The romance and the marriage plans went glimmering as 1974 drew to a close. The end came after the princess spotted Richard in Nice in the company of a beautiful model. Elizabeth Taylor, in a conversation with Max Lerner, had predicted the relationship would break up if Burton "starts wandering," and it did. Princess Elizabeth flew back to London. On her arrival, the *Daily Mail* said that friends had elicited the following comment from her: "I didn't realize it takes more than a woman to make a man sober—I thought I could do it and failed."

Burton denied that the engagement was broken, asserting that he had been on the wagon since June "except for an occasional glass of wine." Nonetheless, he and the princess never resumed their relationship.

2. A Talk with Henry

NOW WAS THE TIME OF HENRY WYNBERG. SUDDENLY, IT SEEMED, HE popped into Elizabeth's life and into the newspapers. Black-haired, handsome, and five years younger than Elizabeth, he had flown to Europe to be with her. Published reports said that his friends had loaned him $15,000 "to bankroll," as one magazine wrote, "his international pursuit of Liz."

Wynberg speaks in a soft, barely discernible Dutch accent. He has avoided discussing his involvement with Elizabeth but reluctantly agreed to talk, and he added new dimensions and insight to the tangled web of Elizabeth's life. To begin, he calls the story of his subsidized romance "pure nonsense," adding, "Reporters always got everything wrong about me. The only thing they ever get right is the spelling of my name."

Wynberg was never taken seriously by Elizabeth-watchers, which included the entire international set, mostly because he was not himself a celebrity of the stature admired by the beautiful people; nonetheless, he was a stabilizing influence on Elizabeth in this ebb-tide period of her emotional life.

He was the other side of the coin from Richard, quiet where Burton came on strong, though both had risen to affluence from low beginnings. Wynberg had been born in Amsterdam and came to California in 1952 after traveling around Europe. He worked as a waiter in a large restaurant in Los Angeles. To supplement his earnings he took another waiter's job in a country club miles away, commuting between the two at breakneck speed.

But Wynberg was not about to spend his life waiting on tables. He ditched both jobs and became an automobile salesman. During lulls, he studied the facts about the used-car business, noting the marked differences between the amount paid to sellers, and the prices for which the used autos were sold. The profit potential, he felt, was great. Soon, he went into the wholesale end of the business, buying from one dealer and selling to another. "I can say I've done well for myself," he says. Since then, he has sold his used-car interest and gone into real estate and other businesses, including managing a pop singer.

In 1960, Wynberg married Carol Russell, a young actress, and had a son, Brenton. In 1967, the couple was divorced, and Henry, by then a wealthy man, bought a home in Beverly Hills.

His proximity to the film colony threw him into contact with movie people. "They liked me and I liked them," he says. He was invited to their parties, they to his. He was accepted. Then followed his introduction to Elizabeth at the Hollywood club. It was love at first sight—on Henry's part.

Wynberg renewed his acquaintanceship with Elizabeth during that summer of her discontent in Rome. Henry insists that he had gone to Rome on business on July 25, 1974 and had asked his friend Peter Lawford where to stay. Lawford, he said, had suggested the Grand Hotel, and Henry registered there under the name of Herman Wynberg, his legal name on his Dutch passport. He had not known, he says, that the Burtons had reserved a suite there, though both were still staying at the Carlo Ponti villa.

It is difficult to believe that Wynberg's presence in Rome at precisely the moment when the Burton-Taylor marriage was exploding into bits was coincidental—yet he insists it was exactly that—and that he did not know Elizabeth had moved into the Grand, following a blowup with Burton, until he read a newspaper in his room at breakfast one morning.

He telephoned Elizabeth, who at this point almost desperately needed someone to talk to and counsel with; she invited him for drinks that afternoon. From that time forward, Elizabeth and Henry were together a great deal.

Wynberg had a local reputation for being a very skillful lover, but now that he supposedly stirred Elizabeth physically, tales of his sexual prowess spread. One story, most likely apocryphal, which illustrated Henry's international notoriety, went the rounds: once in Paris, while walking along the Champs Elysées, a young woman spotted him and immediately ripped off her clothes. Nearly nude, she kneeled before him and pleaded, "Take me! Please take me!"

(When Richard heard about Wynberg's endowments, he reportedly said, "I'm sure that like the used cars he sells, it will fall off just at the psychological moment.")

Elizabeth and Henry traveled to the glamour capitals of the world. In July 1974, a year after they met, they were in Munich watching the soccer match between Germany and The Netherlands for the World Cup. They cruised for weeks along the Cote D'Azur aboard the *Kalizma*, sailing southward to Palma de Majorca, turning northward along the coast and dropping anchor at Monte Carlo, where they were guests at the cinnamon-colored palace of Prince Rainier and Princess Grace of Monaco, moving down Italy's boot to the rocky island of Capri with its breathtaking view of the Bay of Naples, going south to Sicily where they wandered through the ancient towns, marveling at the medieval domes and bells, and gasping at the deep gorges of the countryside.

In the fall, they returned to New York for the social and theatrical season. Friends who saw Elizabeth marveled at the glow in her face; she seemed at peace and radiantly happy. Later, they flew to Palm Springs to help Sara Taylor celebrate her birthday. According to one reporter, Elizabeth's mother, taken with Wynberg, remarked on meeting him, "I think he's a wonderful, considerate gentleman."

Burton, glowering in London, was anything but pleased. Wynberg's father, Nick, also in London, announced, "Elizabeth Taylor and my son are very much in love and will be getting married soon."

In California, Elizabeth's close friend and confidant, Peter Lawford, was reported to have said, "Yes! It's love! It's definitely love between them. And I for one am predicting that they'll get married. I'd be very surprised if they both aren't married by next summer."

Richard, told of the remarks during a pause in the filming of *Brief Encounter* with Sophia Loren for a television movie for Hallmark, exploded. "Over my dead body will Elizabeth ever marry that used-car salesman!"

And yet, as Henry Wynberg tells it, Richard Burton might well have been succeeded by a used-car salesman as Elizabeth's husband. Wynberg talked freely about the depth of his relationship with Elizabeth. He said they were truly in love and that the star herself had proposed they marry.

The information, if true, is surprising, for Wynberg had never been considered by Taylor-Burton watchers as much more than an interval while the stars regrouped. Yet coming from a man who had spent almost three years with Elizabeth, it must be given a measure of credence. After all, she did admit that she had proposed to Michael Wilding, her second husband.

The interview was conducted in late October 1976. Although at times Wynberg's replies were crisp, he sounded sincere. The section concerning the marriage proposal follows:

Q. Was she in love with you?

A. Yes.

Q. During the last year?

A. We were together for almost three years.

Q. When did you meet?

A. In 1973.

Q. And when did you see her last?

A. This year.

Q. Did she tell you she was in love with you during some of that time?

A. Sure.

Q. Why didn't she marry you?

A. Well, I'm still single.

Q. But she told you that she was in love with you at the time she was separated from Burton, did she not?

A. Right.

Q. Did she want to marry you after she was divorced from Burton?

A. Right.

Q. And you refused?

A. Right.

Q. Why?

A. I don't want to be married.

Q. You don't want to be married?

A. No.

Q. Why is that, Mr. Wynberg? You didn't want to be married to Elizabeth Taylor, the reigning queen of the movies?

A. That's it.

Q. Oh, you mean *because* she was the reigning queen?

A. No "because." I just never felt I needed a piece of paper to feel secure.

Q. But you didn't want to be her husband?

A. No.

Q. Did you feel you would be in her shadow?

A. No, that's not it. I just didn't want to be married.

214

Q. Did you have a quarrel about it?

A. No, never.

Q. Did she understand?

A. Sure.

Q. And then, ultimately, it ended?

A. Right.

Q. Do you think you'll ever see her again and be friendly again?

A. Yes, I think so. Elizabeth is a very complex person—but fabulous.

Q. Why does she keep getting married so often?

A. She needs the security of a husband.

Q. Did she plead with you to marry her?

A. No. Not exactly that.

Q. But she did want to marry you?

A. Yes. She sure did.

Elizabeth, through a spokesman, vehemently denied Wynberg's story. John Springer, who has been her press representative for many years, said, "It's incredible! I know for a fact it's untrue! Wynberg chased her and chased her! Again and again he asked her to marry him!"

Is Elizabeth's version the true one?

Or should we believe Henry?

Whichever, the fact remains that they were very close for a long period and that Elizabeth had a special need of him.

Max Lerner, who spent months with Elizabeth working on her autobiography, a project since suspended, believes that in Elizabeth's choice of Wynberg "there were strong overtones of the ultimate revenge, calculated to infuriate Burton."

It is an unwarranted putdown, for though Wynberg was clearly no inspired artist as Burton was, no creative genius, he was a male nonetheless with his own special strengths, a good mind, a gracious personality and—perhaps most important—he offered a broad shoulder to lean on in a time of crisis.

"It's ridiculous to compare me with Richard Burton," Wynberg said. "I never think of myself in those terms. I am me. I don't think it's necessary to be an actor or an entertainer to be part of Elizabeth Taylor's world.

"I am not an actor, but is it holy writ that Elizabeth must only like an individual in show business and that I must only be attracted to someone in the automobile field? We were just two human beings who met at a critical point in the life of one of us. We meshed. We understand one another. We empathized with one another."

Nor is Wynberg the "weak" man he has been pictured. Elizabeth's male-chartists are fond of saying she has an odd characteristic of alternating between "weak" and "strong" men. Thus Hilton was weak, Wilding less so. Todd was strong, Eddie Fisher weak. Burton came on the strong cycle, Wynberg the weak one, and now, her latest husband, John Warner, is strong. A nice theory, but just that.

Elizabeth herself has said, "You know, people are wrong about Henry. They think of him as weak. He isn't. In some ways, Richard was weaker than they thought and Henry stronger."

There were times when Elizabeth, in a depressed mood, would be snapped out of it by Wynberg's no-nonsense approach. He would tell her firmly that tears and self-pity can only feed on themselves and that her outlook must be an optimistic, positive one. And she would listen.

Which is not to say that Elizabeth had turned pliant and self-effacing. Hardly. There were plenty of times when, with old-time tartness, she made Henry squirm. Once, for example, the two were at the Polo Lounge in the Beverly Hills Hotel. Elizabeth, in a pixyish mood, leaned over to the next table and, grinning broadly, pointed to Henry and asked, "Would you buy a used car from this man?"

The Wynberg connection ended, at least in 1976, on a positive note, expressed by Elizabeth in these words, "He is a sweet and wonderful man who was very kind to me when I needed a friend."

3. Cold Turkey

BY THE SPRING OF 1975, A LITTLE LESS THAN A YEAR AFTER THE DIVORCE, Richard Burton was facing a grim choice: Give up drinking or die!

There is a small smile on his face at the recollection, but it radiates no amusement. "The learned doctors told me if I continued to booze, I should be prepared to welcome the end.

"That finally did it," he says.

That, and apparently a number of other factors:

• He felt he was still deeply in love with Elizabeth, and the realization had at last sunk in that he could not hope to win her back unless he stopped drinking.

• He was facing professional extinction as a serious actor. He could have had jobs, of course. "Las Vegas, for instance," he says, "is always kind to fading superstars. But there was nothing really demanding, nothing that dominated me and forced me back to the theater or films."

• His children: His daughter Kate "hates it when I drink," he admits, adding, "All the kids do."

• Still another unpublicized reason: gout. Burton's left foot is affected. (When he gets an attack, he can only hobble about painfully.) Important for control of gout is a high intake of fluids to reduce the precipitation of uric acid in the kidneys, but the fluids recommended are not of the alcoholic variety.

He went to his villa on Lake Geneva in Switzerland, a surprisingly modest little house with simple furnishings but a large library of 3,000 books. There, in the tiny village of Celigny, Burton set about licking the liquor problem.

A tall, beautiful black model and actress whom he had met on a movie set played a key role in getting him off the bottle.

He remembers her with affection and gratitude.

Her name is Jeanie Bell. And she may have saved not only his career but his life. In October 1969, Ms. Bell, who was born in Jamaica, became the first black woman to be photographed for a *Playboy* magazine centerfold. A graduate of Phyllis Wheatley High School in Houston, Texas, she took a job in a downtown men's clothing store, then became a secretary for a steel company.

A former business associate said, "Jeanie Bell is a very intelligent person—I'll bet that if she had stayed, by now she'd be running the entire organization."

Evidently, Richard appreciated both her beauty and brains.

One day, however, Jeanie Bell spotted an advertisement announcing a Miss Houston beauty contest. She entered and won fourth prize. Soon after, she won third place in a Miss Texas contest, was awarded a scholarship to a modeling school, and her new career began. Following a number of modeling assignments and acting parts, she won a role in two Burton films, *The Klansman*, made in California in 1974, and *The Jackpot*, shelved early in 1975 in France because of spiraling production costs.

The villa at Celigny became a one-man alcohol rehabilitation center. Burton wisely began his drying-out under the supervision of a Swiss doctor—and Jeanie Bell.

"The doctor and Jeanie stopped my drinking dead," Richard recalls. "I mean on the spot."

It was not an easy time, even though his detoxification from alcohol was medically supervised. He was given sedatives, tranquilizers and anticonvulsants in the proper amounts to minimize any possible withdrawal symptoms. Along with the medications was a program of recreation, nutritious food and exercise.

Jeanie Bell refuses to take credit for getting Burton to stop drinking. "Richard put himself on the wagon," she insists, though adding, "I assisted him. I suppose I gave him soul. He had to have somebody to talk to and to listen to, and he had to have peace of mind. I helped supply that."

During the hard weeks, Jeanie visited him often at the villa. She lived nearby, in Geneva. Burton spent his days walking and reading.

But Richard Burton is a Celt, and the image of heroes who are victorious while seemingly defeated is a strangely pervasive part of all Celtic folklore in the British Isles. One of the best known Celtic mythic tales, for example, is the story of the warrior Cuchulain,

218

who, while defending his country from invaders, tied himself to a pillar of stone because he wanted to perish while standing. Though mortally wounded, he laughed as a raven slipped and slithered on his blood. Thus, upright and laughing, he won a spiritual victory over death. Richard Burton did not die, though by his own admission, he had come close; and near as he was to defeat, he was to rise to an even greater glory.

By early fall, Richard Burton had won his fight. He was drinking only milk and Perrier mineral water.

When Richard convinced Elizabeth that he had become a teetotaler and no longer had to consume a quart of vodka a day to be able to function, the couple seemed headed for another reconciliation.

On August 20, 1975, Richard told an aide, "Elizabeth and I may soon remarry." And then he added, "This is not a trial reconciliation—this is permanent!"

The associate congratulated Elizabeth and told her how happy he was. She replied, "That makes two of us very happy."

In Switzerland, however, a spokesman for the couple said that Richard and Elizabeth would live together and that "definite marriage plans were premature."

Despite the announcement, there was speculation that the couple would soon be married in Israel, where Richard was scheduled to make a movie.

"After all," said John Springer, the couple's publicist, "Elizabeth is a Jewess."

Richard and Elizabeth arrived in Israel and were greeted by roaring crowds. "It's like coming home," they said—Elizabeth, the converted Protestant, and Richard, the roaring Welshman.

On a pilgrimage to Jerusalem's Wailing Wall, Burton, wearing a skull cap, and Elizabeth, a flowered silk headscarf, made brief appearances; the Wailing Wall has an iron barrier that separates men and women. Although they were again stormed by huge crowds and had to be rescued by police, they communicated their respect for the ancient holy place—and the crowds seemed to sense it.

They left Israel, still unmarried, and made their way to Africa. There, on October 10, in a primitive Botswana village, they exchanged ivory wedding rings. Cost: $40.

Ambrose Masalila, a member of the Tswana tribe, and District Commissioner, performed the ceremony. After pronouncing them man and wife, he, Elizabeth, Richard and two witnesses left in a Land Rover to drink champagne on a nearby river bank—on the way they passed a rhino and hippo.

"Even they seem to be smiling," said Elizabeth. "Everybody is happy now that Richard and I are back together."

Burton offered to buy his new-old bride another million-dollar diamond ring that he would purchase in Johannesburg. She refused, saying, "I don't need another ring. Richard doesn't have to spoil me any more. That African village desperately needs a hospital. We'll use the money for that."

A few weeks after their remarriage, at Elizabeth's urging, Richard decided to return to the stage. He read dozens of plays, but nothing seemed suitable. Finally his agent suggested he read *Equus*, then running in New York.

The role of a child psychiatrist racked by doubts about himself and his profession enthralled him. He stayed up all night reading it, blocking out the role in his mind. He agreed to play it in New York, replacing Anthony Perkins.

Although he had been an actor for more than thirty years and a major star for twenty, Burton was terrified. Would he succeed? Fail? Just be mildly good? "To be blunt," he says, "I was bloody scared! Frightened!"

When he opened in New York late in February, the reviews were ecstatic. Walter Kerr, in *The New York Times*, called his performance "the best work of his life." The critic for *The Times* of London cabled back that "the sounds [of his voice] are as clear and persuasive as they were twenty years ago when every male lead at the Old Vic used to go to Burton." In Boston, Emory Lewis of the *Record* wrote, "It is one of the most magnificent performances of this or any other year." And *Variety*, which a short time back, had compared Burton to the besotted shadow of John Barrymore, now hailed him as a "gifted, galvanizing actor." *Variety* also wrote, "Personal magnetism and energy are the key elements in Burton's gripping portrayal. . . . The actor brings great intensity, admirable clarity and, especially in his climactic final scene, infectious power to the performance."

Richard Burton, written off as a has-been, had come back gloriously, triumphantly. From the day he began appearing, hundreds of persons thronged the stage door nightly, waiting for a glimpse of him. A patrolman who directs traffic on West Forty-fifth Street at showtime has been on the beat for nine years, yet admits he has never seen anything to equal it. Inside the theater, Burton received wild ovations not only after each performance but on his entrance.

The drama was ending—or so it seemed. Richard and Elizabeth's fairy-tale romance would end, as such tales must, with the prince and princess of players living happily ever after.

But that wasn't the way it would turn out. The Burtons have lived their real lives in a series of climaxes, some small, most violent. Another, the most violent and final of all, erupted suddenly and unpredictably just as the story was coming to its happy ending.

Richard had met a former London model, twenty-seven-year-old Susan Hunt, then the wife of James "The Shunt" Hunt, who is popularly known as "the golden boy of British car racing." There were reports that Richard was smitten with the tall blond beauty, stories that soon reached Elizabeth. At the time, the Burtons were staying at the Lombardy Hotel on East Fifty-sixth Street, and the arguments were so loud that they were heard outside the suite. As for drinking, Richard had not returned to his former habits, but on occasion he still hoisted more than a few.

In the last week of February, while Burton was appearing in the pre-opening night previews of *Equus*, Elizabeth had enough. On Monday, February 23, she left Burton and flew out to her mother's home in Los Angeles. That evening, Burton, emerging from the stage door after a performance, confirmed the split, then went on to a restaurant to join Mrs. Hunt and a group of friends. A party, planned at a small Greenwich Village restaurant to celebrate Elizabeth's forty-fourth birthday at the end of the week, was canceled. Later, their lawyer, Aaron Frosch, reported that he had prepared a separation agreement.

Elizabeth had watched Richard's performance only a few days before, had gone to his dressing room and scrawled a message in pink lipstick to him on his mirror, "You are fantastic, love."

Weeks later, the traces were still there. He had not cleaned it off.

And so, once more unto the breach. Elizabeth, imitating the action of the tiger, had summoned up the blood and was in California in furious mood. The great romance was coming to a swift, shuddering end.

4. Fadeout

BURTON, LOOKING BACK UPON THE WRECKAGE OF HIS MARRIAGE TO Elizabeth, searched for an explanation.

"She's an individual and so am I," he says. "We have differing personalities. When we're together, things seem to happen. To put it mildly, we clash.

"When I say 'up,' she says 'down.' My 'white' is her 'black.' My 'night' is her 'day.' "

At the end, there was almost total inability to agree on the basics of day-to-day living. They had drifted a long way from the period in their lives when each was willing—anxious even—to make compromises when he believed (and acted upon) his definition of love. Once he had said, "Love is a high degree of tolerance carried to excess. If you love somebody really, truly, and he or she turns out to be a murderer, you love that person despite everything. You love the faults as well as the things of which you are proud. And if one is intolerant, the other must be tolerant of that intolerance."

Elizabeth had accepted that. "There is no such thing as the ideal man or woman," she had said. "We're all just too human to be ideal. It's the faults one has to accept and love."

When the faults became too overwhelming, she apparently could accept them no longer.

Elizabeth may have thought she would find at least a partial solution when Richard stopped drinking and became, once again, a bulwark of support for her insecurities, a strong person who would meet her openly expressed needs. But she discovered that whether the drinking stopped or it did not, whether the eye for other women stopped roving or continued, there could be no harmony in a marriage to Richard Burton.

Elizabeth and Richard have been portrayed by those who watched their personal lives unfold as two powerful personalities who clashed; the immovable object and the irresistible force that met and defeated each other. This is also how they view themselves.

And yet, after lengthy study and scores of interviews with those who knew them well through the years, the conclusion is probably the opposite: Each was not strong but weak; each needed strength and support that the other failed to deliver; each consumed too much time and energy trying not only to alter the behavior of the other but to control it as well.

Now, looking back on their lives—together and apart—we can see signs that Richard and Elizabeth probably had deeply rooted feelings of inadequacy. When they became man and wife, the symptoms produced by a lack of self-esteem multiplied, and being the Burtons made them even more prone to the inner stress that showed itself in their unusual behavior.

Ultimately, we must ask this question: Was this great love, conducted center-stage as the world watched, really love at all? All those protestations of perfervid attachment—his "we are flesh of one flesh, bone of one bone," her caressing his socks when he was away—was it the love of mature persons genuinely concerned with each other's welfare or a powerful physical attraction combined with a desperate need to be needed? Were they two people deeply in love, or two inadequate personalities looking to one another for reassurance and bolsters to the ego without which they each felt emotionally naked and terribly vulnerable before the world?

Faced with the loss or threatened loss of his loved one, Richard was engulfed by feelings of self-defeat, as evidenced by his admissions to Sophia Loren at the Villa Ponti. Elizabeth's constantly recurring feelings of jealousy were telltale signs.

The quarreling, too, was revealing. "There is no room in marriage for warfare between the sexes," Dr. Polatin has written. The battles that erupted so often, rather than strengthening the foundation of their marriage, as Elizabeth believed, apparently eroded it instead. To survive, a marriage needs cooperation, friendship and trust; this is no less true in a marriage between stars than other individuals. Constant battles no more clear the air between couples than constant wars between countries. Quarrels, on the scale and frequency conducted by the Burtons, are sure signals of marital ill-health.

Significant, too, was Elizabeth's infinitely sad observation after the second divorce. "I suppose," she said, "when they reach a certain age, some men are afraid to grow up. It seems the older men get, the younger their new wives are—so maybe I was just getting too old for him." If true, the remark tells much about the depth of Richard's love for her.

"Love," wrote Dr. F. Alexander Magoun in *Love and Marriage*, "is the passionate and abiding desire on the part of two or more people to produce together conditions under which each can be and spontaneously express his real self; to produce together an intellectual soil and an emotional climate in which each can flourish, far superior to what either could achieve alone." The definition scarcely leaves room for ending a relationship because a wife has become "too old" for a husband!

In the end, Elizabeth and Richard probably failed as husband and wife because they were apparently unable to grant to one another what Dr. Harry A. Overstreet has called "the full right to his unique humanhood." Love, like plants, needs light and air to grow and thrive. The Burtons, feeling alone, lost and worthless without the other, engulfed each other; and love, which perhaps could have grown, was stifled.

It is a measure of their mutual hunger for love that both refused to believe that the marriage had terminated, in spirit if not in the divorce court, until they could no longer avoid the reality. As recently as 1976, after they had rewed in Africa, both said, and doubtless believed fully, that they had never been happier. Incredibly enough, when they separated once again after that remarriage, Elizabeth was quoted as saying, "We can't live without each other," and Richard said, "We're apart now, but for a time. I suppose we'll get back together." It was only several months afterward that Elizabeth, having found another man "to love 100 percent," at last admitted that she and Richard should never have remarried.

Overall, too, the movie-going public must bear a large share of the blame for their marital debacle, for Richard Burton and Elizabeth Taylor were, in a large sense, our creations. We inflated the Burtons and sent them aloft. To alter the analogy, we enthroned them as superbeings and expected them to perform for us, on and off their stages. We have paid them vast sums for the entertainment they afforded us, and they did not disappoint us.

Elizabeth knows this well. "I think it's part of our society to enjoy putting you on top of the ladder and then take an animal delight in tearing you to bits," she says. "The public seems to revel in the imperfections of the famous, the heroes, and to want to be in the position of attacking—which I guess makes them feel a little bit superior."

What she left unspoken was that we play games with our stars far more sadistic and psyche-eroding than the ones George and Martha played on each other and their guests in *Who's Afraid of Virginia Woolf?* If we enjoyed Burton's charade of "hump the hostess," do we recognize ourselves as we play our own game of "hump the stars"?

The rules are simple: "You are our monarchs. So each of you must live up to your rank. Behave like royalty, not the present-day rubber-stamp kind but the crowned heads of old. Do the things they did: Be bizarre, scandalous, wicked. Titillate us, shock us. We'll pay you extremely well." Our motives are not sinister. We mean no harm to our stars, whom we admire, idolize, and even love. But, understandably, we want value for our money, and the value we demand is the excitement of watching them do what we cannot, will not, or fear to do.

Dutifully, they perform for us, those overpaid rock, TV and movie stars, not, of course, in any *quid pro quo* sense. Some, in fact, insist they owe nothing to their fans but an onstage performance. But in every way they are made to feel special, and the feeling confers upon them a license to a life-style unlike the rest of the world's levels below them. Ever present is the realization (which we feel continually) that they are Stars, superior personages inhabiting a strange, wonderful, unreal world. Pleasures, often undreamed of, are there for the reaching out. Money in limitless quantities can purchase anything—anything. Relentlessly, as though by some unseen force, they are pushed into their performances which so excite us in the broad off-stage audiences. There are those who revel in group sex, homosex, and in bisex, all of which is revealed explicitly to us by "new journalists" and by the performers themselves in their memoirs; there are those who engage in drunken brawls, shoot one another, get themselves maimed or killed or arrested, pop pills, squirt heroin into their bloodstreams and occasionally wind up in an emergency ward as an OD. And it's all part of the price of admission.

Burton and Taylor, too, danced to the strings we pull. That they haven't been destroyed as human beings as some of the others we elevated to their special pinnacles—sad human beings like Judy

Garland, Marilyn Monroe, James Dean, Freddie Prinze, and so many others who died tragic victims of stardom—is a tribute to their resilience and refusal to take themselves seriously. Burton came closer to tragedy than many know. Elizabeth has suffered emotional traumas: loss of a sense of identity, a fearsome insecurity and an "enormous" guilt complex about her divorces.

On the basis of all the evidence, the bottom line may well be this: The Burton-Taylor union was not a marriage of two people who insisted upon their own independence, but of two sensitive human beings who needed each other too much and never could give one another sufficient emotional support to face a world that showered too much glory and luxury upon them, and that in the end engulfed them both.

The Roman candles they sent up during their sixteen years together may have finally exploded their last flare and the sky is dark. But while they lasted, they gave one hell of a glow.

Epilogue

She went to Palm Springs to visit her mother and made headlines by telling a reporter that gun-control legislation was essential and that Robert Kennedy would still be alive if we had legislated against Saturday-night specials.

She went on a week-long fishing trip to Baja with Henry Wynberg and caught nothing. "I suppose that I'm too soft-hearted. After all, fish have mothers."

She was the major attraction at the Academy Awards ceremony in Los Angeles, stunning in a strapless dress that designer Halston had created for her. Low in spirits, she had wanted a new look. She had telephoned him from Hollywood. "Is this really Halston?" she asked. "Is this really Elizabeth Taylor?" he responded. Would he come to Hollywood to create a dress for her? Impossible, he was too busy. She pleaded and he agreed to come—"only for you." Halston took her in hand, and a "new" Elizabeth emerged. They became great friends and be began designing dozens of dresses for her, downplaying her earlier dramatic sexiness and remolding her into a more tasteful, understated elegance.

She went to a reception given by the Publicists Guild in Hollywood and so charmed comedian Redd Foxx that he removed a valuable jade ring from his finger and made her a present of it.

She flew to New York, dug in at the Sherry Netherland Hotel and attended parties and openings. She went to Westchester County, a-dazzle with part of her jewelry collection (and protected by eight bodyguards), for a Liza Minnelli performance.

She kissed Jimmy Carter at a fund-raising reception during his campaign and almost eclipsed the man who would become the next President of the United States. *The New York Times* headlined the story of the event: ELIZABETH TAYLOR BRIGHTENS FETE FOR CARTER.

She went to Montauk and partied with the Andy Warhol crowd. In a tee shirt and jeans, she played baseball with a team of residents and ate clams at a seafood bar. She handed out autographs cheerfully and guffawed when a trucker peering for a closeup look said he thought his wife was prettier.

She toured Washington, D.C., as the guest of her old friend, Illinois Senator Charles H. Percy. She met Carl Albert, the then House Speaker, and asked them both to support foreign-aid funds for a hospital in Botswana, Africa, where she and Richard were remarried.

She danced with Senator Edward Brooke of Massachusetts, lunched with the Senate's Majority Leader, Mike Mansfield (since retired), and started worldwide rumors buzzing when she was seen often with Ardeshir Zahedi, the Iranian Ambassador to the United States.

She went to a party in Chevy Chase, escorted by Ambassador Zahedi, and there she met John William Warner, Jr., the dark-haired lawyer who was then head of the U.S. Bicentennial Administration. Virginia newspapers predicted that a political future lay ahead for him, perhaps as governor of Virginia or as the Republican senator filling the seat to be vacated in 1978 by William Scott, who has announced he won't seek reelection. Warner has a reputation in the capital for wit, hard work, kindness, a quiet strength and reliability. (One friend said, "You can count on John Warner. When he tells you he will do something, he does it. The man has that abused word in its best sense: character.")

She fell in love.

Coyly, she denied all rumors of any serious involvement. In late July, she flew to Vienna to star in a movie version of *A Little Night Music*, returning to spend brief vacations with Warner at his 1,000-acre Atoka Farms in Middleburg, Virginia, the heart of the Virginia horse country. On October 10, she and Warner announced their engagement.

Warner, campaigning for President Ford, was often asked about himself and Elizabeth Taylor. He drew upon his background as Bicentennial director for a charming answer. A young school child, he said, assigned to write a brief life story of Benjamin Franklin, turned in the following: "He was born in Boston. He moved to Philadelphia. He met a pretty lady on the street. He asked her to marry him. They got engaged and he discovered electricity."

On December 5, as the sun set below the Virginia ridges, she married Warner on a hilltop at the farm. Fifty friends, family members and farmhands watched the ceremony. Elizabeth wore a fox fur trimmed gray and purple tweed coat and a two-piece dress of the same material. "The color of heather," she said.

The Reverend S. Neale Morgan of the Emmanuel Episcopal Church of Middleburg joined them together. They honeymooned in Israel, England and Scotland.

Washington and Virginia socialites wondered what Elizabeth planned for herself. Some believed she intended to retire soon from the movies and, backed by Warner's high social standing, try to become a new "hostess with the mostes'."

The reigning social queens can rest easy. Betty Beale, a high priestess of Washington society, hardly thinks Elizabeth intends to challenge them. "She is a career woman. That's where her chief interests lie."

On the other side of the country, Henry Wynberg is dubious, very dubious, about the future of the marriage. He does not know John Warner, he says, but when he is asked if he thinks Elizabeth was really in love, he replies, "No chance."

"I just don't see it from a gut level," he adds. He has never discussed the Warner marriage with Elizabeth, but he offers this observation: "If I were you, I'd wait a little while before you close your book." Why? Isn't the end of the story approaching? Is this not the "happily-ever-after stage?"

Wynberg thinks not. "They have two chances," he says. "Slim and none."

Nonetheless, Elizabeth appears radiantly happy. She had thought after the second debacle with Richard that she would never marry again, that she could never again fall in love. During the engagement period in the fall of 1976, she was girlishly giggly as she talked about John Warner. "I want to be buried with him," she told Betty Beale.

229

After the second divorce, Richard kept a low profile.

He continued to give outstanding performances in *Equus* and t[o] spend much time with lovely-looking Susan Hunt. Burton woul[d] return almost every night to his suite at the Lombardy Hotel. "Yo[u] may not believe it," he said, "but I actually read."

He was host at the Tony Awards given for outstanding stag[e] accomplishments. He made a routine presentation, but later in th[e] evening he received a special "Welcome Back to Broadway" meda[l]lion for his starring role in *Equus*. "When my fortunes were low as a[n] actor," he said, "I have been saved by Broadway. The first time wa[s] *Hamlet*, and now *Equus*."

He went to Hollywood in late spring to begin filming *Exorcist II The Heretic*, in which he plays the role of a priest. On June 8, he and Susan flew to Haiti. He was to obtain a divorce from Elizabeth and marry Susan, but lacking the written consent of Elizabeth Taylor, he left without it. The major Haitian newspaper, *Le Nouvelliste*, made much of their visit, publishing a lengthy two-column account on its front page and picturing them with President Jean Claude Duvalier, who entertained the couple at his palace.

Richard returned to Haiti in early July with the correct legal papers. On July 28, he received word in Hollywood that his second divorce from Elizabeth had been granted. Elizabeth, in New York, promptly telephoned him in Hollywood, wishing him well.

He finally married Susan Hunt, who had meanwhile obtained her divorce in a judge's chambers in Arlington, Virginia, after flying from LaGuardia Airport to Washington on a scheduled airline. The ceremony was brief; only a few friends attended. Virginia was chosen because it had no residency requirements. They had their wedding dinner for ten friends at the Laurent Restaurant in the Lombardy Hotel, where they occupied a suite. From Vienna came another telephone call from Elizabeth Taylor, offering her warmest wishes for their happiness.

He has not returned to heavy drinking because, at long last, he has come to the realization that liquor can be "deadly poison." As 1977 opened, he made the blunt statement—once again consistent with the frankness that has marked all his public statements—that he thought he was an alcoholic. "Nobody has actually defined what an lcoholic is," he said, "but from all the various things I've read about lcoholism, I think I qualify."

So months will go by and Richard Burton will not touch a drop, and not just because it is "poison" but because, he candidly admits, he simply can't take the extended bouts as he once did: he doesn't feel well after them. He tries to be careful now about the amount he drinks and the time he spends consuming liquor.

Richard and Elizabeth, apart now and married to other people, entertained us royally for almost a generation, offstage and on. It was a strange, wild, wonderful and certainly unpredictable union, and it is all over now.

Perhaps. But their lives have taken strange twists and turns, so some final lines may be quoted from Burton's beloved Shakespeare. In *Twelfth Night*, the clown Feste sings:

What is Love? 'Tis not hereafter;
Present mirth hath present laughter;
What's to come is still unsure.

Index

Index

235